HARSH OUT OF TENDERNESS

A catalogue record for this work is available from the National Library of Australia

Copyright © 2020 John Taylor

Cover illustration copyright © 2020 Dimitris Souliotis.

All photos in this book are reproduced with the permission of copyright holders. All rights reserved.

Book design by Michael Alexandratos.

ISBN: 978-0-646-81566-4

Published by Cycladic Press, Sydney, Australia.

All Rights Reserved. No part of this book may be reproduced or transmitted in any form or by any means, electronic or mechanical, including photocopy, recording, or any information storage and retrieval system, without prior permission in writing from the publisher. All inquires should be addressed to Michael Alexandratos, Cycladic Press: cycladic.press@gmail.com

HARSH OUT OF TENDERNESS

The Greek Poet & Urban Folklorist Elias Petropoulos

JOHN TAYLOR

CONTENTS

Introduction   ix

Harsh out of Tenderness   1

Photo Gallery   169

Appendix   191
For Elias Petropoulos   193
Two Texts on "Kaliarda": Greek gay slang   197
Benavis ta kaliarda?   199
Kaliarda Revisited   221

Bibliography   227

Acknowledgments   279
Books by John Taylor   281

INTRODUCTION

Elias Petropoulos (1928-2003) was the most controversial Greek writer of the twentieth century. Imprisoned three times during the Junta (1967-1974) and persecuted by Greek judges as late as the 1980s, when Greece had reestablished a democratic government and entered the European Economic Community, this poet and "urban folklorist" (as he liked to call himself) produced a multifarious, groundbreaking, and oft-humorous literary, lexicographical, and folkloristic oeuvre that consistently provoked—and still provokes—extreme reactions from his readers. One intensely admires Petropoulos, or despises him; dispassionate appraisals are rare, almost excluded by definition. This is to say the least, but the purpose of this insider's portrait of the author is, of course, to get beyond this "least."

Petropoulos was the eldest child of Sophia and Nikos Petropoulos, a low-level civil servant. He was born in Athens on 26 June 1928, but he grew up in Thessaloniki after his father was transferred to the northern Greek city in 1934. He had a brother, Soulis (1936-2002), and a sister, Zoista (1932-1936), who died while she was a small child. Petropoulos came to cherish Thessaloniki as his hometown, and he later devoted path-breaking, copiously-illustrated studies to its multicultural history. These books and photograph albums also got him into trouble, by the way, when he insisted that the town should be understood historically and culturally as less "Greek" than "multiethnic" and, notably, Jewish because of the many Sephardic refugees who, once they had been driven out of Spain in 1492, had settled and flourished there (or in Istanbul). During his childhood and adolescence in Thessaloniki, Petropoulos was immersed in and fascinated by this multicultural ambience; as fate would have it, the family settled in a house formerly owned by a Turkish bey. But soon the Second World War loomed, then brutally arrived: the Germans marched into town on 9 April 1941. While barely a young adult, Petropoulos found himself fighting in the underground movement and later, during the bloody Greek Civil War (1946-1949), on the leftist side. Moreover, in 1943, he had watched the large Jewish population of the city being rounded up and publicly humiliated, before they were deported to Nazi extermination camps.

While continuing to live in Thessaloniki in the late 1950s and early 1960s, Petropoulos first established his literary reputation by writing unusual kinds of criticism, sometimes composing erotic poems based on the paintings of his artist-friends as well as, among his several discoveries, penning the first major articles about the avant-garde writer Nikos Gabriel Pentzikis, whom he had met as early as 1948 or 1949 and who had become his mentor. Petropoulos's first book, a pioneering study of Pentzikis, dates to 1958, and he was one of the habitués of the famous pharmacy in which Pentzikis distributed many more literary insights than pharmaceutical drugs. In 1966, after Petropoulos had settled in Athens, the perspicacious critic likewise published the first study of the poet Odysseus Elytis, who would win the Nobel Prize in 1979; and in 1972, he was already arguing for the importance of Nikos Kachtitsis, whose novels would be more widely read only in the mid-1980s.

During this Thessaloniki period, Petropoulos had also endured long years (1949-1957) of unemployment and scraping by, a predicament that many leftists from the underground movement of the Second World War and the Civil War also experienced. Finally, in 1957, a leftist City Council came to power in Thessaloniki, and Petropoulos became responsible for greatly improving the cultural facilities of the town during subsequent years. These labors undertaken by a man who was subsequently often accused, by his enemies, of being a sociopath, a provocateur, and an egomaniac, are very little known. By the next year, he had become a member of the editorial committee of the important review *Diagonios*, which the poet Dinos Christianopoulos had founded; he thereafter wrote art criticism in its pages as well as in other magazines. Above all during these years, Petropoulos began compiling the extensive "personal archives"—a key methodological concept and, indeed, material reality for this ferocious autodidact and indefatigable observer—of notes, on-the-spot drawings, interviews, photos, engravings, documents of all sorts, and sundry objects (like stamps, postcards, and rare records) that would enable him, until only a few weeks before he died from prostate cancer on 3 September 2003, to wield his precise, hard-hitting, and sardonic style on extremely well-documented subject matter ranging from prison life, public hygiene, sexual mores, and the sociology of brothels and newspaper stands to clothing (especially hats), common furniture, canes, mustaches, graffiti, gestures, traditional food, argots and jargons of all kinds, automobile decoration, birdcages, gravestones, what he termed "popular architecture," etc., etc., etc. (The author liked to finish pronouncements with three resounding, and sometimes ironic, *et ceteras*.)

As a folklorist (but he much preferred the Greek term, *laographos*), Petropoulos energetically moved from topic to topic throughout his writing career; one seeks in vain an aspect of Greek daily life and manners that he left uninvestigated. Most importantly, every time that this resourceful independent researcher and incorrigible troublemaker devoted an essay or, even more characteristically, an entire book to a given theme (such as nargileh smoking, condoms, lice, shadow theater, and Turkish coffee, to cite five additional examples), the reader—shocked into anger or enthusiasm—would once again find himself looking at Greek culture and its quotidian in new, sometimes disturbing ways. Petropoulos had wide-open eyes and he opened eyes. He was ever spotting, examining, and meticulously recording facts revealing the authentic contents of what others, but not he, called a "national" culture, even as he cast a skeptical eye on chauvinistic ideas or "daydreams," as he sneered, about that culture. Some of the facts are brutal, it must be admitted; others are amusing or endearing, while still others induce a particular kind of melancholy that also qualifies Petropoulos's prose and poetry. His life's work, which comprises over seventy titles as well as—he claimed—some thousand published articles, is unified by these attempts to pay very close attention and define oft-hidden factual truths. Pushing this intention even further, he also innovated, among Greek field researchers, in using photography as a tool for recording evanescing objects of folkloric interest. He took this rigor to such extremes that it constituted a methodology in itself and, with typical resolution, he never tired of challenging the presuppositions governing much of the academic research that was being carried out in Greece, and sometimes elsewhere, in similar fields. Had he not been such a naughty *mounopsira*, a "woman's crotch louse"—as the expression goes and as he liked to characterize himself—digging down into fine details and pinching the Greek state and establishment where it hurts, he would have been celebrated as a national treasure.

Petropoulos moved from Thessaloniki to Athens in 1965 and, only four years later, that is two years after the Colonels had pulled off their coup d'état, his name became much more widely known. This was because of two books and a long poem that landed him in jail for three successive terms. Many Greek intellectuals, writers, artists, and musicians were imprisoned during this period for political reasons, or were forced into exile, but Petropoulos was convicted as a common criminal for his writings. He was proud of this distinction, for, although his own political thought bordered on anarchism, he belonged to no political party or organization and was wary of ideologies of all kinds. Despite his suffering (a guard once intentionally broke his fingers by twisting them), Petropoulos managed to put his three prison terms to use by adding considerably to "archives" that would later fuel *The Good Thief's Manual* (1979) and several other books as well, ranging from *From the Jails* (1975) and *The Underworld and Shadow Theater* (1978) to *Rebetology* (1990) and *Saint Hashish* (1991). In fact, he graphically and movingly describes prison life in nearly all his studies. Because he was allowed to read only the Bible in his cell, this self-proclaimed atheist translated the Book of Revelations—a "surrealist poem," as he termed it—into Modern Greek. His version was published as *The Apocalypse of John* in 1975. Even more impressively, in his introduction to *The Good Thief's Manual*, Petropoulos poses as a Burglary School professor and claims—half in jest, half in earnest—that he "hopes to offer a new viewpoint on the social status of the Thief." The earnest wins out: he does precisely this, and with compassion.

During the grim years of the Junta, when nearly all the key novelists, poets, and intellectual personalities who had remained in Greece feared to speak out on or write about potentially "immoral" topics, the first of Petropoulos's incriminated books was *Rebetic Songs* (1968), an encyclopedic anthology of the genuine lyrics of Greek "rebetic" songs. These songs had often been censored by governments in the past and were essentially banned during the Dictatorship of the Colonels. Finding no publisher for his anthology, Petropoulos boldly self-published it, thus offering a critical edition of songs that had nonetheless become, ever since the 1950s, popular among lower-class Greeks, who knew scores of them by heart. Deeply influenced by Turkish folk music and played with Turkish instruments (especially the *bouzouki* and the *baglamas*), rebetic songs are sung in the rather obscure argot of the Greek underworld. Petropoulos not only elucidated the slang of the *manges*, the "thieves," "bullies," "rowdies," "tough guys," and other social outcasts who danced to and sang this music (the adulterated versions of which the tourist still hears today in tavernas), but also described the role of the underworld in preserving certain folk traditions and revealed how intricately Greek and Turkish folk cultures were intermingled. This latter, politically inflammable topic would engage Petropoulos throughout his career. By "eyewitnessing" (as he phrased it) the Turkish, Sephardic, and sundry Balkan cultural elements that had permeated Greek life for over four hundred years, he aggressively but also rigorously challenged the narrow ways in which Greek culture was being perceived. Furthermore, the authentic, uncensored lyrics of rebetic songs are similar to those of the Blues in their expression of "immoral" themes such as drug addiction, hashish, crime, prison life, prostitution, and sexual lust. For publishing his unexpurgated anthology, Petropoulos was convicted of pornography and sentenced to five months in prison in 1969.

His second pornography conviction, for a five-month stretch in 1972, was for a long poem entitled *Body*, which Petropoulos had written in 1969 for an album by his artist-friend Pavlos Moskhidhis. The judges objected to one line: "I forget even the fatherland when I see a young naked female body." Such aphoristic phraseology, at once straightforward and ironic, characterizes much of his later poetry (and "anti-poetry") as well, published in volumes such as *Suicide* (1973), *Five Erotic Poems*

(1975), *Mirror for You* (1983), *In Berlin: Notebook 1983-1984* (1987), *Never and Nothing* (1993), and, posthumously, *After* (2004). The conviction for *Body* received some publicity outside of Greece, namely in a long article that appeared in the German weekly magazine *Der Spiegel*. A few foreign journalists were taking an interest in him by this time, but the barrier of the Greek language made it difficult, if not impossible, for them to provide, beyond an anecdotal report on his publications and tussles with the Greek judicial system, a sober-minded appraisal and presentation of his rapidly growing oeuvre. Incidentally, Petropoulos, who was a poet at heart even in his folkloristic writings, called the Greek language "a very old slut" and maintained that his "experiencing of her refinements would never be finished." Few have mastered the modern idiom more sensually or profoundly.

Immediately following this prison term for *Body*, Petropoulos returned behind bars for *Kaliarda* (1971), a dictionary of Greek homosexual slang. Petropoulos was no homosexual (but instead, by his own admission, "a very active heterosexual"), yet he had put together the first such lexicon published anywhere—even before Bruce Rogers's *Queens' Vernacular*, issued the following year and usually, erroneously, considered to be the prototype. As with the anthology of rebetic songs, Petropoulos had dared to self-publish the dictionary with all his exquisite typographical taste. (Throughout his career, even in the many cases where well-known publishers printed his books, this maniacal aesthete insisted on designing everything beforehand and overseeing the entire publishing process.) This time the judges convicted Petropoulos of insulting governmental authorities, the royalty, and the Greek Orthodox Church with the entries of his, once again, "pornographic" dictionary, and for circulating indecent publications. A specific objection to the book was that, in Greek homosexual slang, the term "U. S. Embassy" means the public toilets in Omonia Square, a natural meeting place for homosexuals. The sentence for this "habitual offender" was now seven months. Incredibly, in the months following the end of the Dictatorship, the folklorist continued to run into scrapes with the police whenever they found him photographing and drawing in cemeteries. He notes the several cases in the preface to his album of drawings, *The Graves of Greece* (1979), his "most beautiful book," as he maintained. In 1975, Petropoulos left Athens for Paris, accompanied by his lover, the folklorist Mary Koukoules. He never returned to his homeland. He traveled a few times to Belgium, the Netherlands, and his beloved Italy, spent an entire year in West Germany (and while he was there visited East Berlin), and made one memorable trip to Turkey.

In Paris, Petropoulos was extraordinarily productive. Books that had been building up in his archives, most of which had traveled with him to the French capital, now took shape and flowed from his pen. (Before leaving Greece, he had donated all his rebetic song archives to the Gennadius Library in Athens, as the first of his many subsequent gifts to this library, where nearly all his archives are now housed.)

However, the poet and folklorist's trials and tribulations did not end during his French "exile" (as he viewed his expatriation). *The Good Thief's Manual* appeared in 1979; the police later confiscated copies and the author was finally sentenced *in absentia*, in 1980, to eighteen months of prison. This trial was commented on in foreign newspapers, including *Le Monde* and *Die Zeit*, and extensively in the Greek press, while two other books that Petropoulos had published at more or less the same time—*Lousology: The Book of Lice* (1979) and *The Brothel* (1980) —were becoming bestsellers. Despite their subject matter, the latter were not incriminated, probably because of the writer's ingenious ploy: on their covers were printed respectively "Keep the Americans out of my Country" and "Throw the Americans out of Greece," a reminder that the United States still maintained military bases in the country. Any judicial proceeding against the books would necessarily be a political one, and a rather strange one given the anti-American propensities of the PA.SO.K Socialist government, which had come to power in the meantime. In the pages of this memoir, I have noted other legal ploys conceived by Petropoulos who, having studied law at the University of Thessaloniki in 1949, knew how to draw the Greek state into its own traps and blatantly exhibit its contradictions. (But even without the year of study, he would have known how to do so.) His most compelling personal campaign during these early Paris years consisted of a public appeal, reiterated between late 1981 and early 1983, to convince the PA.SO.K. government, and specifically the Minister of Culture, Melina Mercouri, to commemorate the Holocaust of the Jews of Thessaloniki.

During this prolific period, Petropoulos also produced his photograph albums on the history of his hometown (*La Présence ottomane à*

Salonique, 1980; *Salonique: l'incendie de 1917*, 1980; *Old Salonica*, 1980) and on various features of popular architecture (*Ironwork in Greece*, 1980; *Balconies in Greece*, 1981; *Wooden Doors Iron Doors in Greece*, 1982; *Courtyards in Greece*, 1983). His success and notoriety encouraged publishers not only to accept new book projects—several were already in the works—but also to re-issue earlier books in new editions. In 1979, for instance, appeared a beautiful, greatly expanded edition of the rebetic song anthology, this time cleverly and touchingly illustrated by the artist Alekos Fassianos, with whom Petropoulos often worked. (Nearly all of Petropoulos's books were illustrated by his artist-friends; such collaboration was essential to him.) The rebetic songs anthology remains Petropoulos's best-known book, though he himself considered his work-in-progress of some three decades, *The Cemeteries of Greece* (2005), left not quite finished at his death, as his masterpiece. Throughout his twenty-eight years of Parisian life, the author frequently contributed to Greek literary reviews, magazines, and newspapers, and occasionally to foreign periodicals as well. A pattern developed: he would first write an article about a certain topic, drawing on his archives for a few illustrations and often adding some of his own sketches; and this periodical publication would provide the impetus for expanding the article into a longer piece, and for writing other related articles, that would all be much more richly illustrated when they were gathered into a book with a coherent theme. In the last decade or so of his life, Petropoulos continued to write with a sort of generous rage; he produced an incredible quantity of original work, publishing—to mention only a few examples—poetic evocations of the art and personality of the French artist Roland Topor (1991), a book about the *fustanella* (1993), his own erotic collages (*Mainly That*, 1994), and volumes focused on such diverse topics as chairs, windows, shoe scrapers, bean soup, as well as, in extremis, *The String* (2002). Beginning in 1990, the publishing company Nefeli started reprinting earlier books and issuing many of the new ones in a special "Collected Works" series. Another important publishing company, Patakis, also brought out several books by Petropoulos at the end of his life.

I met Elias Petropoulos by chance. I had arrived in Paris from the island of Samos in 1977. One day, two years later, I tacked up a want ad in the Greek bookshop that was then located on the rue des Patriarches, near where he lived on the rue Mouffetard, because I was seeking a Greek partner for a poetry translation project. Petropoulos answered the want ad, stipulating that the two Greek poets—Kostas Karyotakis and Yannis Ritsos—whom I had mentioned on my card should be disqualified because "one was dead and the other an idiot," and declaring that he was seeking a translator for a book called *The Good Thief's Manual*. We eventually got together at his apartment. During the eight years that followed, I saw Petropoulos at least once weekly (and more often, two or three or four times a week), for an hour or two or three each time. I became his translator, a sort of secretary for him, as well as the foreign critic who was writing the most extensively about his books. In addition, with respect to my own desire to be a writer, I had the inestimable fortune of being his "apprentice"—an odd term in our age of academic creative-writing programs and workshops, but no other word is appropriate. He never read my poems or short stories in manuscript before they were published, but as I was working with him he inevitably turned into my redoubtable mentor. As a mentor, he was exacting, but also patient and generous. Because he was a man of extreme passions and enthusiasms, this equation should be understood as extremely exacting, extremely patient, extremely generous.

Our intense collaboration ended in July 1987. My wife, Françoise, had obtained a teaching position at the University of Angers and we decided to leave the capital. I continued to see Petropoulos after our move to the provinces, on my occasional day trips to Paris, though with increasing infrequency. We would talk on the telephone, but as the years went by our chats became rarer. We still exchanged postcards now and then. He continued to send me photocopies for a while, whenever an article by or about him appeared. With a couple of notable exceptions, I stopped translating his books as well as the work of other Greek poets and writers whom he had recommended to me. With his encouragement, I devoted more time to my own writing. Moreover, as a critic, I turned fully to contemporary French prose and poetry. Once Françoise and I had settled in Angers, this reorientation of my literary activities evolved quickly, if naturally, and had nothing to do with a change in my deep affection for the man who had taught me so much. I felt motivated by Petropoulos to pursue my own path. He never put pressure on me to restore our former working relationship. A near silence settled in between us toward the turn of the century. Our last long telephone conversation took place in September 2002, and he related, all the while dismissing, the problems that he was having with his prostate cancer. I then visited him in the Clinique Geoffroy Saint-Hilaire, where he was dying, and I was present at his final controversial act: in accordance with a poem-testament published in his collection *Never and Nothing* (1993), the original Greek edition of which I had prefaced, his ashes were dispersed in a Paris sewer.

An additional clarification is necessary. In 1981, I began a book about Elias Petropoulos. I ambitiously imagined a critical appraisal of all his writings, as well as an insider's view that would draw on extensive biographical information and elucidate his personality. He knew about the project and, interestingly enough, kept putting off requests for work sessions during which I intended to interview him with a tape recorder about biographical detail from his Greek past. I had drawn up a first list of questions, which I had shown him. Not a single work session took place, but I progressed on certain parts of the manuscript. One day, when my rough draft had reached about fifty pages, I realized that I was up a dead end. I threw the manuscript down the garbage chute of our sixth-floor apartment on the rue Albert-Bayet. I had concluded that it was impossible to arrive at any definitive "truths" about his exceedingly complex personality. This, too, constituted a lesson that I learned from him: it is a writer's books that matter most; there are no single truths emanating from his personality. A human being is full of contradictions, impulses, intentions; one searches for unity in vain. In his case, this is especially true. The positive and negative elements of Petropoulos's character should by no means distract readers from the lasting importance of his countless contributions to Greek culture. This legacy is priceless. Moreover, as some anecdotes that I relate here show, his personality included traits that were quite different from those that a reader familiar only with his books and sulfurous reputation might imagine. An exceedingly complex personality, indeed.

My goal in this memoir is more modest than that of my earlier project. I stick to events that I eyewitnessed. This rule implies that nearly all the events evoked or described in this book took place during Petropoulos's Paris years. (Readers of Greek should consult the special

Petropoulos issue of the magazine *Mandragoras*, brought out in October 1997-April 1998, for more biographical information than I provide here.) I proffer few prolonged psychological analyses about what the poet and folklorist "was like." I avoid hearsay, which is particularly widespread and tenacious in his regard. In fact, I first wrote down many of these memories strictly for myself, beginning only a few days after his death. They were a product of, and an antidote to, my grief. And the form that I spontaneously gave to them on the page somewhat recalls stylistic and narrative aspects of Petropoulos's own writing. Later, I similarly used a collage-like approach to arrange my recollections and, although I came to add more objective critical passages to my original draft, I have maintained this overall scheme here. I want this simultaneous memoir, tribute, anthology, and introduction to resemble his own writings. In his essay "Phallocratic Etymology" (1983), he explains:

> Like all folklorists, I began to write at a rather advanced age. But by an early age I had already begun to observe and to check my observations. In order to verify what I had noted, I naturally appealed to our classic articles and books. However, from these comparisons arose my first doubts about the percentage of truth contained in these articles and books. There are no boundaries between scientific fields. While studying a given topic, you need to leap with ease from local history to proverbs, and from topography to traditional dances. For me, such leaps have never caused any problems.

It is my hope that readers who, in the future, will marvel at or be infuriated by Elias Petropoulos's poetry and folkloristic writings, will also be intrigued by these glimpses of the private man, portrayed in typical everyday scenes at which I was present. Some of them are perfectly banal, and I have retained them intentionally: a writer's life, and Petropoulos's own career displayed these qualities par excellence, necessarily consists of drudgery, long solitary hours, reading, typing, fact-checking, methodical proofreading, preparing manuscripts, dealing with editors and publishers, and so on. Petropoulos's life was extraordinarily full and indeed often "colorful," though perhaps less so than some readers imagine. The qualities that emerge above all are hard work and determination. In order to give English readers a sampling of his style, I have interspersed my reminiscence and commentary with translated excerpts from his books; that is, passages on which I worked with him yet which were never published. I have also rendered several short poems for this memoir. Finally, I have adapted, revised, and sometimes expanded passages from my published articles about his books in an attempt to outline his ideas and critical methodology as clearly as possible. For the record, I have reprinted, in an appendix, the poem that I read at his cremation in the Columbarium of the Père Lachaise Cemetery, during an afternoon in which poets and writers from at least ten countries and languages also read tributes; and I have added my two studies of *Kaliarda* and Greek homosexual terms: these two articles are particularly hard to find. In accordance with how the mentor himself wrote, I have embellished nothing.

I would especially like to thank Mary Koukoules for her constant help and encouragement on this project, and for her careful reading of successive drafts of the manuscript. She enabled me to pin down elusive facts, correct errors, add names or details to some of my memories, improve my bibliography and, not least, tidy up my Greek. She also increased my already extensive "archives" by providing copies of books and articles that I did not have. Katharine Butterworth, Dimitris Souliotis, Veroniki Dalakoura, Elias Papadimitrakopoulos, and Françoise Daviet-Taylor likewise helped me to verify dates and descriptions. Heartfelt thanks are likewise due to my editor and publisher, Michael Alexandratos, whose enthusiasm for, and attentive work on this project was motivating from the very onset.

Although I began to write this book long before reading and then reviewing, in the *Times Literary Supplement* (20 August 2004), Rosmarie Waldrop's *Lavish Absence: Recalling and Rereading Edmond Jabès*, I felt encouraged by the affinities between Waldrop's open-ended approach and the one that I had spontaneously adopted for my memoir. Waldrop and I later discussed these affinities in Le Sorbon, a café in the Latin Quarter, on 25 October 2004. Similarly, a long conversation, on 28 February 2006, with the French novelist Florence Delay about our respective mentors (hers being the Spanish writer José Bergamín) provided a firm amicable impetus to finishing this book. See the vivid portrait that she draws of Bergamín in her memoir *Mon Espagne, or et ciel*. He, too, was tender, generous, melancholy, and full of a rage that kept him looking hard at the world, and at words.

Saint-Barthélemy d'Anjou,
26 June, 2019

Note: To facilitate the reading of this book, I have used English titles for Elias Petropoulos's books. The Greek titles and full references to the original books can be found in the Bibliography. In cases where Petropoulos published a book only in France, I have used the original French titles. Similarly, I have transliterated the many Greek words that Petropoulos analyses in the passages that I have quoted and translated. I have chosen not to place accents on these transliterated Greek words, once again in an effort to simplify the visual presentation of the text.

HARSH OUT OF TENDERNESS

It was a Saturday afternoon in May, 1979. Elias Petropoulos had started laying a stone walkway behind his and Mary Koukoules's country home in Coye-la-Forêt, a village located north of Paris. It was my first visit to him there. I helped him to continue the path. The heavy flat stones were piled at the back of the yard. We carried them one by one toward the house. Petropoulos was fifty-one years old. I was twenty-seven. I kept insisting—to no avail—that I alone do the carrying. Taking turns with the shovel, we knifed through the grass into the hard ground, slipped the shovel blade just below the roots, removed large flat pieces of sod, then shoveled out a little more dirt so that the stones could be placed firmly in the ground. Using a watering can, Petropoulos poured a little water onto the shoveled space. I would place the stone there in the exact position that Petropoulos had determined—a maniac in this respect as in so many others. Then he would stand on the stone, wiggling slightly, using his weight to fix the stone permanently. The labor in the hot sunshine made us grimy and sweaty. When we finished, Mary served glasses of cold lemonade.

The next morning, we decided to walk in the nearby forest. Petropoulos brought a camera, supposedly so that we could take a few pictures of each other in the woods. As we were walking out of the village, he stopped in front of the half-opened iron gate of a mansion and adjusted his camera for a picture. He stealthily pushed the gate open, informing me that such undertakings in wealthy neighborhoods were dangerous because of the watchdog that would attack if a pedestrian stepped past the gate's threshold.

"But you don't want your picture taken here, do you?" I asked, still unable to understand why we had stopped so soon.

Petropoulos chuckled, began focusing his camera on the roof of the mansion. "I saw this the other day." On the gabled roof I noticed the simple black weathervane that had attracted his attention. I was perplexed.

"You aren't going to take a picture of that, are you?"

"Sure. Why not?" he replied. "People put up all sorts of weathervanes. Why should I eliminate certain weathervanes from my collection for personal aesthetic reasons? A conscientious folklorist does not have personal preferences."

Petropoulos was "collecting weathervanes," as he put it, for an album that he had planned about this aspect of French popular culture, even as he had already produced albums (with French translations) on Greek kiosks (*Le Kiosque grec*, 1976), birdcages (*Cages à Oiseaux en Grèce*, 1976), and automobile decorations (*La Voiture grecque*, 1976). Five similar albums whose introductions and captions I was soon to translate into English had already been long in the works: *Ironwork in Greece* (1980), *Balconies in Greece* (1981), *Wooden Doors Iron Doors in Greece* (1982), *Courtyards in Greece* (1983), and *Windows in Greece* (1996). This weathervane album, like the one that he projected about French cemeteries and gravestones, was never finalized and published.

Petropoulos told me that, as a writer, he was "always at work and always on vacation." In the years that followed, I constantly saw the work side of the equation; as for the vacation, I have doubts. I saw him more or less relaxing only one other time.

II

It was seven years later, in mid-May, 1986. I had to drop something off at the rue Mouffetard apartment in Paris, where Petropoulos and Mary Koukoules lived most of the time once Mary's children, Phaedon and

Katia, had grown up. I think that I needed to give Petropoulos a photocopy of a letter that I had received from a professor in Israel, concerning *The Jews of Salonica / In Memoriam / Les Juifs de Salonique* (1983), the album of memorabilia that Petropoulos had printed in 202 copies and donated to university and national libraries worldwide. That same afternoon, Françoise and I also intended to browse for books at the Gilbert and the Presses Universitaires de France bookstores on the boulevard Saint-Michel. (The latter, the PUF bookstore, has now disappeared, replaced like so many other Latin Quarter bookshops by a retail clothing outlet.) So she accompanied me to see Petropoulos, which was rare. That afternoon, too, was warm and sunny.

We rang the outside buzzer at No. 34. This automatically opened the first door. We entered the ground-floor corridor, found Petropoulos's name on the intercom board to the left, with the second group of buzzers. For several months, it was actually not "Petropoulos" that was visible there, but rather "Fassianos." The prank had not been made, needless to say, by the famous Greek artist, with whom Petropoulos had long been friends. (Alekos Fassianos had illustrated the fourth edition of the enormous *Rebetic Songs* anthology, which had first been published in 1968, and several other books by Petropoulos as well.) Françoise and I rang the buzzer, heard after a moment Petropoulos successively asking in Greek and French: "Nai?...Oui?..." I replied, simply saying "Maître...," the respectful French title for lawyers and notaries that, for our mutual bemusement, we employed when greeting each other. The lock clicked. I pushed open the door. We climbed the dark narrow spiral staircase, with its exposed wooden beams, finding the door to Petropoulos's study open when we arrived at that level. (He no longer worked in the living room, but rather in the one-room studio apartment to the right, as one climbed the stairs; the two apartments were connected to each other, and from the inside of this study he could reach the upstairs bedroom by means of an inner spiral staircase.) Petropoulos had opened the studio door, but, as usual, he was already back behind his desk, gluing something. I gently rapped with a knuckle on the door. We entered.

Petropoulos's desk was large for the size of that small room, whose walls were covered with books and a few drawings. Knowing that

Françoise and I were both coming, he had already placed two chairs in front of the desk.

After greeting me and especially Françoise, whom he had not seen for several weeks following upon a sadly memorable dinner in Paris with the short-story writer Elias Papadimitrakopoulos and his wife Niobe—about which more below—, he immediately started talking about the female pubis, explaining that certain erotic fashions had come and gone, "that there were times, during the Ottoman Empire for example, when pubes were shaved or depilated with hot caramel, like women's armpits and legs are shaved today." He had discovered engravings proving this. "In some men's magazines today," he reported, "you can also find pictures..."

I wondered if he were going to search for samples in a large folder, to his immediate left, on which "KAPOTA" ("condom") had been marked in bold capital letters. He did not do so. This file was to become, a decade later, one of his biggest book-albums: *A History of the Condom* (1996).

After we had listened to these and other details, then—once I had managed to change the subject—chatted about the letter that I had brought or perhaps about a Russian film that he had seen (at the time, he was religiously attending a retrospective of films by Sergei Eisenstein), I explained that we would be leaving, that we wanted to head for the bookstores, to be followed by Luxembourg Gardens, where Françoise and I planned to work a little more on the translation, into French, of my first book, *The Presence of Things Past*. We stood up. To my great surprise, Petropoulos asked if he could come along. "I'm weary," he avowed.

From the rue Mouffetard, we turned left onto the rue Blainville (where there was a small newspaper shop with a photocopying machine that he used often), then headed up to the rue de l'Estrapade, to the place de l'Estrapade (where army deserters were tortured in the seventeenth century, as Petropoulos pointed out, asking: "vous savez ça?"), and from there we attained the rue des Fossées. Photocopying, torture, ditches (as the street name "Fossées" suggests)—the sewers. At this point, instead of taking the rue Malebranche before angling left onto the rue Le Goff, as Françoise and I would have done, Petropoulos directed us up the rue Saint-Jacques slightly, before turning down the rue Royer-Collard. He mentioned that he had recently had dinner not far from there with the French poet, writer, and translator of Greek literature, Jacques Lacarrière, who was the first French writer whom Petropoulos had befriended after arriving in France in 1975. In fact, not long after his arrival in Paris, Petropoulos had gone to visit Lacarrière at his home in the Burgundy village of Sacy. Coincidentally, Lacarrière was correcting the galley proofs of what was to become his best-known book, *L'Été grec* (1975); despite his intimate knowledge of Greek culture, he had remained unaware of Petropoulos's *Rebetic Songs*. This explains the footnote that was inserted at the last minute, on page 350 of Lacarrière's book, and that rectifies his initial sentence stating that "the history of rebetic songs remains to be written, and I am sure that it will be one day—by foreigners or Greeks—for this music created by common people has a universal value."

Just when we reached the main entrance of Luxembourg Gardens, Petropoulos suggested that we first cross the place Edmond-Rostand and buy some pastries. Which we did. Éclairs, surely.

Then we returned to the Gardens, finding a shady bench near the bandstand.

Petropoulos was in a mood that surprised me. He did look weary. He was more subdued than usual. He relished his éclair, but then he leaned back and seemed content to be outside in a beautiful garden, in the balmy spring weather. Perhaps he was trying to concentrate on the sensations provoked by the balmy weather, on the way the warm air touched the skin on the back of his hands. Petropoulos was indeed a sensualist. He eventually told us that he sometimes felt that it was not really a life, a writer's life, always shutting himself up in a study and "not living."

"But such is my life," he added sternly after a moment of silence. With this confession, all his rage and determination returned.

III

When I began working with Elias Petropoulos in late March, 1979, Françoise and I did not have a telephone in our apartment located on the sixth floor of the high rise at 17, rue Albert-Bayet. Having a telephone line installed in a house or an apartment was expensive in

France back then—about seven hundred francs. Petropoulos sent me notes whenever he planned to be in Paris for the day or the weekend. He was then living most of the time in the Coye-la-Forêt country home.

I have kept all these handwritten notes except, apparently, the first one, which I have been unable to find in my files. This was his reply to my want ad (posted in the Greek bookshop that was then located on the rue des Patriarches, not far from the rue Mouffetard), in which I expressed my interest in finding a Greek collaborator for translating Modern Greek poetry into English. I had mentioned the poets Kostas Karyotakis and Yannis Ritsos on my card, which Mary Koukoules read one day while she was in the bookshop. I remember the essence of what Petropoulos wrote to me, probably in mid- to late-February, 1979: "Karyotakis is dead and Ritsos is an idiot, but if you are interested in Modern Greek literature, I have a book that needs translating: *The Good Thief's Manual*." I replied to this intriguing, intimidating missive. Petropoulos's second letter, dated 26 February 1979, mentions that he has just been in Paris and that he will again be in the city in a few days. He adds that he "speaks French like an Armenian." But we must not have met until late March. A third letter is dated 27 March 1979 and specifies the stairway and floor of the rue Mouffetard apartment.

The Good Thief's Manual is his funny, learned, and compassionate "guide" based on his conversations with common-law prisoners while he was himself imprisoned during the Dictatorship of the Colonels, for five months in 1969 and for five months and then seven more months in 1972, respectively for the *Rebetic Songs* anthology (1968), for his erotic long-poem *Body* (first written in 1969), and for *Kaliarda* (1971), his lexicon of Greek homosexual slang—the first dictionary of homosexual slang to be published anywhere. On 23 October 1980, Petropoulos was sentenced *in absentia* to eighteen months in prison and a large fine for *The Good Thief's Manual*.

IV

On 26 August 1980, Petropoulos sent me this message in French, telling me that he is in Paris and waiting for a phone call from me. He is using what he called "phonetics":

TZON,

ZE SUY A PARI.
  Z' ATAN EN COU-DE-FYL!

YIA-XARA
  YLYAS
  [de N° 34, MOUFTAR]

[AKH! PARDON POUR LE
  PHONETIKS]

V

A new (undated) letter written in Greek and probably posted in early October, 1980, mentions that he will be in Paris between the 16th and the 20th of October. And so on. I would call him from the phone booth on the boulevard Vincent-Auriol or—if it had been vandalized—from another one located near the Galaxie shopping center on the place d'Italie. It was at this time that Françoise and I finally had a telephone line installed in our apartment and rented our first telephone, a cream-colored one with an extra earphone on a cord. These extra earphones (or ear receivers) were typical of French telephones back then and enabled a second person to eavesdrop, sometimes dangerously, on a conversation. After that date, Petropoulos no longer mailed brief notes about upcoming appointments, which is not to say that he stopped sending me other messages, documents, and especially photocopies of articles by or about him.

VI

During one of these first work sessions, I asked him about a strange word in a rebetic song, the genre of underworld song whose lyrics he had compiled in his anthology. He hopped up, held a felt pen out to me and with a gesture showed me that it was a knife. Opening his mouth, he passed the pen slowly back and forth across his tongue. "The tough guy has just stabbed someone," he related. "Now, according to an old underworld custom, he's going to lick the blood off his knife. That's what your word means."

Here is the overall picture, as depicted in one of the countless fascinating short texts of the *Rebetic Songs* anthology:

> The Greeks are a rather vindictive people. But revenge became a well-established institution only on the islands of Crete and Mani. On Mani, revenge or feuding was a family affair defined by a series of severe, inflexible rules. There it was believed that a murdered man's blood howled for revenge. On Mani, murderers could circulate freely as long as they were accompanied by a nonpartisan chaperone (*ksevgaltis*). This was because taking revenge by ambush (*khosia*) was considered to be an ignoble act. The rival clans often made truces (*treva*) or mutually forgave each other (*psykhiko*). As for the rest of Greece, revenge, at least as it is evoked in demotic songs, is a personal affair. And with only one sentence levied: murder. This is not the case, however, in rebetic songs. A *rebetis* or *mangas* (the underworld hoodlum) will more typically take law into his own hands during tempestuous love affairs. He will threaten to cut his lover's hair off, to abandon her, to go away or, allusively, even to kill her. *"Sighoura tha pame, aphou phtasame os eki, / esy sto khoma ki egho sti phylaki"* ("Sure, we'll be a-goin', since we've come this far, / you into the ground an' me behind bars"). Beatings rarely appear in rebetic songs. But beatings are mentioned in several songs evoking the police knocking the hell out of some poor thief. Murders are also mentioned. *"Mana mou me skotosane / dyo makhairis mou dosane"* ("Oh, ma, they've killed me / stabbed me twice") —one example of several such lines. The murderer's weapon is usually a knife. Noteworthy is the underworld custom of "eating" or "drinking" the victim's blood, whence the colloquial expression: *"Tha sou pio to aima"* ("I'll drink your blood"). This occurs immediately after the stabbing. The murderer simply licks the bloody blade of his knife clean.

VII

Petropoulos always explained words and expressions by acting them out or making small drawings. Most of these drawings were ephemeral aids, sketched quickly on a piece of scratch paper, then wadded up and thrown into the wastepaper basket near his desk. I simultaneously took notes on my translation manuscript, sometimes finding the appropriate English word immediately or at least having gained enough understanding to find it later, at home. Petropoulos strictly distinguished between these disposable drawings and those he made to illustrate his books. He gave me a few originals of the latter genre of drawings, notably a series depicting the typical Jewish chests that he had seen while growing up in Thessaloniki. One of the drawings bears a dedication to Françoise. We framed the drawing, and it hung in the kitchen of our apartment in Paris. After we moved to Angers in July, 1987, it hung in the entryway of two successive apartments, then a house. Now it hangs on the wall of my study upstairs, beneath a painting-collage by Louis Calaferte and above an engraving depicting the Protestant village of Dormillouse, in the Hautes-Alpes. By the way, did Petropoulos ever read Calaferte's erotic novel, *Septentrion*, or his sequence of short erotic texts, *The Way It Works with Women*?

As for the quick translation-drawings, I still have a few that I took back to the apartment when I was unable to find an immediate equivalent for the Greek word. I would keep the drawing nearby when I was poring through dictionaries. Here are examples:

— a drawing of the side of a roofed house, with an arrow pointing to the *khatilia*, the "rafters."

— a drawing of a minaret, as well as the rampart of a castle or tower, with the *mazgali* ("loopholes") specified.

—one twelve-page and two ten-page stapled booklets that Petropoulos prepared in advance for one of our work sessions on

Wooden Doors Iron Doors in Greece: he had anticipated all sorts of translation problems by making dozens of little drawings and noting the specific terms. Among these are sketches of an archway with three terms for the "keystone" noted; a *sefer-tasi*, a sort of porringer carrier, with a note reminding me to eliminate the dot over the "i" when I reproduce the Turkish etymology (and I forgot to do so on the proofs); several kinds of locks and doorknobs or handles; all sorts of castle features; a Byzantine chapel with a front entrance for men and a side entrance for women; various shoes, sandals, and slippers; a four-story house with a *mesopatoma* ("mezzanine"); two pigs with a triangular wooden structure around their necks; and, last but not least, knuckles rapping on a door, accompanied by the caption *"tak-tak!"*

— a note with a drawing, on which Petropoulos inquires whether I have understood what the word *bagdhati* means. (It is a construction method whereby walls are formed by nailing thin wooden strips to both the inside and outside of wall beams.) This note was mailed.

— a page listing my questions about the words *khaghiati* ("open space under a roof"), *sakhnisi* ("corbelled or enclosed balcony"), and other technical terms, with Petropoulos's drawings in the margins. On one of the sketches, he has taken the time to pen in curlicues representing smoke rising from a chimney; on another, he specifies the "ears" of "balconies with ears" (*balkonia me aphtia*).

— two well-sketched balconies, one a *tzelouzia*, the other a classical balcony with a "railing" (*kighklidha*) and "console" (*phourousi*). On the same page are drawings of an "ax" (*aksina*), a "poughshare" (*yni*), a "hammer" (*sphyri*), a "trivet" (*pyrostia*), a "steelyard" for weighing objects (*kantari*), a "balance" (*palantza*), a "pair of scales" (*zygharia*). On the second page of these notes, Petropoulos again sketches a balcony railing and specifies the words *pritsinia* and *kolara* (respectively "rivet" and "weldment"). He must have mailed these two stapled pages to me, for at the bottom of the second page is a question: "John, do you have any more doubts?"

— similarly, a list of Petropoulos's rules (that differed from the official international system used by scholars) for transliterating these three Greek letters: χ = kh, δ = dh, γ = gh.

VIII

One of Petropoulos's pet peeves was the French word *périple*; another was *orthographe*, which means "spelling." More than once, he gave a Frenchman (or woman) an etymology lesson, in more or less this tone of voice:

"You French don't know anything about the Greek language. Take 'orthographe.' You think the word means 'spelling.' In fact, 'orthographe" should mean 'speller', as it comes from our word 'orthographos': a person who 'writes straight.' You should say 'orthographie' for 'spelling'. Another error is 'périple.' The roots of this word clearly indicate that the trip in question is made in the water, in a boat. You cannot take an inland 'périple'! These are just two examples of the thousands of errors you make when you borrow words from our language."

As to modern demotic Greek spelling, which was still not standardized in the 1980s, he had several original (and stubborn) ideas about how it should be done, especially when it came to slang words. Petropoulos's departures from common orthographic practice were based on his etymological research and his extremely fine ear for pronunciation. On manuscripts prepared for publishers and printers, he would note that certain words needed to be spelled accordingly, little matter if they seemed misspelled. I remember articles published in Dimitris Yiakoumakis's review, *Tomes*, and there were others brought out in other magazines, accompanied by a disclaimer: "The editor has respected the author's spelling."

Yiakoumakis, the former Naval cultural attaché at the Greek Embassy in Paris, had participated in the heroic Naval Mutiny against the Junta and was at the time a high-ranking official in the Defense

Department. He had taken over Dimitris Doukaris's review, *Tomes*, and published it on the side. He was one of Petropoulos's consistent supporters, and notably issued *Courtyards in Greece* at his small press, Phorkys. Because he also published some of my own articles and stories in his review, I corresponded with him regularly. Françoise and I met him once, at his Athens apartment on Mithymnis Street. (I remember a large and magnificent painting by Fassianos that hung in the parlor.) Yiakoumakis took us to an excellent taverna that evening. At one in the morning, he broke off our conversation about literature, recalling that he needed to report to the Defense Minister early the next morning. "There's tension again in the Aegean," he explained. Petropoulos had friends and supporters from all walks of life, even as he had enemies from all walks of life.

IX

Of his generation, few knew more about the Greek language. He was prouder of this knowledge than of his other accomplishments. One day he declared that the poet and 1979 Nobel laureate Odysseus Elytis was "one of the five people in Greece who know Greek," the implication being that he was included in the remaining group of four (and perhaps *was* the remaining group of four—as I teased him). Petropoulos wrote the first study of Elytis's work in his *Elytis Moralis Tsaroukhis* (1966). Yiannis Moralis and Yiannis Tsaroukhis, whose paintings Petropoulos also admired and analyzed, were well-known Greek artists.

For Petropoulos, words were living, tangible, evolving, multidimensional entities. He made me aware of this fact in countless ways, most of all by pronouncing the same Greek word several times in a row, each time differently according to the context that would be established by a given social group or period of time. These various pronunciations of the same word were naturally accompanied by appropriate gestures, similarly associated with social groups and historical periods. Petropoulos loved etymologies. He ever wanted to get back to that first solid sense. For a man who often thought about death, who had written a long poem entitled *Suicide* (1973) with the line "Death, you take what you cannot give me" and had added in parentheses "(O long inner dialogue with the frightful end)," who would focus on death before returning with rage to the chores of observing and writing, and who called himself a "thanatologos," the roots of a word implied roots in Being. His folkloristic search for and study of tangible objects, and his devastating stylistic factuality, participated in the same quest for roots in Being. Yet Being, if he truly imagined it so, was ever perched on the brink of nothingness, extinction, disappearance. On a photocopy of his article on mud and shoe scrapers (*Ikhneftis*, May-June 1986), which eight years later had characteristically grown, along with other articles, into an entire book (*Iron. Mud. Canes.*, 1994), he noted the date "26 June 1986" and added in parentheses: "(= 58 years...)."

X

Saturday, February 6th.
It's cold.
But even colder is the silent telephone.
At sixty-five, everything is melancholy.
At sixty-five, everything is shit.

(From *After*)

The posthumously published *After* (2004) is one of his three collections —*Never and Nothing* (1993) and *In Berlin: Notebook 1983-1984* (1987) are the other two—that often comprise Martial-like short verse and epigrams. Greek and Latin scholars: read these poems and compare them to those by Martial and some of the Greek epigrammatists! In fact, Petropoulos translated into Modern Greek twelve "little songs" from the *Palatine Anthology* for a volume illustrated by Alekos Fassianos in 1980. These songs were put to music and recorded by Notis Mavroudis in 1985.

XI

Whenever I told Petropoulos about a foreign novelist or poet with whose work he was unfamiliar, he always demanded descriptions of the man's style—of his "language," as he put it. When I told him that I was writing stories about my childhood in Des Moines, he asked: "And the language?" He was not inquiring whether I was writing my stories in English or French, but rather about the stylistic perspectives that I had adopted. As a prose writer, he wrote clear, hard-hitting, sometimes savagely ironic sentences. As a reader, he liked Greek poets and prose writers with complex diction: Elytis, as well as Andreas Embirikos and, of course, his own mentor, Nikos Gabriel Pentzikis, about whom he wrote the first book (*Nikos Gabriel Pentzikis*, 1958) published anywhere; moreover, it was the first literary study in Greece to use statistics. And he admired the moving and stylistically refined stories written by his close friend, Elias Papadimitrakopoulos.

XII

> Also gone my cherished mentor,
> Pentzikis, who never managed
> to convert me.
> Pentzikis has died—
> a great Greek mind
> who was disgusted by his imitators.
> When my mentor died
> those rats of Athens
> who hated him treacherously
> listened to the news in silence.
> Go to hell, worthless bastards!

(from *After*)

XIII

We spoke in Greek, we spoke in French. Sometimes we misunderstood each other.

One day, Petropoulos called and I understood that he wanted me to drop by and see him on my way to the language school, located on the boulevard Saint-Michel, at which I was then teaching English. I replied with something like "All right, we can see each other right now." I put on my jacket and left the apartment, deciding to walk to the rue Mouffetard, an itinerary (rue Albert-Bayet—place d'Italie—avenue des Gobelins—rue Mouffetard) that I took nearly every day. (I think now of the tiny haberdasher's, on the avenue des Gobelins, at which I bought a black hat with a large brim...)

When I arrived at 34, rue Mouffetard, and rang the buzzer, I discovered that no one was home. I waited outside the building entrance, thinking that Petropoulos had run a quick errand: to the post office, surely, as he was wont to do.

As it turned out, he had taken a taxi to the place d'Italie, because he had actually said that he was going to drop by our apartment—which he rarely did.

As I was waiting in the rue Mouffetard and was about to leave a note on the door and walk on to the language school, I saw him coming up the rue Mouffetard.

"Why weren't you at home?" he asked.

"Why weren't you at home?" I replied.

We shook hands.

XIV

The phone rang at eleven o'clock at night, waking us. It was Petropoulos calling from La Vieille Grille nightclub. A group of Greek musicians, led by the bouzouki player Nikolas Syros, was playing and singing rebetic songs "à l'ancienne," Petropoulos specified. "Come immediately!" he ordered when I hesitated.

Françoise had to teach the next day, so she went back to sleep. I of course could not refuse. In addition, I had never heard rebetic music played live, and I had begun to translate the lyrics of rebetic songs for a new and enlarged English-language anthology that Petropoulos hoped to publish in Greece. In 1975, in Athens, he had already published Katherine Butterworth and Sara Schneider's versions of fifty songs, *Rebetika: Songs from the Old Greek Underworld*. My anthology, which was to offer new versions of the fifty songs comprised in their book, plus add one hundred fifty more lyrics from the over one thousand four hundred songs included in the fourth edition of Petropoulos's anthology, was eventually published in 1992 by the London-based, now-defunct, Alcyon Art Editions run by Dimitris Sabatakakis.

So I dressed, put on a tie, then headed for the métro station at the place d'Italie, which was just three stops from the place Monge, near which La Vieille Grille is located. I did not wait long on the platform. After a quick ride, I arrived at the nightclub in short time.

I entered the dark smoky club and found Petropoulos and Mary Koukoules sitting at a small round table with the three musicians, who were taking a break. We shook hands, uttered greetings in Greek. There were not many customers, just couples or groups of friends sitting at five or six other tables. Almost as soon as I sat down, the owner came over, shook my hand, too, and asked what I would like to drink. I must have ordered a *ballon* of red wine, as was my habit back then.

When the musicians began playing again, I noticed Petropoulos singing along softly, murmuring the lyrics. I glanced at him only once, though. It seemed to me that I should not invade his quiet melancholy and ask him about the songs. Many were sung during the next hour or so, until the musicians decided to call it quits. The owner decided to close down as well; he turned on the overhead lights. I reached for my coat, "a Royal Air Force pilot's jacket," as Petropoulos had specified in great digressive detail one afternoon, at his apartment, when I had showed up wearing it. As on so many other subjects, Petropoulos was a walking encyclopedia on details from the Second World War. These details were not only book-learned, but also and especially eyewitnessed, experienced. Petropoulos, his brother Soulis, and his mother had first fled from, then suffered in, Thessaloniki during the war; beginning in 1943, the writer had participated in the United Panhellenic Organization of Youth (E.P.O.N.) and had worked in the underground movement. His father, who was also a member of the Greek Resistance, had first fled to Albania and then, in 1944, disappeared, probably murdered; but the corpse was never found and, although Petropoulos later had a few leads and hypotheses, he was unable to elucidate the mysterious circumstances under which his father, aged forty, had vanished forever from his life.

It was only at this point, after the concert was over, that Nikolas Syros explained to the owner of La Vieille Grille who Petropoulos was: not only a famous Greek writer, but specifically *the* specialist of rebetic music. The owner, who was a gregarious, jolly chap sporting a beard, asked Petropoulos if he could say a few words about rebetic music in front of the customers. Chuckling, and very politely, Petropoulos refused. "C'est fini tout ça," he added. The owner did not really understand the refusal, all the more so because the atmosphere in his club was friendly and informal. As for myself, I perceived for the first time that Petropoulos could be prone to secret moments of sadness and, moreover, was sometimes shy at heart.

XV

Before first-class cars were eliminated from the Paris métro system by the Socialist government in 1982, Petropoulos always rode in them, never in the second-class cars. He would buy a *carnet* of ten first-class tickets. I don't remember ever seeing him using a monthly first-class pass. Whenever we took the métro together, he gave me a first-class ticket because I had a second-class monthly pass; if my pass were checked by a ticket controller and I were in a first-class car, I would have to pay a fine. In the underground corridors of the métro, Petropoulos often bent down and gave a coin to beggars. He rode in first-class cars not out of snobbery, but rather because he would stand a better chance, if he had to walk by a policeman making a routine identity check, of not being stopped and asked for his foreign resident's permit. After six or seven years in France, Petropoulos no longer had a *carte de séjour* (the French equivalent of a Green Card), and this was one of his constant worries.

I took a bus with Petropoulos only once. It was on the bus line No. 62, which ran down the rue de Tolbiac. We got off near the Lycée Claude-Monet, reached the avenue Edison, stopped at No. 42, paid a visit to Alekos Fassianos. (The avenue Edison runs into the rue Albert-Bayet, the street on which Françoise and I lived; we saw the artist rather often, and a few times he came up to our apartment on the sixth floor to sample one of Françoise's herb teas.) After Petropoulos and I had entered Fassianos's small apartment and while we were standing amidst large luminous canvases in progress, Fassianos looked at Petropoulos and stated ironically: "Someone has been giving me anonymous phone calls." Petropoulos answered devilishly, smothering a laugh: "Oh really?"

Above all, Petropoulos preferred taxis. This likewise had to do with his fear of falling prey to a routine identity check. In preferring taxis, he also resembled many well-off Parisians, yet his use of taxis went beyond practical and administrative considerations.

One day, we were returning by taxi to the rue Mouffetard apartment from the Mérat brothers' printing shop at which all his bibliophilic projects were carried out. (The shop was located at 21, rue du Vieux-Colombier, at the back of the same building that houses the theater in which Antonin Artaud gave his famous lecture on 13 January 1947.) Petropoulos got into a discussion with the driver about the man's job. Petropoulos wanted to know everything: the work hours, the wages, the percentages, the tips, the taxes, the anecdotes. He acquired an insider's knowledge of all sorts of trades in this way. He always tipped taxi drivers generously. And he was delighted whenever the taxi driver turned out to be a true Parisian *mec* with a sinister, hoarse, mocking, tough-guy accent—the *gouaille* that has now almost completely disappeared.

In *The Underworld and Shadow Theater* (1978), Petropoulos reports: "On 16 September 1972, accompanied by the Modern Greek specialist Stathis Gauntlett, I went to Plaka, to the house of Panayiotis Mikhopoulos, and began to ask him minute questions about the tough guys (*koutsavakides*) who appeared in shadow theater. (...) On 20 August 1973, I went up to Maroussi, to the home of Evghenios Spatharis, a Karagiozis player... We began to speak about the relationship between shadow theater, the underworld, and rebetic songs..." In *Turkish Coffee in Greece* (1979), he mentions that his cellmate in the New Prison of Thessaloniki was a Gypsy named Niko M. who, on 31 August 1969, told his fortune by reading the dregs at the bottom and along the sides of his coffee cup. Petropoulos quotes the at once ominous and auspicious verdict—one part of which is "a Feminine Face will be sending you definite Words in a sealed Letter"—and describes the technique in detail (for he, too, could tell fortunes in this way). He was constantly seeking out such people.

XVI

He never passed the Greek driving test, and thus had no driver's license, but he was an indefatigable walker. "An automobile can bring on the death of a folklorist," he would say. "A folklorist has to be out in the street, walking slowly, observing, taking in everything, every last nook and cranny." Taking a stroll with Petropoulos implied an intensive course in observation. Subtle architectural details, odd shop windows, sundry objects, vehicles and pedestrians (especially women). Looking closely but also obliquely at things animated all his folkloristic research and writing. And his kind of looking, as transcribed in his books, is contagious. Merely leafing through his albums, let alone perusing his writings, enables one to see Greece anew. "Vision means ideal possession," he writes in *Body*.

XVII

Françoise and I had invited Elias Petropoulos, Mary Koukoules, and Katharine Butterworth (who was visiting Paris) for a noon lunch. Butterworth was a close American friend of Petropoulos's who lived in Athens. At the time, she owned and ran Study in Greece, a study-abroad program for American students interested in modern Greece. It was the first such program to give importance to contemporary Greece and especially to the Modern Greek language. She had also co-translated the aforementioned first English-language anthology of rebetic songs and, after Petropoulos's emigration to France in 1975, she continued to help him in many ways.

Noon was much too early, as it turned out, for they all had gone to bed very late the night before. (We should have known better: Elias and Mary often went to bed late, after attending a gallery opening or watching a film.) In addition, we had no proper dining room; our living room was rather small, had a couch and a wicker armchair, and was otherwise crowded with plants, books, and Françoise's long desk; we ate in the kitchen. The kitchen faced south through a large bay window and the kitchen table was squeezed in between more plants, a radiator and the stove. That day, it was very hot. Beads of sweat appeared on Petropoulos's forehead.

We had prepared *osso buco* and intended to cook up some tagliatelle. Françoise dropped the nest-like clusters of tagliatelle into a pot of boiling water, but when she had finished she saw that there was not enough water. She filled another pot with hot water from the tap, then started pouring the extra water into the pot in which the tagliatelle were cooking. Watching all this intently, Petropoulos started shouting: "Stop, Françoise! Stop! C'est une catastrophe! You never add water to pasta that is cooking!"

The pasta turned out perfect. Petropoulos had three servings.

XVIII

We also, naturally, had pasta with him when Wayne Dynes was in town for a few days in late April, 1986. Dynes was the jovial and erudite professor of art history at Hunter College who published *Gay Books Bulletin* (later renamed *The Cabirion*), a scholarly review which was devoted to Gay studies and in which I had published two articles about Petropoulos's *Kaliarda*. That evening, Petropoulos showed up with an enormous bouquet of roses for Françoise and two bottles of champagne, though he himself never drank alcoholic beverages.

This evening occurred a few days after the explosion (on the 26th) of the nuclear reactor at Chernobyl. On the day following the meal, or perhaps on the day after that, Wayne, Françoise, and I strolled in Luxembourg Gardens during the afternoon, then sat on a bench for a while near the sailboat pond. As we later learned, it was one of those days when an unusual east wind was pushing radioactive clouds from Ukraine over France, a meteorological phenomenon that was being denied daily by an eminent physics professor, an expert in nuclear catastrophes, who had been solicited by the French government to explain the situation on radio and television. This kind of professorial subservience absolutely infuriated, but did not surprise, Elias Petropoulos.

XVIX

He loved pasta. He could be a connoisseur of fine foods. Once, quite late in the evening, he took Françoise and me to an Armenian restaurant near the country home in Coye-la-Forêt. Françoise and I had actually already eaten a salad and a pizza in Paris before taking the train to Coye-la-Forêt from the Gare du Nord, not having understood that Petropoulos was expecting us for dinner as well. (This may well have been another of those instances when, talking on the phone, he and I misunderstood each other slightly but significantly.) Of course, we could not tell him that we had already eaten when, as we got off the train, he told us that a dinner reservation awaited us. Luckily, though there were few customers in the restaurant, the service was slow, enabling us to build up our appetites again. When the time to order finally came, Petropoulos took over. He knew so much more than the Armenian waiter about the Armenian culinary arts, that the old chef and proprietor had to be called out of the kitchen to confirm that what Elias was requesting could be made. The old man knew Elias well. The two of them had become friends and occasionally played backgammon together. Telling us that we had been invited by a true connoisseur, he served us up rare, complicated, savory dishes.

XX

Above all, Petropoulos loved pastries. Sometimes, when we had finished working at the Mérat brothers' printing shop, he would say that he was hungry. Leaving the rue du Vieux-Colombier, we would head for the Sèvres-Babylone métro station, near which was a bakery and pastry shop that also had a few tables. We would enter, stand in line, then Petropoulos would order two chocolate éclairs for each of us. We would both have a large cup of hot chocolate as well. This was typical.

XXI

Sometimes, when I dropped by the rue Mouffetard apartment to work with Petropoulos in the late afternoon, I brought two chocolate- or coffee-flavored cream puffs—*religieuses* or "nuns," a pastry name that delighted him. Back then in French bakeries, the young woman working behind the counter would first take an appropriately sized sheet of gift-wrap paper and place it underneath a small piece of white cardboard; then she would arrange the pastries on the cardboard, finally folding up the paper around the pastries so that a four-sided pyramid was formed. If the folding was done carefully, only a little of the whipped cream on the cream puffs would be touched by the paper. The last step was to close up this paper pyramid, at the pinnacle, by tying a thin, usually blue, ribbon in such a way that the customer could carry the pastries home by slipping the knot around his index finger. Petropoulos untied such packages very carefully, with all his folklorist's admiration for this dying technique. (His books are full of technical descriptions; he loved explaining methods in step-by-step fashion.) Going to the kitchen, he would prepare some "European coffee." At least for me, he never made Greek coffee, which he called "Turkish coffee," anyway.

XXII

By telling these anecdotes about Petropoulos and eating, I do not wish to give the impression that he was obsessed by food. He adored hearty food, but it was ever associated in his mind with folklore, nationality, ethnicity, sociology, population migration, aesthetics, and the changing world. He often explained recipes and cooking techniques because of their folkloric interest. Above all, food was connected in his mind with language. In *Turkish Coffee in Greece*, the reader not only learns how to make and serve a good Turkish coffee, but also forty-six different ways to order it, and ways to insult the coffee maker if it is not up to his standards:

> Weak coffee is called "water-broth" (*nerozoumi*) or "water-gruel" (*neroproutsi*), whereas a flubbed coffee is termed "black-broth"

(*mavrozoumi*). For the same disaster, the word "burbling-water" (*nerobourbouli*) may be used. "Burbling-water" is also employed to characterize thin, tasteless soups. When a Greek wants to say that his coffee is too bitter, he exclaims: "Poison!" On the other hand, when his coffee is too sweet, he will express his disgust with a "Pffff! Sherbet!" In prison, "plain coffee" is called "rowdy-dowdy" (*daidikos*). Some coffee drinkers will insist that their coffees be "settled" before they are served. With such eccentricities, we have already broached the legendary folklore of the coffee fiend's finicky whims.

The coffee fiend usually drinks extremely strong coffee. The coffee fiend wants his coffee in a thick cup, which will keep it warm yet at the same time not burn his lips. Before drinking his coffee, the coffee fiend will drink down a glass of cold water in one gulp. This not only washes the phlegm down his throat (which common folks mistakingly call the "larynx"), but also rinses his stomach so that the flavor of the coffee may be wholly appreciated. The slang expression "five puffs and a long sucking sip!" (*pente physa kai mia roufa!*) shows how underworld hoodlums used to drink their scalding hot coffees. Another proverbial expression ("sip an' let'er come," *roufa ki erkhetai*) states, on the other hand, that a first sip of coffee is sometimes all that is needed to blow a fart. It is to be noted, however, that to fart in prison while someone is drinking his Turkish coffee is considered to be a deadly insult (with unforeseeable consequences). The coffee fiend usually sighs deeply ("...ahhh!") after his first sip, and then immediately lights up a cigarette. (...)

Every coffee fiend has his own personal way of drinking his coffee. If the thick cup has a little crack in it, the coffee is sent back. Some coffee fiends insist that their coffees be brought to them at once. If the waiter tarries, the coffee fiend begins to grumble: "What's going on with that coffee?...What's the snag?" Other coffee fiends will wait for a while before ordering their coffees (but it is not known why). Most coffee fiends sip their coffees slowly, delicately, serenely, voluptuously, soberly, or thoughtfully—to gladden their hearts.

Petropoulos ever skillfully inserts vivid sociological—or rather, "laographic"—remarks into objective, yet nonetheless often humorous, descriptions:

The way a coffeehouse customer sits reveals his social origin. Roughnecks from tough neighborhoods cross their left leg over or under their right one. Whether over or under, the left leg is kept in a horizontal position, with the left ankle touching the right thigh, just behind the right knee. This is the typical Turkish way of crossing legs. Turkish rowdies crossed their legs this way, leaving their left *katsari* (a slipper-like shoe, either heelless or with the back of the heel, the counter, broken and tucked in under the foot) on the floor and balancing a cup of coffee between their ankle and their heel. This custom was adopted by the Greek underworld. In prison I often observed old convicts knitting while keeping their coffee cups poised on their foot in this manner. (...)

For parties, little desserts designed to accompany coffee came in great varieties: liqueurs, sherbets, jams, cookies. Sherbets were made from several kinds of fruit (e.g., apricots, strawberries, blackberries) and served frozen. Another refreshing sherbet, typically Peloponnesian, was made with currants soaked in rose water. *Bozas* (from Turkish *boza*) was a sweet-and-sour decoction of ground barley. There were sweet wines with chunks of fruit in them. There was orgeat. The range of sweet jams that could accompany a cup of coffee was endless. *Triantaphyllo*, rose jam, is considered to be one of the finest jams. It is made in Chios; also on Mount Athos. The Chios islanders used to make excellent jams out of lemon blossoms, pistachio nuts, and naranjillas. In Thessaloniki, the favorite dessert used to be that fantastic *dolma*, made from grated pumpkin. Anatolians loved sweet fragrances: coffee flavored with jasmine blossoms, sherbet made with lemons or violets.

These little desserts were prepared for visitors by housewives or servants. The housewife would arrive with the platter and set it down in front of the hapless visitor—hapless because the visitor would immediately have to:

1) eat a spoonful of the jam, then leave his spoon inside the glass of water (the spoon is never put back into the jar because the remaining jam will candy);

2) drink the water, trying not to choke, while repeating several sober benedictions ("May you live long. . . And may the new year bring you a son...And may you live a hundred years...");

3) take the cup of coffee in hand, whereupon the housewife usually scurried away at last.

The ritual described above is a relatively simple one. In a nobleman's house, there was a much more complicated ritual through which visitors had to go, even if they were relatives of the family. Dimitris Kabourghlou, the renowned specialist of the history of Old Athens, writes that as soon as the master of the house awoke, the maid "would bring the *magiouni* (a sweet jam made of honey, pine nuts, and naranjillas) and then his coffee." When the French voyageur Antoine-Laurent Castellan reached the house of a Navarino nobleman, he was bathed, sprinkled with orange blossom cologne, served coffee and fragrant desserts, then sherbet, and finally a chibouk. If the guest was a friend of the head of the family, the housewife would serve the coffee, then disappear. The coffee would be made in the kitchen or over the fire in the fireplace. The cups were set on the sofa or on one of those many-cornered small tables inlaid with pearls and fine wires. Sometimes the coffee was made over a brazier, one of those round, copper braziers with circular trays around them for the *briki* [Turkish coffee pot], the coffee box, and cups. In his story "Rodina akroghiala" (1907), Alexandros Papadiamantis mentions how convenient it was "to make coffee over an alcohol burner." Alcohol burners, however, were often the cause of fires. Guests who belched dramatically at coffee time especially flattered their host. Farting was strictly forbidden, but not spitting. Clearing the throat ostentatiously after spitting was considered a sign of nobility and authority until the beginning of this century.

XXIII

Next door to the coffeehouse is the hash den and, unsurprisingly, this major locus of folklore also fascinated Petropoulos. He was an expert on the history, use, and social significance of hashish. He expatiates on the subject in *Saint Hashish* (1991), as well as in several studies of "Hashish Rebetic Songs". Here is an excerpt from one of these latter short texts, written by this folklorist who, as he claimed, never once smoked hashish:

There are hashish drinkers, hashish eaters, and hashish smokers. This is because hashish can be put in coffee, mixed into an electuary, or smoked in cigarettes or in a nargileh. Raw hashish powder is stirred into coffee. In electuaries, the hashish is mixed with honey, dry figs, and nutmeg. There are two techniques for smoking hashish in cigarettes: the *sphina* ("spike") and the *tsigharliki* ("reefer"). The "spike" is the easiest: with a match, the hashish smoker carefully makes a tiny hole in the cigarette and then stuffs a "spike" of hashish into it. The dose is enough for one or two people. A reefer is rolled into a cylindrical shape with two cigarette papers filled with both tobacco and tiny bits of hashish. The reefer's mouthpiece or "clip," which is made out of a small piece of cardboard, is called a *tzivana* (also: *tziovana* or *tzovana*) in Greek. The lighted end of the reefer is called the *fourfouri*.

Hashish users usually smoke reefers because they are easily and quickly rolled and take up no particular space. However, a nargileh, which in Greek is called *arghiles* (singular) as well as *mapas* ("blockhead"), *kalami* ("reed," "shinbone"), and *o Thanasis me to trypio to kephali* ("Thanassis with his head full of holes"), requires suitable surroundings and certain preparatory and precautionary measures. At first, nargilehs were smoked in *tekedhes* ("hash dens"; singular form: *tekes*), a Turkish term that originally referred to the mausoleums of pashas, dervishes, and generals, or to monasteries. When it became impossible to use nargilehs in public, they were smoked in caves, on deserted beaches on the outskirts of towns, and sometimes even in taxis. Inside the hash den, peace and quiet prevailed. Order reigned. As well as a specific, well-established, hierarchy. Veteran old-timers of the hash den were revered by the younger hashish users. The most important personages of the hash den were the *teketzis* ("hash-den owner") and the *tzaktsis*, the person responsible for packing the nargileh bowl with his thumb and serving them to customers. The rebetic song composer Tsitsanis, in a banned song, compares the hash den to a church. Since real nargilehs were expensive and difficult to hide, makeshift ones were fashioned out of small crocks, coconuts, clay boxes, tin cans, bottles, and even eggplants, pumpkins, melons, bread loaves, potatoes, or apples.

The passage then precisely describes nargilehs, nargileh smoking techniques, and getting high.

XXIV

Despite his love of homemade food and sweets, Petropoulos was not obese. However, at one point during the mid-1980s, he decided to lose a few pounds by not eating lunch. In front of me, he gripped his gut, showed me the fat by squeezing it, and declared that he would go on a diet by eating only in the evenings. Back then, for several weeks, he would work through the lunch hours, smoking cigarillos one after another.

Inversely, sometimes he stopped smoking for a few days or even a week or two. It is hard to say whether this stemmed from a secret fear of lung cancer. He had a theory, which he expressed publicly with characteristic vigor, that lung cancer was not necessarily caused by smoking. In this he was as stubborn as he was wrong, and in addition he knew perfectly well that my own mother, who had been a chain-smoker, had died from lung cancer in 1981. It was not possible to discuss the topic of smoking very long with him. In *After*, he observes: "I smoke like a chimney. / Thus I am free / while vanquishing my own cancer."

In *The Good Thief's Manual*, he remarks somewhat similarly in a passage about Junkies: "When Drug Addicts stop taking drugs and start eating well, they get their strength back quickly, without any extra care or therapy."

Of course, this same pigheadedness—his adamant refusal to accept and repeat commonplace truths—had enabled him to make deep insights into Greek folk culture. His attraction to overlooked or scorned objects revelatory of genuine folk culture stems from this incorrigible stubbornness. In *Lousology: the Book of Lice (*1979), for instance, he notes on the first page: "Lice and bedbugs have their own folklore. The hour has come for the louse to get its book." "Authenticity" and "truth" (by which he essentially meant rigorous factuality) were key goals for his research, which was carried on in fields as diverse as music, architecture, literature, history, sociology, folklore, and lexicology. His forte was an ability to discover and document previously ignored or disdained material and declare it to be an *objet d'étude*: homosexual slang, bedbugs, tattoos, door lintels, prison beadwork, birdcages, shadow theater, outhouses, coffeepots, condoms, desserts, kitchen sink design, old-fashioned locks, brothel furniture, grave lanterns, "etc. etc. etc." Petropoulos indeed liked to break off lists like these with three emphatic *et ceteras*—a habit that cropped up often in his books (especially *The Good Thief's Manual*) and that he associated, if I am not mistaken, with the Greek novelist Nikos Kachtitsis, whose writings he and Elias Papadimitrakopoulos had been the first to discover. (See their pioneering tribute, *Nikos Kachtitsis in Memoriam*, published in 1972.)

Petropoulos unceasingly and courageously pursued his vision of Greek culture, going to whatever extremes were necessary—and he relished extremes—to collect, document, and describe diverse manifestations of Greek folklore before it was too late, before the onslaught of industrialization, the apathy of the general population, and police and governmental oppression caused them to perish forever. From his albums to his slang dictionaries, from his books about criminality and prisons to his anthologies of underworld art forms, from his books and albums about his hometown of Thessaloniki to those devoted to sexuality and eroticism, his basic subject remained urban folklore in Greece. It is obvious that this appellation must not be understood in its narrow academic sense. Petropoulos preferred the Greek word *laographos* for "folklorist." Although he sometimes searched for other possibilities by groping with his hands in the air, he would ultimately shrug his shoulders and declare that no suitable French or English equivalent existed.

XXV

A final perspective on eating:

> All alone at home
> for the past two weeks,
> I have received few telephone calls.
> I empty out a can of mushrooms into the frying pan
> and heat them up
> without butter, without salt, without a sauce.
> I eat them, standing in front of the television set,
> while watching Blacks looting stores in Los Angeles.

The United States is rotting away slowly but surely.
How the devil to get rid of my melancholy!

(from *Never and Nothing*)

XXVI

Most of the topics that he examined now crop up in standard courses taught in American or European sociology, history, gender studies, gay studies, popular culture, and literature departments. But remember that Petropoulos was investigating such subjects by the early 1950s, and writing about them by the end of the same decade. He had an uncanny ability to grasp the essential facts and ideas of a text written in a language that he did not understand very well; that is, all foreign languages until he started learning French in 1975, at the age of forty-seven, becoming fluent in the language only in the early 1980s. I know that his knowledge of English grew during his work with me: I certainly noticed constant improvement, measurable by the increasing number of times he put his finger on mistakes! He long had little access to foreign research because of the lamentable state of Greek libraries. Because he was working alone, his accomplishments as a pioneer in several fields are astonishing.

"But Elias," I once chided him, "shouldn't you use footnotes now and then, or at least give more precise references for literary quotations? That would make it easier for scholars."

"No!" he thundered, "It's ugly stylistically!" "Footnotes would clutter up the text for the common reader, and scholars should know their field well enough to locate my quotations. I defy them all to find an error, a misquotation!"

Can any Greek academic folklorist or sociologist match Petropoulos in erudition, storytelling prowess, or, more appropriately, in both at once?

XXVII

For both brothel owners and the police, the choice of Angelakis Street as the location of a few brothels was a good one. Angelakis Street was a virtually deserted street that was found outside of the Old Salonica district. The street ran downhill from the top of the Avenue of the Army (*Sidrivani*) to *Skamnies*, "Mulberries," as the gardens and their mulberry trees were called in those days, before they were replaced by the YMCA building and its grounds. At first, Angelakis Street had a few houses on its western side; on its eastern side, there was nothing. After the Asia Minor Disaster, the extensive vacant lot alongside Angelakis Street (where the International Fair would be located in later years) was soon overrun with slums, constituting what was called the *Kato Aghias Photinas* neighborhood. This slum neighborhood was eventually razed during the dictatorship of Metaxas. At the time, the *Kato Aghias Photinas* neighborhood consisted of dilapidated shacks, common toilets, a common washhouse, and so on. These slums were, however, the privileged site of three prospering bawdyhouses. The setting up of these brothels did not bother anyone in the least; not even the Archbishop complained. Moreover, their favorable location suited customers, who were able to slip, sight unseen, into the houses. The only element of worry and potential risk came from curious tram passengers riding down the Avenue of the Army. For this reason, brothel customers in Angelakis Street would keep their backs to the trams, both when going down the street to the brothels and when leaving them. This was because the tram tracks on the Avenue of the Army crossed Angelakis Street diagonally.

No. 19, Angelakis Street, was a house with an upper storey. It had neither a lawn nor a garden, however. The front door of this particular brothel did not open out directly onto the street; instead, it opened out onto a sort of driveway that was roofed over by the upper storey. This driveway could be closed off with a second door, made of iron, which faced the street. No. 19, Angelakis Street, was thus secured by two outer doors. The driveway would be lit by a lamp at night.

As soon as the customer had passed through the first outer door, he would cross the narrow driveway, open the second outer door (this one made of wood), and enter the brothel parlor. A communal whorehouse without a parlor is unimaginable. In brothel parlors such as this one, one would always find chairs and sofas for the customers and prostitutes, one or two small tables with ashtrays, the *madam*'s desk, and a bulletin board with the girls' photos tacked up on it. Like prisons, barracks, hospitals, and monasteries, brothels have their own particular odor, which can be qualified as being neither pleasant nor unpleasant.

No. 19, Angelakis Street, had a parlor, three rooms, and a kitchen on its ground floor. On the upper floor, there was a second parlor, plus four more rooms and a bathroom. Seven rooms were thus available for seven "live-in" prostitutes. *Madams, bouncers,* and *housemaids* did not live in brothels. In the case of No. 19, Angelakis Street, the *madam* (none other than Dhédhes, a close friend of General Vardhoulakhis and godmother of Chief-of-Police Mouskhoudis) lived near the White Tower. The housemaid lived with her only son at No. 49, K. Melenikos Street. Every prostitute had a bed, a closet, a dresser, a table, and one or two chairs in her room. I remember that Lela (today an upstanding, respected citizen living in Patriarch Joachim Street) had a gramophone in her room. In rooms such as these, there were no radiators, but rather stove heaters. The proverbial washbowl, water pitcher, and bottle of potassium permanganate would be found on the dresser. Several rugs would cover the floor. The bed would always be a double bed and it would always be made. On the bed, one could see a small, well-stuffed, cushion. A prostitute worked and lived in her room, which, incidentally, was always kept spotlessly clean. Customers would never be allowed to sit in the upstairs parlor. It was in the downstairs parlor that the prostitutes would put on their show. (...)

Many whorehouse customers, after entering the parlor, would plop down on a sofa, with no intention whatsoever of picking out a girl. They did not run the risk of being thrown out of the place. At least half of the men sitting around in a brothel would have come for "non-sexual" reasons. Some men would go to a whorehouse to get out of the cold and warm up, others to take a bath or shower, and still others to while away the time. There were, however, *serious* customers who would remain in the parlor for at least a half hour before making their move. The *madam* was capable of picking such men out of the parlor crowd in a flash. This is why she would soon urge such customers on, with the courteous exhortation: *Ade, pandreveste* ("Hey, come on, marry her..."). The *madam* kept order in a dictatorial manner. Any troublesome or drunken customer would be chased off the premises.

Madams knew how to use their stern, harsh appearances to the utmost, not to mention their even sterner, harsher, tongues. The brothel *bouncer* was only rarely obliged to make an appearance and, even more rarely, to intervene (in a fistfight, for example). Brothels usually opened in the early evening and closed at midnight. The *bouncer* would lock the outer door and go home. Sometimes, an excited or excitable customer would beat on the door after midnight; but it was never opened. If the customer kept up his ruckus, one of the prostitutes would call the police. A few well-known expressions—*bourdello to kanat' edho mesa?* "What have you turned this place into? A brothel!" or *ti to perasate edho bourdello?* "What's this? A brothel with a wino inside!"—do not evoke the order and decency that always reigned in whorehouses... (from *The Brothel*)

XXVIII

Petropoulos reoriented contemporary Greek folklorists' concentration on obsolete or virtually nonexistent pastoral aspects of Greek folklore toward the city and town and, within towns, toward unusual, bristling, loci of folklore. As he states in his introduction to *Birdcages in Greece*:

Greek popular culture today is a set of habits and simple things—for example, underworld songs, plastic toys, flower pots on balconies, the curses you can hear everywhere, decorated automobiles, expressive gestures, words tossed to passing women by guys hanging out in the street—also birdcages with their gaudy singing birds—but Greek folklorists do not seem to care very much about the rich significance of reality.

Petropoulos went out into the streets and documented just that significance. His insistence on urban rather than on pastoral or rural folklore also had the effect, in numerous ways, of pointing out what we do not know or refuse to see, namely that not only ancient Greek temples, Byzantine basilicas, and tumbledown Frankish castles provide interest for architectural studies, but also simple doors, kiosks, balconies, windows, gravestones—"etc., etc., etc." This is not to say that he was unaware of village folkways and the architecture of simple village houses; on the contrary, numerous passages in his books show how closely he had studied non-urban folklore as well. In *Balconies in Greece*, for example, he describes the "balcony-outhouse" common to mountain villages:

> The *balcony-outhouse*, which took up all the space of a small balcony, was often enclosed with branches and ferns. A triangular hole enabling the excrement to fall into the courtyard below was found on the *balcony-outhouse* platform. *Balcony-outhouses* did not stink in the slightest since the pigs and hens in the courtyard would instantly gobble up any excrement falling from heaven....

In *Wooden Doors Iron Doors in Greece*, he similarly evokes how, in mountainous regions, "fences were sometimes made out of a row of Christ's thorn bushes (or holm or kermes oak)." He adds that this was to:

> keep hens, tortoises, pigs, goats, and other animals out of a vegetable patch that was much to their liking. These vegetable patch fences also had a sort of primitive gate made out of thin branches. Pigs were able to push the branches apart with their snouts and enter the garden. In order to prevent this from happening, peasants would put a triangular wooden frame around the necks of all the pigs in the area. But at least forty years have gone by, I daresay, since I have seen a pig with one of those frames around its neck…

Yet above all, Petropoulos's albums and books discuss or "eyewitness"—as he would also insist—the urban, popular, aspects of modern Greece, and notably the Turkish or Ottoman cultural influence on such aspects. This was another deep-rooted, intricate, historical phenomenon that most academic writers failed or refused to notice before Petropoulos showed them the way. In his album of old photographs and postcards, *Old Salonica* (1980), for example, after raking "chauvinist historians" over the coals in his introduction, Petropoulos portrays Salonica as a "multiethnic city from its very birth": not only Greek, but also Turkish, Armenian, Albanian, and especially Sephardic Jew. As he concludes, "a photograph shows what it shows; it is difficult to deny it." In *Ironwork in Greece*, he concludes his brief introduction with an even more striking remark: "Photography assassinates the author." In *The Underworld and Shadow Theater*, he analogously observes:

> Modern Greek historians still do not understand that history is also written in the tiny want ads of lonely hearts newspapers, and not just in battles or the list of prices on the stock market. Modern Greek historians, sociologists, philologists, and folklorists deeply disdain the trivial events of our more unimportant everyday routines, and refuse to study subject matter deriving from dime novels, vulgar customs, public hygiene, sexual idiosyncrasies, slum architecture, homosexual slang, types of insults, local food, etc. etc. etc.

Petropoulos liked to insist, half in jest, half in earnest, that Greek Americans were secretly disappointed when they traveled to Greece for the first time because "they had thought that we were all still wearing chitons!"

XXIX

His search for the truth about the genuine makeup of Modern Greek culture and folklore made him the most provocative cultural critic in his homeland. His quest was specifically motivated by an interest in Turkish culture, and in the cultural influence of Turkey on modern Greece, that was almost unique among the Greek intellectuals of his time. This interest in the cultural exchanges between Greece and Turkey comes up time and again in his books. *The Underworld and Shadow Theater*, for instance, traces this kind of folk theater back to its Turkish roots and examines its intimate relationship with the underworld. The same book also relates certain aspects of shadow theater to subjects such as public hygiene, a juxtaposition that once again invokes Turkish culture in a provocative, yet perfectly justifiable way:

> It is thought that no outhouses ever existed in Greece. Peasants used to ease nature in the farmyard. The hens and pigs would gobble up the excrement instantly. In the village of Kastraki (near the Meteores),

there was not a single outhouse, at least until 1952. Soap and running water belonged to realms of the imagination. Naturally, nothing more needs to be added here about the cleanliness of the genital organs and the rectum. The colloquial expression "he has ants in his ass and swallows in his ear" perfectly illustrates the situation.

Toilet paper began to be sold in urban grocery stores only toward the end of the 1950s. Until then, old newspapers were used by city dwellers. In villages, a peasant would wipe his ass with leaves, wild fruits, or stones. Nonetheless, there was always a simpleton who, urged on by friends, would wipe his ass with fig leaves: the results would be tragic.

The Turks lived alongside the Greeks. I do not really wish to point to their spotless hamams or bright-white turbans. I would simply like to recall the Turks' extremely well-known habit of washing after every defecation. Greeks considered this habit effeminate. Krystallis has his hero, Captain Kostantara, insult a Turk with the word "clean ass!" (*koloplymeno*).

Petropoulos's *Lousology* also comprises long illuminating passages about the public hygiene and personal cleanliness that derived from Turkish customs:

> The word *lousimo* (washing, bathing) mainly refers to the washing of the head. Most of the time, our Greek houses did not have bathrooms. Only the big houses of [Ottoman] *aghas* had water closets. These water closets (as well as a thousand other types of Turkish toilets) have not yet been studied by our ever-competent Greek architects and folklorists. That's the way it is. Mothers used to wash their little boys in a basin, that is until they had attained the age when "their balls got covered with hair" (*emalliazan t'arkhidhia tous*). In the old days, mothers could touch their sons' privates—such was their relationship. This is no longer the case. Let me only mention this problem, which would otherwise lead us deeply into psychoanalytical considerations. (...)
>
> Every city in Greece had Turkish bathhouses, called *hamams*. When the Turks left, the Greeks furiously destroyed the hamams. Yet the Turk is not hidden in mosques and hamams. The Turk lives on in

the hearts of Modern Greeks. The sooner we understand this fact, the freer we will be. (...)

Washing in the hamam proceeded in a rather strict fashion: you paid > you took three towels and a bar of soap > you went into a dressing room and undressed > you put the largest towel around your waist and put on a pair of special wooden sandals > you passed into the main hamam room > you spent a short time in the cold room, where there were also lavatories, so as to get accustomed to the suffocating atmosphere > you opened the door and went into the central hall > you entered the cabin of your choice and sat down near the water basin with its fountain > you washed, washed again, finishing with a good scrub > you returned to the cold room, where you took a nap for an hour or two > you woke up, ordered a cup of coffee, dressed, and quietly left the hamam.

The bathman (*loutraris*) or bathwoman (*loutrarisa*) was a scornful, shadowy professional. There is a pertinent insult concerning him: "I'll see you ending up as a bathman!" (*Pou na se idho khamamtsi!*). The bathman worked in the hamam fourteen hours per day. He came to work at dawn and left at sunset. Like the tripemaker's fire, the fire of the hamam never went out. The bathman strolled around the hamam wearing only a towel and wooden sandals. If you didn't want to wash yourself, you made a sign to him and received a priority number. The bathman worked in a little room with a low marble bench, exactly the size of a tombstone. The customer waiting in line would wet his hair and then lie down near the scalding hot *omphalos* in order to work up a sweat. When his turn came round, usually indicated by a gesture from the bathman, he would go into the little room and lie down on the marble bench. (...) Literally speaking, the cracks in the marble bench were filled with *spaghetti*—such were called the incrusted lines of dirt. (...).

In the old days, men and women went to the same hamams. Men washed early in the morning or late in the evening, women between noon and early evening. The *changing of the guard* was signaled when the hamam-owner rapped two goblets together. The bathmen would wake up the men as the bathwomen were coming in for the women. Little boys were allowed to come into the hamam with their mothers. Later, another solution was found for the problem of separating men and women. A wall about four meters high was built, dividing the central room and its *omphalos*. The adjoining rooms were consequently divided as well: men and women could bathe at the same time. The acoustics in hamams were amazing. Nastradine Hodja rightly complained that a hamam should be built *above* his minaret so that he could hear "Allah is One" better. Men remained quiet in hamams. From the women's side, however, could be heard shouting, screaming, loud laughing, children being bawled out, and even fighting. Men would listen to all this with resignation....

XXX

Always concerned about cleanliness, Petropoulos would wash his hands several times a day. When I arrived, he would ask me if I wanted to wash my hands before we started to work together. Often I went into the kitchen and did so. Then we would drink a cup of "European coffee."

XXXI

Petropoulos loved to dismantle something "typically Greek" (a word, habit, costume, gesture, kind of food—"etc. etc. etc.") by showing that it was Turkish in origin; or Slavic, Albanian, Bulgarian, Armenian, or Jewish. He was fascinated by all the national and ethnic groups that entered into the cultural mosaic of modern Greece. Almost all the Greek words—*briki* ("coffee pot"), *flitzani* ("cup"), *yedeki* ("water boiler"), *tabis* ("man who prepares the coffee"), and so on—associated with coffee and coffeehouses are Turkish in origin, as the etymologies in *Turkish Coffee in Greece* prove. The *Rebetic Songs* anthology is full of information about the Greeks and Turks of Turkey, for Petropoulos knew how strong was the influence, on this music, of the one and a half million Greek refugees who had flooded into Greece during the 1922 Asia Minor Disaster. In *The Underworld and Shadow Theater*, as well as in other books, he notes in passing: "The *fustanella* is considered to be the national costume of Greece and is thus worn by the Royal Guards as their official uniform. In fact, the *fustanella* was originally the national dress of Albania." He relished pointing out this contradiction whenever the topic of Greek nationalism or chauvinism was raised. He ended up devoting an entire book to the *fustanella* in 1993.

This at once harsh and humorous skepticism is fully deployed in a second book published in 1993, *National Bean Soup*. The list of Petropoulos's other books and articles which, in at least a few passages, fustigate nationalism would essentially mirror his entire bibliography. In the introductions to his photograph albums of "popular architecture"—*Ironwork in Greece, Balconies in Greece, Courtyards in Greece, Windows in Greece*, and *Wooden Doors Iron Doors in Greece*—he evokes the Ottoman origins of much of what is viewed as typically Greek architecture: the "Macedonian" house, the "Aegean" house, the low doors of Greek Orthodox monasteries, the various types of locks, and much more. Writing in *La Présence ottomane à Salonique* (another album of photos issued in 1980), Petropoulos outlines his own critical methodology, all the while criticizing that of academic researchers: "Greek historians search for documents relevant to their country's recent history in Paris, Venice, and London. Greek historians write books with titles like 'Greek History' when in fact they should be writing 'The History of Greece.' It is in the archives of Istanbul that the secrets about the recent history of Greece are found. In Greece, 'Turkology' is an unknown discipline. But no Greek, be he historian, folklorist, linguist or sociologist, can be competent in his field if he has not studied Turkology." Once he had arrived in Paris in 1975, and until about 1978, Petropoulos, accompanied by Mary Koukoules, attended seminars in Turkish studies at the École Pratique des Hautes Études. However, most of his knowledge came from his vast reading, from his friendships with Turkish writers, artists, and intellectuals, and from his gift for observation. He would ask countless questions once he had found a reliable informer. He was a ferocious autodidact.

XXXII

In the early part of his career, he took advantage of any friend's excursion out of town to borrow a camera and roam about the streets of towns and villages all over Greece. He managed to visit over a hundred sites in this way. He looked for and photographed birdcages, decorated automobiles, wrought ironwork, kiosks, doors, windows, graves, and all sorts of other revelatory folkloric objects. Often he was the only researcher interested in such objects at the time, despite the fact that, as he remarks in the introduction to *La Voiture grecque* and repeats often elsewhere, "in Greece, as in all underdeveloped countries, Western Civilization brusquely arrived during the period 1945-1975, destroying every manifestation of local folklore." While his friends were lying out on the beach or seeing more typical tourist sights, as he would tell me, he began compiling his extensive files, archives, and collections, which I saw and leafed through in his upstairs study in the Coye-la-Forêt country home. Most of these files, archives, and collections were eventually donated to the Gennadius Library in Athens. (Petropoulos's first donations began in 1974, before leaving the country for France, when he gave the library his rebetic song records and archives.) A few other documents, such as the photos reproduced in *La Présence ottomane à Salonique*, were given to the Bibliothèque Nationale in Paris. The University of Thessaloniki has about 1500 postcards from his collection. This kind of collecting was not without dangers. In his introduction to *The Graves of Greece* (1979), an album which consists of his own black-ink drawings on brown paper and which he considered to be his most beautiful book, he writes:

> In opposing my attempt to print the mortuary remembrances contained therein, the Greek government and Greek universities displayed an unbearable hostility. Let it suffice to say that I was arrested by the Greek police while I was sketching and photographing in the cemeteries of the island of Thassos, Amynteo, Khrysoupolis, Didymoteikho, Dhrama, Alexandroupolis, and the island of Samos.

In *Ironwork in Greece*, he reports, not without irony, that he was arrested "high up on the mountain of Hymettus" by the Navy military police as he was photographing examples of wrought ironwork such as balconies, railings, and shoe scrapers.

XXXIII

Generation after generation of folklorists and musicologists continued to research Greek demotic songs, and Petropoulos was also extremely knowledgeable about this kind of folk music, even if he characteristically tended to focus, not on the music per se, but rather on the taboo subjects that occasionally cropped up in the lyrics. In *The Brothel*, for example, he studies demotic-song lyrics containing the word *poustis*, which means "passive homosexual" in the pejorative sense of "fag" or "queer." He uses these lyrics to show that there is a "long history" behind "Anatolian pederasty," which he strictly distinguishes from European and North American homosexuality. "The unique victim of Anatolian pederasty is the *poustis*," he writes. "All the abuse is heaped on the *poustis*'s back, as it were. The *poustis* is considered to be guilty of everything. The *poustis* always has to pay the consequences." After analyzing demotic-song lyrics, then passing in review various rebetic songs and colloquial expressions, Petropoulos devotes a typically erudite, precisely documented, and oft-humorous passage to the buttocks, the passive homosexual, and sodomy:

> In underworld slang, the "bottom" is also called the *kardan* (from French *cadran* "dashboard") or the *diaforiko* "differential", both of which are derived from automobile terminology. The expression *kolos trifasikos* "three-phase ass," that is "an ass that can electrocute you," comes from electricians' jargon. Often we hear *tha pari to maghalo vravio yiati ekane to kolopaidho!* "he'll get the big prize because he took on the role of the passive homosexual!" (i.e., he was a butt-licker, licked the judges' asses). Here, the word *kolopaidho* literally means "child newly born of the asshole." The same meaning is implied by Yiannis Skaribas when, in his book *Gorilla and Gorillas* (1979), he writes: "They aspired to the big prize...that Switzerland granted to those 'achievers.'" I shall not examine the origins of the word *poustis* (from Turkish *puşt*) here. In mundane parlors, a synonym is employed: *tioutos* "one such." Emmanuel Roïdis, however, did not mean this when, in his story "His First Duel," he wrote: "Three elegant young men were sitting there, *kai eis proin tioutos meta dhyo kryrion* ("and the 'ex-young man' [an older young man] with two ladies." The word *bines* has a very specific meaning. It refers to a homosexual who can take on either the active or the passive role. The lexicographer N. P. Andriotis associates the term with the verb *binevo* [in his classic *Etymological Dictionary of Modern Greek*, 1951, 1983]. The verb *binevo*, meaning "to

mount a horse," "to ride a horse" (from the Turkish *binmek*), is well known because of a line in a demotic song: ...*binevoun t' alogh tous, siet' i mavroghis*... ("...they mount their horses, the black earth trembles..."). I believe, however, that the word *bines* anagrammatically derives from the Turkish word *ibne*. Other synomyns of "passive homosexual" exist: *digi-dagas* (of onomatopoeic origin, suggesting swaying, effeminate gestures) and *floros* "greenfinch." Homosexuals abhor the word *poustis*. As for the cruising methods used by *poustides* and *epivitori* "stallions" (that is, active homosexuals), Periklis Sfyridhis's story "The Exit," published in the literary review *Diagonios*, may be consulted. I have no desire to go into the homosexual life of Greek monasteries. Themos Kornaros once wrote on the subject and was then sentenced to five years in prison....

When I discussed the translation of this passage with Petropoulos, he completed the above etymology of *bines* as follows: the Turkish word *ibne* is a synonym of *puşt* ("poustis"), and the former comes from the Arabic *ibn* "son." And he explained that Kornaros's imprisonment both during and after the Greek Civil War, because of his descriptions of homosexuality on Mount Athos, ruined him as a writer. He vanished from the Greek literary scene completely. Readers aware of Kornaros's fate can thus be affected, not only by the humor of Petropoulos's disquisition, but also by its implicit melancholy. This sometimes tense emotional dichotomy, as embodied in his style and the intricate information that it relates, is typical of all the folklorist's writings.

XXXIV

Beginning as early as the late 1940s, Petropoulos especially went out and collected *rebetika*, which were disdained at the time by nearly all academic researchers, both in Greece and abroad. In *The Underworld and Shadow Theater*, he had already warned (in 1978) about the narrow, anachronistic scope of contemporary Greek folkloristic studies, and cited the influence of the famous folklorist Nikolaos Politis:

> Modern Greek folklorists work according to the methodology established by Nikolaos Politis, who, both rightly and wrongly, is called

the "father of Greek folklore." During the last decades of the nineteenth century, Nikolaos Politis laid the foundations of a broad research project, the main aim of which was to derive contemporary Greek folk culture from that of ancient Greece. Already during his lifetime, a radical social transformation was taking place in the country. Already during his lifetime, the folk culture that he was describing had actually died. The little pupils of Nikolaos Politis are still busying themselves with the corpse. Contemporary Greek folklore studies continue to "demonstrate" that, in the Balkans, only the Greek people are of cultural interest. Modern Greek folklorists have essentially worked on the Greek demotic song alone. (...)

I am obliged to grope my way forward. In Greece, the absence of [a serious] bibliography [of folklore studies] is surprising. We have a good anthology of poetry, but no history of art. We have several histories of literature, but no suitable dictionary of the Greek language. Nor do we have a satisfactory etymological dictionary (the same holds true for Turkish), nor a history of Greek music, nor a general work on modern Greek architecture. (...) Books touching upon religious matters or on ethnic groups in Greece are tacitly forbidden, as are those that would deal with the influence of the great Turkish civilization on Greece. The archives of the Police, State, and Church are closed to researchers. The National Library of Greece is nothing less than a heap of manure and the National Art Museum began to function only three years ago.

Harsh words, indeed. But no one worked harder than Elias Petropoulos to improve the state of what he called "our bibliography," by which he meant the corpus of books and research, on all subjects, that could be procured and read in Greece. It is telling that he never sold anything that he had collected, but rather bequeathed all his archives to libraries. More generally, Petropoulos was not someone who needed to own or possess things.

He often complained about glaring gaps of knowledge, about the impossibilities of having access to certain forms of knowledge, and about academic misprision as regards the knowledge available. This time Petropoulos is laying the empirical and conceptual foundations for the study of the underworld and shadow theater:

The reader will have observed that I use the word *hypokosmos* (underworld). I am not doing this out of eccentricity. The Greek word "hypokosmos" (hypo + kosmos) expresses the notion of a social "basement." The prevailing ideology unfortunately disparages this term. I employ "hypokosmos" straightforwardly. It is not necessary to categorize the Greek underworld.

It is unimaginably difficult for anyone to penetrate the mentality and lifestyle of the Greek underworld. In our bibliography there is not one study—not even one description—of the Greek underworld. A member of the Greek underworld is usually called a *koutsavakis* or a *mangas*. This is not entirely correct. The notion of *koutsavakis* ("tough guy," "bully") does not have the same meaning as the notion of a member of the underworld. To be specific: a tough guy or a bully usually belongs to the underworld, but not necessarily; a member of the underworld can be a tough guy or a bully, but not necessarily. In other words, we are dealing here with two superposed circles that intersect over their greatest part. (...)

There is no noteworthy book on the street layout of Old Athens. In fact, there is no book whatsoever on how the streets of Old Athens were laid out socially. From the few extant references, we know that the Psiri quarter had the following advantages for *koutsavakides*... [Etc., etc., etc., as Petropoulos goes on to outline a social street layout for the study of Old Athens.]

In the introduction to *Kaliarda*, Petropoulos adds the essential notion that "the *hypokosmos* is not only the main bearer of Greek traditions, but it also continues to create new traditions." Because of this conceptual shift, his folkloristic methodology differs markedly from that of every other researcher in this field.

XXXV

Through his monumental anthology of over seven hundred pages and some one thousand four hundred rebetic song lyrics, Petropoulos was to the rich and ethnically complex culture of modern Greece what Meleager was to the ancient Greek poets—a master anthologist, collecting and preserving for posterity an exceptionally vivid and moving literature. Many rebetic songs are masterpieces of folk poetry, not to mention their interest for historians, sociologists, and musicians. Without Petropoulos, many of the scores and lyrics would have been lost forever.

The rebetic songs, whose lyrics resemble urban Blues music especially, but also those of country music and even Negro spirituals in certain respects (and, of course, those of other European urban folk musics such as the Portuguese *fado*), constituted an oral cultural heritage in Greece long before Petropoulos's anthology was published in 1968 (in a privately printed edition because he had found no publisher for his manuscript). Petropoulos was later arrested on charges of "pornography" and sentenced to five months in prison. The irony of his stay in prison is that it enabled him to gather many more song lyrics that were totally unknown outside of the Greek underworld. Similarly, when Petropoulos was incarcerated in Korydhalo Prison during his stretch for *Kaliarda*, he ran into the very person—a homosexual named Perla— who had helped him on the first edition of that lexicon. Perla subsequently furnished 150 additional terms and expressions that were eventually included in the 1982 edition.

Since the 1950s, rebetic songs had been very popular in Greece, and most Greeks knew scores of them by heart by the time Petropoulos began collecting the lyrics. Nevertheless, as he writes in his introduction to my translation, *Rebetika: Songs from the Old Greek Underworld* (1992), the songs were long despised by the upper and middle classes. The songs were highly influenced by Turkish folk music and played with Turkish instruments (especially the *bouzouki* and the *baglamas*, but also the *outi* and the *santouri*). They were sung in the rather obscure *argot* of the Greek underworld and expressed "immoral" themes such as drug addiction, hashish, crime, prison life, prostitution, and sexual passion. However, the lyrics represent no particular ideological or political stance toward modern Greece. In fact, the lyrics were sometimes criticized by the Greek Left on account of their political inapplicability. Rebetic songs advocate neither social change nor revolt; like the Blues or Negro spirituals, they reflect the melancholy, despair, and desires of a people hopelessly and perpetually bound to the lowest socioeconomic class in society. The pornography conviction stemmed from the "immorality" of the rebetic themes, especially those concerning hashish. Beginning in 1936, recordings of rebetic songs had to pass through a government censorship office. For example, in this strophe of the song "Manolis the Hash-Head," first recorded by Kostas Nouros in 1929 the word "pipe-bowl" was suppressed by the government when Dalaras recorded it in 1975:

> You didn't expect, Manolis, to be caught red-handed,
> To have your pipe-bowl broken, to be sent to the hive.
> If you're a fine ace, where're your beads?
> If you're a rumbler, where're your knives?

In his extensive commentaries on the songs, a typical provocative aspect of Petropoulos's writing appears. In his annotations about esoteric slang words and underworld customs, Petropoulos never shirks from raw detail. Some hashish song lyrics are impenetrable if certain techniques for hiding hashish (in a prophylactic pushed up into the rectum, or a small quantity slid underneath the foreskin of the penis) are not explained: Petropoulos explains them. A careful perusal not only of the rebetic song lyrics themselves but also of the annotations and Petropoulos's lengthy introduction to the anthology offers a wealth of information about an obscure, despised, social subgroup. It is also important to look up his "Rebetic Glossary" (first available in the original edition of *Rebetic Songs*, then re-published in his 1980 collection of articles, *Short Texts 1949-1979*), *The Underworld and Shadow Theater*, *From the Jails* (1980), and his *Rebetology* (1990). Petropoulos had even planned a new collection of articles about rebetic songs, but this volume, tentatively entitled *Para-Rebetology*, was left unfinished. In any event, his penetrating curiosity and search for facts about the underworld and prison life and, by extension, the judicial and penal system, also motivated the indictment for his anthology. Petropoulos's trial and imprisonment for *Rebetic Songs* anticipated his indictment for *The Good Thief's Manual* twelve years later.

Petropoulos put to work certain tools that Meleager did not possess. The anthology includes an extensive introduction; a "Photo-History" section (containing some 1500 memorabilia such as autographs, notes, manuscripts, identity cards, passports, and instruments, as well as diverse drawings, photos, and engravings of the *manges* or underground tough guys, the hash dens and taverns, the singers, dancers, composers, and musicians); and a third section comprising articles written by other writers about rebetic music, as well as sketches, stories, memoirs, and even a movie scenario. The entire book is cleverly and touchingly illustrated by Alekos Fassianos. It is an indispensable encyclopedia, and a prime example of Petropoulos's lucidity about and compassion for the downtrodden.

XXXVI

Petropoulos's second pornography conviction, for a five-month prison term in 1972, was for a long poem entitled *Body*, which had been written in the spring of 1969 and first published in an album by the artist Pavlos Moskhidhis. The judges objected to one line: "I forget even the fatherland when I see a young naked female body." The case received some publicity outside of Greece, namely in a long article that appeared in the German weekly magazine *Der Spiegel* (5 February 1973). The *Spiegel* article, which also mentions the indictment for *Kaliarda*, discusses the intimate relationship between sexual morality and politics in Greece: not only the censoring of *Body* and Petropoulos's dictionary of homosexual slang, but also the censoring of novel passages and magazine advertisements (showing plunging necklines); the deportation of tourists wearing long hair or mini-skirts; the breaking up of the International Hippie Convention on Crete; and the arrest of nudist bathers on the island of Mykonos. This puts the attack against *Body* in perspective, for, like the *Rebetic Songs* anthology, it is not a political poem.

The pornography verdict nevertheless leaves one puzzled. Without entering into an analysis of this difficult poem, it appears that the incriminated line could be interpreted in such a way that it would even be pleasing to the judges, given the moral-political positions described above. As in any good poem, most of the lines and passages defy a one-sided interpretation. A journalist reporting on the poem in the French daily *Libération* (25 October 1980) even called it "très sage"—sensible, reasonable, well-behaved. In the June 1976 issue of the Greek literary review *Tram*, the poem was announced as appearing, but the corresponding pages were left blank in protest against censorship. A French version, *Corps*, became available in 1976 and was illustrated by the COBRA artist, Corneille, who also became Petropoulos's friend. This was a bibliophilic edition produced at the Atelier Michel Cassé, a lithograph and engraving workshop at which Fassianos also often worked when he was living in Paris. The original Greek poem became generally available in Greece only in 1980, when Nefeli brought out a collection including *Suicide*, *Body*, and *Five Erotic Poems* (1975). A second, non-bibliophilic, Greek-French edition of much of Petropoulos's poetry was published in 1991 by the Éditions du Griot, in a translation done by the author and Frédéric Faure. An even more complete edition of Petropoulos's poetry was published by Nefeli in 1993.

XXXVII

How did Petropulos become acquainted with Greek homosexual slang? He was not a homosexual. To a later revised edition of *Kaliarda*, he added a text entitled "Story of a Book":

> In October 1944, my father was murdered. I was forced to quit school and go to work. I found a job as a road construction worker....During the first part of the year 1946, I was a guard in the big park of Salonica, where I worked until September 1949, going to night school at the same time. In September 1949, I accepted a transfer to the Public Library of Salonica, but I was fired a few days later for being a Communist. How well I understand today that the big park in Salonica (and its environs) was a Great University for me. It was there that I first became acquainted with whores, junkies, bullies, fags, and thieves. It was there that I first smelled the sweet smell of hashish. (I have unfortunately never smoked hash.) It was there that I learned rebetic songs, even if I had already heard them at home. And it was there that I was first impressed by Kaliarda.

Just after leaving prison for the *Body* indictment, Petropoulos went back in for *Kaliarda*. This trial took place on 8 April 1972, and Petropoulos was accused of insulting governmental authorities, the royalty, and the Greek Orthodox Church with his "pornographic" dictionary, and for circulating indecent publications. The sentence—by now he was a "habitual offender"—was for seven months. As the *Spiegel* article points out, a main objection to the dictionary was that, in Greek homosexual slang, the term "U. S. Embassy" means the public toilets in Omonia Square, a natural meeting place for homosexuals. In fact, the word *presvia* ("embassy") means "public toilets" in general in Kaliarda. Other entries found in Petropoulos's dictionary are "The Embassy of the United Arab Republic" (the toilets behind City Hall) and "The Embassy of Great Britain" (those in Constitution Square). Similarly, "Germanogreko" refers to Syntagma Square, since many German tourists were found there. Whether or not these dictionary entries were likely to put Greek foreign policy in jeopardy, the citing of the example of the U. S. Embassy in the accusation suggests what political pressures may have lurked behind the scenes. Moreover, as with the annotations to the *Rebetic Songs* anthology, the entries in *Kaliarda* spare no details that might help the uninitiated reader to better his understanding of Greek homosexual mores. As in his other books, Petropoulos gathered proverbs, expressions, and curses that are not found in other dictionaries of the Greek language. (Several Greek homosexual imprecations, from Petropoulos's lexicon, were translated by Steve Demakopoulos in an article brought out in *Maledicta* in 1978.) It must also be remembered that, at the time, no Greek homosexual dared to "come out." Petropoulos adamantly believed in freedom of speech; this is, of course, an understatement. He supported the notion that homosexuals had the right to speak as they wish, freely and in public, and his lexicon created at least one of the conditions for the realization of this right. Incidentally, when Petropoulos was imprisoned, his dictionary received favorable reviews outside of Greece, notably by the preeminent American translator of Modern Greek literature, Kimon Friar, in *Books Abroad* (October, 1972). Friar was also among Petropoulos's early supporters.

XXXVIII

During the autumn of 1979, I was translating *Enkhiridhion tou kalou klephti* (*The Good Thief's Manual*) from Petropoulos's manuscript. On the first page, Petropoulos's name had been scratched out, and the following pen name had been noted alongside in his impeccable penmanship: E. Pietro Polo. Instead of Nefeli, a fictitious publishing house had been devised. *The Good Thief's Manual* was, moreover, set not in Greece but rather in "Antiqua," whose capital is "Adina." Petropoulos explained:

> As everyone knows, Antiqua is located in southeastern Europe, near Greece and Turkey. Understandably, Antiqua is considered to be a strange country. In spring and summer it is a Colonial Kingdom, whereas in fall and winter it metamorphoses into a Colonial Democracy. In both cases, Antiqua has been ruled by Dictators for the past 150 years. The first king of the country, Toto the Idiot, was a Dictator, as was the first pseudo-democratic prime minister, Beni Zelo.

When the Greek edition appeared—a last-minute decision had been made to leave both Petropoulos's name and Nefeli's on the cover—it looked as though no legal problems would occur. The book became a bestseller overnight and went through a number of printings quickly. However, one day the storm broke: the police confiscated copies in bookshops, and Petropoulos found himself accused of slandering the judicial authorities and the police, as well as, once again, of blaspheming against the Greek Orthodox Church. This came as a surprise to many of his friends in Paris, but not to Petropoulos himself, who had been telling me all along that he was expecting trouble. One evening he called, asked if he could drop by our apartment; he had a stack of photocopies of Greek newspaper articles about the banning of the book and he wanted me to read them. He had given out the same stack, meticulously stapled as usual, to numerous French and foreign journalists in Paris as well. Petropoulos's American friend in Athens, Katherine Butterworth, estimated at the time that for every copy of the book that was sold, as many as five readers could be counted as having read it, as it circulated from friend to friend to friend.

Petropoulos had been anticipating trouble as early as 1976, when he was quoted by Kimon Friar (in *The Athenian*, November 1976) as describing the manuscript of *The Good Thief's Manual* as "a book dagger about jails whose cutting edge will be turned against those who serve the Establishment." (Petropoulos had begun the manuscript immediately after arriving in Paris in 1975.) Friar continues: "Petropoulos assures us that by the time he publishes it (in a foreign language, naturally), he will be a thousand miles away from his fatherland." As it turned out, Petropoulos published the book in his mother tongue and paid the consequences. But he would have had it no other way.

Friar's interview with Petropoulos took place three years before the Greek Press Law was passed in 1979. The Press Law suppressed the journalistic right to unnamed sources and made certain subjects, such as the armed forces and foreign agents, taboo. Publishers and journalists ran the risk of severer sanctions than in the past. The Press Law also reiterated legal stipulations going back to a Press Law promulgated during the extreme right-wing dictatorship of Metaxas in the late 1930s.

As in the cases of the *Rebetic Songs* anthology, *Body*, and *Kaliarda*, the Greek government's continuing interest in suppressing any manifestations of "immorality" was a determining factor in the censorship of *The Good Thief's Manual*. After Petropoulos was sentenced *in absentia* on 23 October 1980—the same year that the country entered the European Economic Community—to eighteen months in prison and a large fine, three other censorship trials took place and were won by the government during the following two weeks: on 24 October, a trial against a publisher who had published *Betty*, the autobiography of a transvestite; on 26 October, a trial against the homosexual magazine, *Amfi*; and on 3 November, a trial against a well-known avant-garde publisher, Exantas Press, who had brought out translations of the Marquis de Sade's classic novels, *La Philosophie dans le boudoir*, *120 Journées de Sodome*, *La Nouvelle Justine*, and *L'Histoire de Juliette sa soeur*.

These trials received some publicity outside of Greece, but to no avail. Petropoulos devised a ploy for potential future indictments. On the covers of two books published just after *The Good Thief's Manual*, *The Brothel* and *Lousology*, were printed respectively "Throw the Americans out of Greece" and "Keep the Americans out of my Country," a reminder that the United States still maintained military bases in Greece. Any judicial proceeding against the books would necessarily be a political one, and a strange one at that, given the anti-American propensities of the newly elected PA.SO.K. Socialist government. Although in light of what had previously been censored, *The Brothel* would have been a prime candidate for a new trial, no governmental action against either book was taken.

Petropoulos remained a wanted man in Greece, because of *The Good Thief's Manual*, despite the action undertaken on his behalf abroad. Articles appeared in *Libération* (25 October 1980); twice in *Le Monde* (14 December 1979 and 19 December 1980, both written by Jacques Lacarrière); in *Die Zeit* (28 November 1980, written by the poet Oswald Wiener); and in *Afrique-Asie* (22 December 1980, written by the American political journalist Schofield Coryell). I wrote what I believe were the only English articles; they appeared in *Maledicta* and the *Journal of the Hellenic Diaspora*. Three months after the trial verdict, the French P.E.N. Club unanimously made Petropoulos an honorary member (on 22 January 1981). A Swedish translation of "Lesson 21" of *The Good Thief's Manual* appeared in *Amnesty International Bulletin* (10 October 1980), with a short introduction by Britt Arenander, Secretary of the Swedish P.E.N. Club. On respectively 3 March and 9 March 1981, the Belgian and Danish sections of the International P.E.N Club sent letters of protest to Konstantinos Karamanlis, the President of Greece; and the Swedish section addressed a letter to Dimitrios Nianias, the Minister of Culture, noting that "the publication of this book would not cause any legal measures to be taken in any country which claims to be a democracy." None of these letters were answered.

XXXIX

The general accusation of blasphemy against the Orthodox Church was most likely founded on passages in the last section ("In Prison") of the book. Elsewhere, little about the Orthodox Church is to be found. In Lesson 34, Petropoulos describes how prisoners respond to the prison regulation that they must attend church services:

> Prisoners call the church the *priest shop*. Prison churches are very small. Not all Prisons have churches. In all cases, most Prisoners attend the service standing outside. For a helper, the priest has a Convict who was once a priest or monk. (There are always a few defrocked priests or monks in Prison; their usual offense: homosexuality.) The real priest and the Convict-ex-priest hate each other.
>
> During the service, the Prison coffeehouse is closed. Convicts who have not gone to the service are locked up in their cells and get really

edgy. Now and then a Convict cries out through his window: "Come on, priest, get it over with!" The priest pretends not to hear and continues his psalmodies. But the Guard Captain turns to the agitator's window and shouts that he will punish him after the service. The agitator-Convict restrains himself and answers: "You fart on my balls!"

Convicts never listen to the psalmodies. Usually they start chatting. Here and there laughter breaks out. On the candelabrum only a few candles burn; Convicts have no money to buy candles. Some Prisoners attend the service in pajamas and slippers; this is considered quite stylish. Other Prisoners, apparently in religious ecstasy, pinch the asses of their pious fellow convicts in the first row.

From time to time a priest decides to preach a sermon at the end of the service. The moment he begins his sermon, a loud collective "OHHHHH!" can be heard, expressing more disapproval than admiration. But the priest drones on.

Another, perhaps more opprobrious, passage occurs towards the end of "Lesson 37," where Petropoulos recounts how prisoners deal with their basic needs:

Grubbing, fucking, and shitting should be done neither hastily nor nervously.

Prisoners run into obstacles when performing these basic needs. In New Prison, cells and dormitories have no toilets. Prisoners must piss into a tub. If a Prisoner wants to shit at night, he must climb up to the window and call the Guard in order to get his cell unlocked. The Guard refuses; the Prisoner starts swearing; the Guard tells him that he will have to wait until morning; finally all the Prisoners are roused and the Guard, accompanied by two other Guards, opens the cell door.

In Souvarov Prison, every cell is furnished with a huge stinking chamber pot. On North Prison Farm, the toilet stalls have no doors. Prisoners defecate as their fellow Prisoners, washing off their plates over the bathroom sink, look on. In all these cases, Prison toilet stalls are horrible. The walls are covered with shit smudges and erotic beckonings. Sperm on the floor. As you are taking a shit, a rat frightens you. But it is only in Prison toilet stalls that you feel lonely. Prisoners spend a long time in the toilet stall; they leave only when they have smoked at least two cigarettes. This is not because of constipation. Not one toilet stall in a Prison of Antiqua has a toilet stool. The usual Prison toilet is a mere hole in the floor. The shitter's position over such toilet holes is physiologically natural, but also tiring. Sick Prisoners have an especially tough go in Prison toilets.

In Seven Tower Prison, the unwritten Convict Code (which is very severe there) requires two buckets of water in the hole after pissing and four after shitting. Moreover, a Convict who goes to the toilet at night must wear rubber-soiled clogs so as not to awake his fellow sleeping Convicts.

A Political Prisoner who wants to shit in his cell hangs a little card on his cell door with the word *NO*. He does this to prevent someone from entering unknowingly. Such finesse is unthinkable among Members of the Mob.

After defecation, Prisoners wipe themselves with common toilet paper or with pages torn out of the Holy Bible.

Another provocative passage is located in the last lesson, which is about prison homosexuality. Petropoulos relates that because religious (but no other) images are tolerated in the cells, some prisoners cover their cell walls "like a chapel" with reproductions of sacred (but naked) scenes, and then masturbate in front of them.

When Petropoulos was dying from prostate cancer in August, 2003, and was confined to a clinic room, many friends sent him postcards of naked women. To cheer him up, Mary Koukoules taped the postcards to the wall just in front of him; but nurses eventually protested and the postcards were removed. Elias Petropoulos managed to provoke controversy even from his deathbed.

XL

The charge that Petropoulos insulted the police is certainly understandable—if "insulting" means making numerous revelations and disturbing analyses. Much of the book is aimed not only at police corruption, but also at the police-underworld war for the control of the hashish, prostitution, and gambling monopolies. Also described are tortures at the Security Police Headquarters and feuds fought between rival police forces. Petropoulos argues that the various police forces, as well as other "respectable" elements in society, combine in forcing the ex-convict back into criminality. The violent attacks levied against Petropoulos show that *The Good Thief's Manual* touched sore spots. This passage appears in "Lesson 20":

> The Police aims to obtain the Prostitution monopoly. In Antiqua, whorehouses were abolished twenty years ago. Whores were forced to rent small isolated apartments, paying their most gracious landlords ten times the usual rent. Any Whore who wants to get an apartment is obliged to ask help from a Policeman. The Policeman gets his kickback, but he always wants more. The Pimp, in other words, is pushed to the sidelines. To put the Pimp in Prison, the Whore (his girlfriend) has to file a complaint. The Policeman summons the Whore to his office. There he asks her to *denounce* her Pimp. Often the Whore gets off by offering him a round sum and promising to fork over the same sum every month. But if the Policeman is too greedy, he will force the Whore to file a complaint against her Pimp. The most convenient ways of putting pressure on a Whore are snatching her tit and twisting it, grabbing her by the hair and beating her head against the wall, or burning her nipples with a cigarette. At the end, even the most stubborn Whore yields.

Lessons 21 through 23 are devoted to tortures at the Security Police Headquarters and offered some of the most difficult passages to swallow for the authorities in power, not because of the author's aggressiveness, but rather because of a hard-hitting cynical humor that hits home:

> TORTURE No. 3. A *billy club up the ass* can be understood only as a humiliating punishment. The Policeman who rams a billy club up the ass of a Suspect Held in Custody has lost control of himself. In this Torture, and it has been proven, Vaseline is not used.
> In 1969, in Saverov Prison, I met a Convict who had had his ass plugged with a billy club, which was then yanked out violently: his

intestines hung out like a worm. The doctor (a real bastard) at Saverov Prison was treating him for a stomach ulcer.

In any event, when they ram a billy club up your ass, know that breathing deeply in and out helps a lot. Some Policemen try to ram various other objects, like pipes or stakes, up the Tortured Suspect's ass. *Never* let them ram a stake up there. If the Policemen insist, threaten them with recourse to the Human Rights Commission or Amnesty International. This threat has about a 0.003 % chance of working.

Of course, some Policemen could not care less about their careers. If the Tortured Suspect is a woman, the Policeman will not hesitate to ram pointed objects up her vagina.

TORTURE No. 7. As a Torture, *Cigarette burns* probably do not go back further in time than the cigarette. (...) Although they are not medical doctors, Policemen who give cigarette burns know the sensitive parts of the body: on a man, they burn his balls; on a woman, they burn the lips of her cunt and the nipples of her breasts. Thieves find even more horrible the burning of their *fingernails*. It is obvious that the Policeman uses high-quality cigarettes for this Torture.

TORTURE No. 9. *Testicle-twisting* and *nipple-twisting* cause unbearable pain. (A single test will convince you). (...)

TORTURE No. 13. *Hanging by the bangs*: two Policemen grab you by the bangs, on each temple, and lift you into the air. That's all.

TORTURE No. 16. *Ice* is an extremely effective torture. It is also cheap, easy, quick, and clean. Moreover, it does not leave any marks on the body.

TORTURE No. 17. *Boiled eggs*...The Torturer boils two eggs well. As soon as they are boiling hot, he thrusts them under the armpits of the Tortured Suspect, who squirms convulsively. After the Torture, the Torturer peels the eggs and eats them...

Petropoulos spends Lessons 18 and 19 describing how a vicious feud is fought out between the "twenty police forces." Surely irritating for those responsible for the judicial system in Greece was Petropoulos's lucid demonstration, in Lesson 24, of how a criminal is forced back into criminality despite intentions of turning over a new leaf. This occurs by means of the "verification game" (as Petropoulos calls weekly registration at the police station) and through police pressure on an ex-convict's employer. The chapter concludes: "Thus, thanks to Police pressure, the Bad Thief once again becomes a Good Thief. The Police gives out a deep sigh of relief when the Thief returns to the bosom of the Underworld."

XLI

The third charge against Petropoulos was that he had insulted and slandered judicial authorities in *The Good Thief's Manual*. As should already be clear, among the weapons in his arsenal are humor, parody, sarcasm, and indeed invective (in a manner recalling the style of ancient Greek and Roman writers)—as stylistic means of revealing facts about thieves, prisoners, the police, and the judiciary. This quality was neatly formulated by Evghenios Arantsis in an enthusiastic review of the book in *Kyriakatiki* (5 April 1981): "To speak about crime is not prohibited, but to speak about crime with poetry and humor is to let all Hell break loose."

The title of Lesson 27, "The Judge: A Sacred Person," already prepares the desacralization, as humor turns to invective:

> Anyone with a Law Degree can become a Judge, provided that he obtained his degree with *bad* grades. In Antiqua, the worst law students become Judges. In Antiqua, the most perverted law students become Judges. As a rule, the Judges of Antiqua are terrified little buggers who tremble at the thought of transfers and unfavorable administrative evaluation reports, who tremble at the thought of ministerial circulars and reprimands by their Superior Magistrate, and, especially, who tremble in front of their wives.
>
> The Judges in Antiqua are completely uneducated, malicious and vengeful, idiotic and hung up. Almost all the Judges in Antiqua are *fascists*.

Or this passage:

> Not all Trials are the same. There are Trial-Comedies, Trial-

Tragedies, Trial-Farces. Trial-Ballets are rare. During the Trial, *imperceptible* factors also play their role. Often the Defendant is convicted simply because he has a strange face. This phenomenon is *extremely well-known* among Underworld Thieves. When a Thief has been sentenced to an exaggerated Punishment because of his face, the other Thieves say: "His map gets it." This same Thief, sentenced to a long prison term, says: "I'm taking Christ's rap." It is noteworthy that Our Savior Jesus Christ was crucified at 33. Judges dislike seeing poorly dressed or unshaven Defendants. Judges have a sergeant's mentality. Thieves are brilliant psychologists. They show up in court well-dressed, well-combed, clean-shaven.

In Prison, you often meet people sentenced out of utter injustice. Convicts treat such innocents with lightly ironic tenderness.

In Lesson 30, Petropoulos delves into the problem of corruption in the Justice Ministry, going so far as to publish a list of the various types of corruption available and the corresponding bribes. Not only is the prosecutor attacked, but also the defense lawyer, commonly considered to be a champion of the oppressed:

Eventually the Thief is taken into Precautionary Custody. He notifies the Defense Lawyer. The Defense Lawyer comes. The Thief tells the Defense Lawyer his story. The Good Thief does not babble on. He tells the Defense Lawyer what he *must* tell him. If he reveals that the Goods are stashed away somewhere, the Defense Lawyer will demand a higher fee. If he confides that there was a strike that the Police have not yet suspected, the Defense Lawyer might turn himself into a Squealer.

The Defense Lawyer's technique is simple:

I. At the beginning, he gorges the Defendant with hopes abounding.

II. On the eve of the Trial, he tells the Defendant: "We're in tough shape."

III. At the beginning of the Trial, as soon as the Judge and Prosecutor have climbed onto the podium, the Lawyer turns to the Defendant and whispers: "This Judge is a real prick—if you get off with five years, consider yourself lucky."

IV. Immediately after the Trial, if the Defendant is sentenced to less than five years, the Lawyer says: "It was a battle, but I managed it." If, however, the Defendant is handed a sentence of more than five years, the Lawyer says: "Didn't I tell you that this Judge is a shit-hole?"

V. The day after the Trial, the Lawyer shows up in Prison and sadly tells the poor ex-Defendant, who is now a Prisoner: "Be brave. Tomorrow I'll file an appeal. We'll win the second time around."

VI. At the same time, the Lawyer skins the Defendant and his family for all they are worth.

Petropoulos boasted that some of the readers most infuriated by *The Good Thief's Manual* were defense lawyers.

XLII

By publishing his vast personal archives of postcards, old photographs and various other documents about Thessaloniki, Petropoulos was far ahead of his time. In Greece, this type of historical documentation had rarely been used by academic historians. The thrust of albums such as *Old Salonica, La Présence ottomane à Salonique,* or *Salonique: l'incendie de 1917,* all of which were issued in 1980, was to offset the nationalistic approach of Greek historians toward the history of the town. This approach was, of course, vintage Petropoulos, who never tired of pointing out that something "typically Greek" was in fact Turkish, Albanian, Bulgarian, Armenian, Slavic, or Jewish—or a mixture of some of the above. "The Greeks do not like to admit that they are Greek," he quips in the introduction to *Cages à oiseaux en Grèce.*

On 5 May 1981, a right-wing deputy demanded in the Greek Parliament the banning of all of Petropoulos's books on the local history and topography of Thessalonki, and especially the book *Old Salonica.* The claim was that the albums were "unpatriotic, un-Greek, and Turkophilic." I interviewed Petropoulos at the time for an article that later appeared in the American magazine *Greek Accent.* He observed:

> I was just beginning to think that for once I had put together a totally inoffensive book, just old photographs and postcards. But now you see

why I cannot go back to Greece. Most of my friends in Athens have been telling me that nothing would happen, even after the conviction for *The Good Thief's Manual*, if I went back. They seem to think that Greece's being in the Common Market would protect me. No way! I've got a bad habit of discovering and then writing about things that mustn't be written about—not from any political party's point of view. Most of the time I can sense when there's going to be trouble, but sometimes even I'm surprised. This goes for almost any subject in folklore. You'd better not write, for instance, that the folk music of northern Greece was influenced by Slavic folk music or that Thracian weaving adopted Bulgarian patterns. Don't bring up the subject of the thousands of Turkish words that have "somehow" slipped into everyday use in the Greek language. In Greece, discussion of these matters is prohibited. It is a fact, however, that, culturally speaking, the Balkan and Anatolian peoples have much in common. By turning the Albanian, Bulgarian, or Turk into a scapegoat, the true sources of the Greek people's problems are obfuscated or ignored. From a political point of view it is very convenient to have a hereditary enemy.

A month after the incident in the Greek Parliament, on the morning of 2 June 1981, Petropoulos stopped in front of a Greek restaurant located on the ground floor of a very old building in the rue Mouffetard. The building, like others on this historic street, had been classified as a national historical monument. Yet the restaurant owner was painting over some centuries-old exposed beams. Petropoulos simply told him that the paint would permanently destroy the grain of the wood and that the wood should be preserved as such. The owner jumped down from his ladder and gave Petropoulos a good thrashing, accompanying his kicks and punches with cries of "dirty communist!" and "friend of the Turks!" (Petropoulos had not been a communist since the days of the Second World War and the Greek Civil War, yet the restaurant owner was aware of the aforementioned, well-publicized, incident in the Greek Parliament.) Injured, Petropoulos had to be transported to the hospital "in a police ambulance," as he was pleased, despite his pains and very black eye, to tell me later that afternoon when I dropped by to see how he was doing. In fact, it was the author of *The Good Thief's Manual* himself, not Mary Koukoules, who had called the police. The American journalist Schofield Coryell and his wife Rosette, who was of Turkish origin and related to the Turkish novelist Yaşar Kemal, were also there in the living room. Coryell reported on the incident in the magazine *Afrique-Asie*. Petropoulos must still have had a foreign resident permit at this point, for the police surely asked him for his papers.

XLIII

Had Petropoulos's troubles with Greek authorities exclusively occurred during the dictatorship of the Colonels, his case could be classified with those of other Greek political dissidents: many intellectuals, writers, poets, artists, and musicians were persecuted and sometimes imprisoned during the Junta; other Greeks, like Petropoulos's friend, the composer Mikis Theodorakis, were forced to flee the country. What is puzzling and troubling is that Petropoulos's trials and tribulations—the expression is to be taken literally—continued after the fall of the Junta. Explaining how and why he ran into so many conflicts with his fellow Greeks and the Greek judicial system is no easy matter. Politics and political history must be taken into account; the initial persecution levied against him partly occurred as a logical consequence of the type of totalitarian regime in power; but it was probably above all the writing "style"—its devastating precision and humor—with which Petropoulos treated so many at once risqué and overlooked topics, as well as his indefatigable collecting of documents and images related to those same topics, that were absolutely unbearable to authorities with interests and reputations to protect, both during and after the Junta. The rigorously documented, multifarious, indeed overwhelming factuality of his books makes them extremely difficult to refute. And the questions that he raises are deep and embarrassing.

XLIV

In *The Brothel*, Petropoulos delves into brothel types, madams, pimps, slave traders, customers entering a brothel for the first time, experienced customers, sodomy, syphilis, gonorrhea, male prostitution, and much more. (Etc. Etc. Etc.) Equally important is his demonstration that we know little, if anything, about the true nature of prostitution:

> We cannot formulate a definition of prostitution because we are unable to perceive clearly what exactly happens between the prostitute and her customer during sexual intercourse. The prostitute delivers her body for a price, but we do not know if this is, legally, leasing an object, transient self-sale, or the simple use of an animate good. We do not know, legally speaking, if the relationship between the prostitute and the customer consists of a one-sided or two-sided agreement. We do not know if paid coition is the same thing for the prostitute as for the customer. Finally, we do not know if paid coition is a legal fact or simply a practical condition.

The same kind of argumentation demonstrates our ignorance of the true nature of a house of prostitution. Amidst the humor and the sarcasm, amidst the learned discussions of etymologies and evanescing techniques, it must never be overlooked that one of the most original and enduring aspects of Petropoulos's writing is his attempt to delineate, for nearly all the topics he studies, what we do not know or, more simply, *that* we do not know.

This recalls, once again, his attacks on the Greek judicial system. His display of the dubious presuppositions underlying it were surely as effective in provoking the attacks made on *The Good Thief's Manual* as his more empirical assaults on judges, the Ministry of Justice, the Government, or the Police. In no other book is his attempt to perceive what we know and do not (or cannot) know, what we understand and do not (or cannot) understand, pushed to more extremes of rigor and devastating ironic clarity. The questions raised at the beginning of Lesson 26 ("Who Designates Crime?") are serious and remain unanswered:

> I doubt that the notion of Crime exists for Minerals, Plants, or Animals. According to our Wise Legislators, only Human Beings commit Crimes. The instructive academic definition speaks of *Crime as an act (or the omission of an act) that is unjust, imputed to its Perpetrator, and punishable by Law.*

The chilling schematization of this definition imposes these questions:

Who defines the type of Crime?
Who is represented by Legislator?
Who is protected by the Penal Code?
What is a human act?
What is Injustice?
Who is the Perpetrator and why does he act?
Why is the Perpetrator punished?
Who punishes the Perpetrator?
What does Punishment mean?
How much does Punishment sting?
Why is there a Punishment for every Crime?
Why is the Perpetrator identified with the Punishment?
Is the Perpetrator born a Perpetrator?
Why does the Judge hate the Perpetrator?
Does the Perpetrator control himself?

XLV

Such questions provoke new ways of looking at justice and the judicial system in Greece (and elsewhere), even if Petropoulos is not usually interested in traditional philosophical discussions of these problems. He is always immersed in concrete details, and his aphoristic declarations ("Theft is the crime par excellence against property," for example, or "I consider a Thief to be more revolutionary than a Communist") are essentially aimed at re-considering reality: real acts, real situations. He makes an assault on pretentiousness, presumption, illusion, and even widely admired noble sentiments by means of eyewitness testimony, with all hearsay evidence barred from his investigative procedure. He ever wants to force the reader back to reality. Tellingly, one of his stylistic tics is to begin a sentence with *"stin pragmatikotita,"* literally "in reality"—"in fact," "in truth," "actually." Another, even more pervasive tic is his use of negative verb phrases.

XLVI

However, an important nuance needs to be added about Petropoulos's *seeming*—his use of Greek words meaning "so-called" or implying "seeming" constitute a third stylistic tic—eschewal of traditional philosophical discourse and dialogue. In *The Good Thief's Manual*, his attack on our sometimes sympathetic, often haughty, and ever-unrealistic preconceptions with respect to thieves and prisoners is carried out by means of a deft parody of professional and professorial discourse. His style blends the "purist" *katharevousa* language with crass criminal slang. The intentional misspelling of famous names (the French philosopher Michel Foucault becomes "Fouceaut," the French novelist Marguerite Duras become "Durat") and the satirical manipulation of *ex cathedra* pronouncements by famous personages (especially Karl Marx) are no gratuitous acts. Petropoulos is no system builder like Marx, and much less a Foucault, whose writings on the history of incarceration Petropoulos considered to be the epitome of professorial gobbledygook, a compilation of pages of indecipherable historical data from which lofty ratiocinations and erroneous generalizations were dubiously drawn, notably when it came to the history of incarceration in Europe. "Fouceaut thinks that Prisons took root three hundred years ago," notes Petropoulos in *The Good Thief's Manual*, adding: "This does not surprise me at all; every Frenchman sees the entire world in his navel. Fouceaut should reread the Myths of Anatolian Peoples." Petropoulos had attended several of Foucault's seminars on prisons. He once stated:

> Let's leave all penitentiary semiology to the side for the moment and simply try to consider the prison from the prisoner's point of view. Suppose mirrors are prohibited in prisons, as they often are. Can you imagine not being able to see yourself in a mirror for years and years on end? Suppose, as is the case in modern prisons, that the cell walls are totally spotless, scrubbed and disinfected as in a hospital every day; that little television cameras watch your every move; that your bed is a block of cement since old-fashioned cots used to be broken up and used as lethal weapons during prison riots...Imprisonment in itself is a punishment. During imprisonment one's punishment can be increased by torture or solitary confinement. But how much discussion has there

been about the daily, constant, and very brutal punishment invisibly emanating from the prison's very architecture and interior design, from its most harmless appearing regulations and enforced customs?

In both *The Good Thief's Manual* and *From the Jails*, Petropoulos presents the stark reality of Greek penitentiaries: the savagery and ribald comedy, the soporific boredom and frenetic liveliness, the various "governments" and "clans," the interior architecture and design, the love life. As opposed to, say, Aleksandr Solzhenitsyn, Petropoulos describes incarceration not from the standpoint of a political dissident but rather from that of a burglar, pickpocket, junkie, or murderer. For Petropoulos, political prisoners are the "guests" of the prison. On account of his pornography indictments, he spent his three stretches in the company of common criminals and was able to make friends within the tightly closed underworld "mob"; he describes in straightforward fashion how one eats, drinks, smokes, sleeps, defecates, urinates, makes love, plays games, communicates, works, and jokes inside Greek prisons. This angle on prison and underworld life is unique and shocking. Few people object to sympathizing with the plight of a political dissident in a Siberian camp or on a Greek island during the reign of the Junta. But how many readers are willing to put themselves in the smelly *pantoufles* ("slippers") of a tough Greek jailbird? Or view the burglary of their apartment from the point of view of the burglar? Or eyewitness the tortures that take place every day, not in Siberia, but just down the street in their precinct police station? In *The Good Thief's Manual*, Petropoulos pokes a salty finger into several secret sores of a *noli me tangere*: private property.

This difference in style and approach has its consequences. Like an album of photographs (one unifying aspect of Petropoulos's multifarious work), his laconic, precise style brings the reader close to reality. At the same time the author's irony, through distancing effects, obliges the reader to re-focus more carefully on reality and the way it is conceptually construed. In the first section —"Thievery Theory"—of *The Good Thief's Manual*, Petropoulos parodies and, at the same time, seriously examines abstract legal categories and their applications by speaking through the persona of a "Burglary School professor":

Hence Things can also be distinguished as Animate or Inanimate. An Animate Thing is a beautiful woman suitable for sale at a brothel. An Animate Thing is the chicken that you will swipe, shortly before wringing its neck. Inanimate Things are gold bracelets, watches, banknotes, etc.

Wide disagreement prevails among venerable Burglary School professors as to whether eggs should be classified as Animate or Inanimate Things. Of course, the kidnapping of a child is a Theft of an Animate Thing, with the overriding objective of obtaining, not the body, but the Ransom. Yet the kidnapping (?) of a corpse is a Theft of an Inanimate Thing. (Common in Italy, such kidnappings are still unusual in backward Antiqua.) And what happiness to be able to steal and sell your own body (= Subjective Theft of Animate Thing + Selfsale). Only whores are capable of such a feat, and for only as long as the paid fuck lasts.

Once purged of false, misleading, or edifying abstractions, the discourse is no longer *about* thieves and prisoners, but rather *with* them in the street, in the pilfered pocket, in the burglarized apartment, in solitary confinement. Most readers did not intend to keep company with such bedfellows. Often the humor intensifies the reader's uncomfortable feelings. One is shocked when one expected to be entertained:

> Many Convicts *starve*.
> I have seen a Convict stash stale bread crusts under his bed.
> I have seen a Convict eat apple peelings left by another Convict.
> I have seen a Convict eat a buttered slice of bread that another Convict had dropped on the toilet floor.
> I have seen a Convict (who is not too bright) swipe and then eat an entire can of NIVEA skin cream. When I asked him why he was eating it, he answered: "I really like vanilla pudding."

XLVII

A further nuance. Even when Petropoulos sticks closely to a photographically realistic style and precisely transmits insider's information that he has gleaned, he is not writing "sociology," at least in the academic sense of the discipline. Once again, the Greek *laographia* is the more accurate word and concept, with its emphasis on "writing" as opposed to a rationalizing "logos." Petropoulos's style often affects the reader literarily, as it were. The form and style of his books recall, if not entirely reflect, genres like the personal essay or even the novel. In an interview given to *Pantheon* (1 April 1981), Petropoulos went so far as to claim: "Unknowing critics should realize that I have written (with *The Good Thief's Manual*) a novel with all the telltale signs of the genre."

Of course, there is no central, prolonged, detailed plot in *The Good Thief's Manual*, so the book is not a traditional novel in this regard. The book is indeed a manual, even if it also essentially chronicles the trajectory of a main character (the thief) from his theft—the various kinds of which are delineated in the second section—to the police station (third section), the courtroom (fourth section), and the prison (fifth and final section). It is likewise impossible to classify the book exclusively as documentary prose or even eyewitness testimony, although typical elements of these genres are also strongly present. Note the author's own distinction between "description" and "narration" at the beginning of the chapter "Kaleidoscope": "Prison life is so multifarious that no pen can describe it. I have tried to *narrate*, in a rather methodical way, the relationships that exist between Guards and Prisoners. I have tried not to yield to the temptation to *interpret* facts." However, Petropoulos subsequently implies that even continuous narration is also sometimes an unsatisfactory vehicle of both factual and more general truths. "In today's lesson," he characteristically notes, "I would like to bring forth, in raw detail, several isolated incidents, facts, and habits of Prison life. I assure you that they are all *true*. After today's lesson, you will perhaps understand Prison life better." The chapter entitled "Kaleidoscope" accordingly consists of a series of scenes and vignettes that are mostly unrelated thematically—for prison life itself cannot be grasped wholly or summed up in any coherent, overarching way.

These are some of the tensions and beneficially heterogeneous literary qualities that inform Petropoulos's style. And they especially shine forth in Lesson 40 ("Pordology, or On Farting") of *The Good Thief's Manual*. An anthology piece, the chapter narrates one of the most basic phenomena of prison life in a style that Rabelais, himself a writer who brought together heterogeneous literary qualities, would have enjoyed:

> Farting is a most personal event, like masturbating. Some people take pleasure in making personal events public. In the normal course of events, a fart is emitted in solitude. If, contrary to expectation, there is an audience, then the fart will (it has been demonstrated) assault the senses of sound and smell—especially that of smell. *The individual who farts in public is called a farter.* From the Bronze Age down to our own times, not a single fart blown in public has occurred unobserved.
>
> Personally, I defend the viewpoint that men fart more than women. The leader of the Women's Liberation Movement, Miss Marguerite Durat, has an opinion diametrically opposed to mine. I would like to add, however, that a beautiful woman who farts *in public* loses much of her charm. Male Chauvinists and Feminists (and, I hope, Homosexuals as well) agree on one point: *a fart is, fundamentally, a musical event.*(...)
>
> In the Prisons of Antiqua, Prisoners work assiduously at cultivating farts. In our times, no form of *energy* should go to waste. A fart provokes laughter. Laughter is absolutely essential to a Prisoner's survival. In Prison, farting often attains the summits of Genuine Art.
>
> Romain Rolland called Panayt Istrati *A Gorky of the Balkans*. An authentic French windbag, Romain Rolland never realized that he was far surpassed by Istrati as a writer. Panayt Istrati offered humanity the most beautiful descriptions, full of thunderous farts and rumbling belches. "Only the dead do not fart," wrote Clement Lépidis. Prisoners are not dead. I am not Panayt Istrati, but I will try to describe the indescribable.
>
> Farts vary in intensity of sound and smell.
>
> Bullies and braggarts fart thunderously. These farts, which boom like cannon blasts, are called *manly* by the Convicts. *The sonority of the fart varies in direct proportion to the personality of the farter.* Fags, hypocrites, and Stool Pigeons blow *hollow* farts, just like an old lady's. In Prison, the familiar sound of a fart spreads joy. There, all sorts of farts can be heard: some powerful like thunder; some whiny, feeling sorry for themselves; some modest and unpretentious; others timid, yellow-

bellied. In Prison, never make bets with farters, not even with one who claims he can blow eighty in a row. You will lose the bet for sure. (...)

Farting also has its folklore.

Sometimes a Convict will wake up another Convict by farting in his ear. Some Convicts fart at the table while eating, exactly like animals (this, I'll refrain from describing). When a Convict farts loudly, all the others shout: "Open up!" The more remarkable farts are christened; thus, in Prison, deep, coarse farts are termed "hoarse." In farting contests, contenders fart standing up with the left leg slightly raised. Convicts often make holes in a common cell wall in order to communicate with the neighboring cell; through these holes they also treat their neighbors to free farts. When a Convict farts, he usually says to the others nearby: "There you are! Sniff it up!" This innocent joke, however, is considered to be a deadly insult to a Convict who is sipping Turkish coffee. In Maximum Security Prisons, farting is forbidden by tacit agreement. Long-Timers fart only when in the toilet. A fart blown impudently in the Long-Timer's dormitory is equivalent to signing your own death sentence.

Petropoulos gets us laughing about things, acts, events, and people about which and whom we are not supposed to laugh. Well, whereas we might laugh about farting, we will certainly not laugh about, let alone feel sympathy for, the kind of burglars whom Petropoulos evokes: they are no romantic, aristocratic, or gentlemanly Arsène Lupins, Robin Hoods, or Billy the Kids. Or will we?

As we have said, a Burglar forces doors and searches through everything at top speed in order to steal money or jewels.

Consequently, he leaves the house in a complete mess. *The Burglar, as opposed to the Picklock, could not care less about how the house looks when he leaves.*

Such indifference sometimes attains the epitome of indiscretion. Some Burglars have the habit of opening the victim's refrigerator, and thus lighting up the kitchen. Some take a nip out of various costly beverages that they find. Others secretly spy on an unsuspecting girl who is asleep and jack off. Some flop down on a spongy bed and fall asleep. Some hang loueys on the Persian carpets. Others destroy precious objects that they cannot carry off.

The epitome of indiscretion, however, is a habit that many Burglars have: *shitting* in the house that they have just burgled. And when I say *shit in the house* I do not mean in the bathroom. These unscrupulous Burglars shit on a silk cushion, or in the middle of the parlor, or even climb up on the dining room table and shit there!

During the past three years, our School, along with the Police Department and the Prison Board, have made a survey of some 1287 anonymous Burglars of Adina. It was found that 496 (out of the 1287) have the habit of shitting in the victim's house during the Theft. Of these 496, 72% shit because of *hyper-emotiveness* (or unacknowledged fear), whereas 28% shit because of *class hatred*. It is significant that among the *class-hatred shitters*, the vast majority climb up and shit on tables. *Such Burglars shit during almost all their Burglaries, and always on tables.* This topic perhaps requires a psychoanalytical study. In any event, no conscientious Burglar would ever think of using such vile means to satisfy his vengeance.

XLVIII

Petropoulos's humor derives from a literary vision encompassing and assimilating all kinds of personalities and activities without prejudice. "I am a man," remarked Terence, "nothing human is alien to me." The same adage stands out defiantly in *The Good Thief's Manual*, *The Brothel*, *Kaliarda*, and ultimately all of Petropoulos's books. It is the impetus of his curiosity and compassion. And this curiosity and compassion near Petropoulos to "real life" to an extent that most writers and artists never dare to experience. "I feel sorry for writers who have not fallen into Prison," he observes with troubling irony in *The Good Thief's Manual*. At the same time, he is able to observe human life and activity with an objective, analytical detachment. This dual quality in his writing would not have been possible had he not been tolerant and unjudgmental, at this level, in his personal life. An intellectual, Petropoulos befriended members of the closed circles of the Greek underworld; he maintained friendships among Greek homosexuals. Neither *Kaliarda* nor the *Rebetic Songs* anthology would have been possible without these friendships, without this respect. Without these friendships (which were thus more than journalistic "contacts"), many of his other books, so rich in human experience and in specialized, often esoteric or taboo knowledge, would have resembled other studies on similar topics: ultimately disappointing because the writer has inevitably remained outside his subject matter.

Tolerance, detachment, straightforwardness, and insider's information create the *style* of this passage from *The Brothel*:

> I am obliged to provide more specific explanations. At the beginning, the prostitute always lies on her back, putting under the small of her back a round cushion that raises her pelvis. Then she spits into her right palm, applying the spittle to her *pudenda*—spittle is a neutral, slippery substance. Then the coition begins. Sometimes, after a short while, the customer will ask the prostitute to change positions to satisfy him more completely. The prostitute will agree to change her body position two or three times, but in general will get angry if a customer demands too many twists and turns, or affection.

Petropoulos's critics would call the above passage "pornographic." Social-ill bewailing moralists or politically correct ideologues might miss the point or demand that an outright attack against prostitution, the prostitute, the pimp, the customer, or men in general, be made. But more about Petropoulos's approach can be ascertained by meditating a moment longer on the phrase "applying the spittle to her *pudenda*—spittle is a neutral, slippery substance." The detail not only gives direct access to the prostitute's world, but also reveals much about the human relationships involved: much is contained in the word "slippery." Petropoulos was no moralist, but he was never uncompassionate. He was amoral and compassionate. Or to put it differently by citing a line in *Body*: "Art has its own morals."

By means of this carefully perceived detail, we pass through documentation and return with a new force and realism to the often too abstract or "second-hand" depictions and descriptions of literature and art. Petropoulos boasted that the most enthusiastic readers of *The Brothel* were the Athenian and Thessalonican prostitutes themselves, who proclaimed that the book described them and their lives perfectly. According to Petropoulos, *The Brothel* was even handed out after the trick in many brothels. His claims cannot be verified, but they are not excessive. In my files, I have a clipping of an erotic film advertisement in which a line from *The Brothel* is quoted.

XLIX

What, once again, is the relationship between this penetrating, far-reaching, curiosity and the persecution that this writer who obviously contributed so much to Greek culture suffered throughout his career? In one sense, he was definitely a *mounopsira*, as I called him in my *Maledicta* article and as Petropoulos himself liked to repeat, a "woman's crotch louse," which in Greek also means a person who digs down into the finest details to uncover startling aspects of reality. It is clear that Petropoulos pinched and bit right where and when the Greek State and Establishment did not expect him. Yet he was also much more than bothersome, troublesome, or meddlesome. He was practically omnipresent, like the tentacles of an octopus, in Greek culture and folklore. Although most academic writers ignored him, or even plagiarized him (see the introduction to *Old Salonica* for an example) as if he did not exist, no genuine scholar can go very far into the fields of lexicography, folklore, architecture, history, or sociology, without running into his looming silhouette. He was no fuming pamphleteer of sedition, as his enemies made him out to be and as a superficial acquaintance with his "scandals" might suggest. However, Petropoulos was subversive and his extensive writings remain so. He was subversive because of the frankness, humor, and "Byzantine"—as he phrased it—rigor that he brought to his studies. He was subversive because he went all out, in aspects of Greek life that were and remain taboo, in his search for the truth. The subversive writer, after all, tears the shroud of our preconceptions, prejudice, blindness, and ignorance, not with screams and propaganda, but rather with a far sharper weapon: a relentless search for truth. This is the quality, *the incriminating quality*, that made Petropoulos so controversial.

It cannot be repeated often enough: he was as brave as he was bold.

Often his search for truth was carried out in the prisons to which he had been confined because of his search for truth.

He was a natural antagonist of bourgeois morals and political correctness, well before the latter term was invented; to wit, the tone of his juxtaposition of women's liberation and underworld behavior in this passage of *The Underworld and Shadow Theater*:

> *Manges* (underworld tough guys) consorted with prostitutes and molls. (...) In both Old Athens and Piraeus, underworld molls were the most liberated Greek women of their time. Molls went about whenever and wherever they pleased, smoked, spoke freely, dressed simply, could scorn men, and were completely indifferent to the institution of marriage. Hoodlums (*koutsavakhides*) never married. They often lived with a woman, but under no obligations. They had a word for this illegal cohabitation: *kapatma*, from the same Turkish word meaning "mistress."

In *Rebetology*, he reiterates the point: "The *rebetissa*, the underworld "moll," is the most liberated woman...in contemporary Greece."

But even bolder are his passages about pederasty, an Anatolian tradition that is not to be confused with contemporary pedophilia (though, I daresay, he might have studied this topic as well, had he lived longer). In The *Underworld and Shadow Theater*, he writes:

> The English archeologist, historian and traveler W. M. Leake [1777-1860] mentions that Mouchtar Pasha, the son of Ali Pasha [the Pasha of Ioannina, 1741-1822], built a seraglio in the Anilios quarter of Metsovo for one of the good-looking local boys. Leake visited the seraglio in 1809. In 1806, Leake had already seen another large house, this one in Tyrnavos, built by the same pasha. Once again, some young Antinous was the cause.
>
> I shall not speak here about the famous *yiamakia* (*yiamaki* [singular], from Turkish *yamak* "helper," "young servant," "border inhabitant," "janissary") or *kioutsekia* (*kioutseki* [singular], from Turkish *köçek* "young male dancer dressed like a woman") who danced wearing bright red skirts and offered their love to whomever paid the most. In their insignificant, superficial article "Le Théâtre Karagöz en Turquie" (1964), Louis Gaulis and Albert Rodrik captioned one picture of a *köçek* thus: "Turkish girl dancer"!
>
> The Greek rebetic song composer Markos Vamvakaris reminisced

how, when he was a boy working in Syra, "his cheek was stolen and his ass was stolen" by a mechanic. Old-time shadow theater puppeteers were reputed to be both great pederasts and great ouzo guzzlers. Equally renowned were the pederasts of Ioannina.

In Greece, pederasts despise passive homosexuals (*poustidhes*). Nor do the latter ever mix with pederasts. Pederasts hunt handsome boys who, themselves, are not necessarily passive homosexuals. In Greece, there used to exist trades typically composed of pederasts: boatmen, shoemakers, and dealers of small wares were often pederasts, for example.

Pederasts by no means violently forced their boys into lovemaking. On the contrary, they would woo the boy and try to win him over. During the sexual act, pederasts would use masticated quince pulp as a lubricant. Pederasts exhibited fetishistic propensities toward *coprolatria*, dung worship, but the relevant details I shall not add here (despite the interest that they would hold for psychoanalysts and criminologists) so as not to disgust my reader.

Pederasts never viewed the boys whom they have won over as *poustrakia* "little queers, fairies." The same was true in the Greek underworld and is still true in Greek prisons. The underworld expression *tin vghazo kathari* "I pull it out clean" (i.e., I manage to meet my expenses or obligations" or "I flee from the penal consequences of the situation in which I was entangled"), now used in colloquial Greek, is derived from homosexual eroticism. Old-time tough guys used to dance the *zeïbekiko* [a solitary type of dance that is performed in a tense, melancholy manner] while holding their genitals. In the underworld, obligatory homosexual acts were often levied as punishments. In Piraeus, underworld hoodlums would often capture one of their enemies and take him to the then-deserted Kallipolis area, where he would be gang-sodomized. The expressions

malli khoristra kai kolo koudhounistra
    "a part in [his] hair and [his] ass like a rattle"

matia klista, kolos anikhtos, oti thelis vlepis
    "eyes shut, ass open, what you want you see"

alia 'po to ghamimeno kai to dharmeno
  "woe [is he] from the fucking and beating"

most certainly derive from the homosexual tradition of the Greek people. The same is true of these two underworld expressions:

mangia, klania ki eksatmisi kai kolo filistrini
  "lingo, farts, and a lot of exhaust [i.e., a big bag of wind, a lot of hot air], and an asshole round like a porthole"

ti mera palikari kai to vradhi maksilari
  "a roughneck by day, a cushion by night."

In the latter expression, the word *maksilari* "cushion, pillow" puzzles one at first; but in fact the explanation is quite simple: during the sexual act, the boy lies on a pillow placed under his abdomen.

Tough guys were usually accompanied by a *psykhoghio* "adopted son." In Istanbul, every tough guy had his *oghlani*. But the meanings of the two terms need to be kept distinct.

Eventually the homosexual tradition timidly appeared in Modern Greek literature. In his text "Paidos! Paidos!" (1940), Menelaos Loudemis describes a group of bricklayers, at least one of whom sodomizes a young Gypsy boy. In V. Mesolonghitis's *Akouma* (1929), an underworld figure relates: "Later I showed him my knife, a dagger given to me by an Anatolian bandit. He was killed by his apprentice. The two of them, as evil tongues say, had something special about them, something so very special that, oh God, you try not to think about it at all."

In my files, I have found the notes that I took when I asked Petropoulos about the distinction between *psykhoghio* and *oghlani* in the above passage. "*Psykhoghio* means 'adopted son,'" he explained, "and by extension 'aide-de-camp' or 'grocery shop assistant,' 'grocery boy.' The word *oghlani* (from Turkish *oğlan* 'boy') first referred to the boy servant whose job was to serve a pasha his coffee. The term carries negative connotations; every underworld boss has his *oghlani*, his 'minion.'" Tughlaci's *Grand Dictionnaire Turc-Français* (1968) gives the fourth definition of *oğlan* as "giton, jeune homme servant à de honteux plaisirs," in other words a young passive homosexual used for "shameful sexual pleasures." In Turkish, the term also means "jack" in cards.

L

Besides the battle for free speech that is implied and is literally, dangerously, at stake in such passages, Petropoulos also initiated and engaged in battles that were not strictly literary or folkloristic. During the Dictatorship of the Colonels, he challenged the Greek law stating that only marriages consecrated in Greek Orthodox churches were valid. Claiming to be a practicing atheist, he petitioned the Council of State, the highest administrative Greek court, over the following dilemma: a practicing atheist cannot be married in a Greek Orthodox Church and a Greek cannot be married anywhere else. Petropoulos's argument—since all Greeks are equal before the law, Greek atheists should have the right to marry—was eventually dismissed on a technicality involving fiscal stamps. He also waged a long administrative battle to obtain a Greek identity card with the words "atheist", not "Greek Orthodox," designated as his religion. He finally obtained this card on 1 January 1979. He was very proud of it: he gave me a photocopy.

When the Colonels banned the public broadcast and playing of rebetic songs, Petropoulos organized rebetic concerts in Athenian nightclubs. After the Greek Army had engaged in a stint of cannon firing from Lykavitos Hill, he sued the General Staff of the Army for "disturbance of the peace." In the appendix of *Kaliarda* (in which several other illustrations of his personal "war to ridicule the fascist mentality that governs every form of social life in Greece" are given), he offers this explanation: "I did not do these things just to scandalize Greeks unworthy of the name. I also wanted to demonstrate to *the enslaved* that even the prevailing fascist laws had loopholes in them." In *Underworld and Shadow Theater*, he had already argued: "It is impossible to comprehend the behavior of modern Greeks if you do not constantly remember that the Greek people were enslaved for at least twenty centuries…"

LI

Anything that is against the Church
rejoices me.
Anything that damages the Established Order
appeases me.
Anything that opposes Morality
Is good for my health.
And because Shit is smeared over everything
I say I'm going to write,
starting right now,
diabolical poems!

(from *Never and Nothing*)

LII

Family, Country, Flag, and God,
Scabies, rabies, cholera, and a cod.

(from *Mirror for you*)

LIII

After the PA.SO.K. Socialist government came to power in 1981, Petropoulos by no means turned his attention away from public issues. In one specific case, he showed that a major historical issue had scandalously been ignored. He began a one-man crusade to get the Holocaust of the Jews of Salonica commemorated in Greece. His project was a crucial one in a country that had "forgotten"—his oft-repeated, accurate, claim—and in a city which did not wish to recognize its complex ethnic origins.

Indeed, during the spring of 1943, over 50,000 of the approximately 57,000 Salonica Jews were exterminated in Nazi concentration camps. The Holocaust marked the abrupt, brutal death of one of the most flourishing Jewish communities in Europe. At its height towards the beginning of the twentieth century, the Jewish community of Salonica numbered over 100,000 members. There were forty synagogues and dozens of Jewish schools and institutions. In 1981, when Petropoulos initiated his project, only about 1250 Jews inhabited the city; one synagogue remained.

The roots of the Jewish community of Salonica go back as far as the Hellenistic period. The Apostle Paul preached in the synagogue there. Towards the end of the Middle Ages, many Jews reached Salonica from Central Europe and Italy. In 1492, Ferdinand and Isabel drove thousands of Jews out of Spain. Between 10,000 and 20,000 of them settled in Salonica, between 20,000 and 40,000 in Istanbul. The commercial activity of Salonica was soon dominated by these newly arrived Sephardic refugees.

The Jewish population of the city increased again in 1536 and in 1650 when new waves of Sephardic refugees arrived from Spain and Portugal. In the middle of the seventeenth century, victims of the Hmelnitski pogroms in Ukraine reached Salonica, and in the years 1720-1730 many Italian Jews settled there. Salonica became Greek only in 1912 (as Petropoulos never wearied of pointing out), after the defeat of the Turks in the Second Balkan War. At that time, many Jews, still grateful to Turkey for providing a haven from the Inquisition, felt obliged to leave the city, which explains the decrease in population between 1900 and 1943.

This is the rich historical background implicit in Petropoulos's widely published open letter, in December 1981, to the Greek Minister of Culture, Melina Mercouri, concerning the Holocaust of the Jews of Salonica. Petropoulos suggested that two projects be carried out in memory of the Salonica Jews deported and then exterminated by the Germans in 1943: the printing of a series of Greek commemorative stamps bearing the inscription "1943-1983 THE HOLOCAUST OF THE JEWS OF SALONICA"; and the raising of a memorial on the University of Thessaloniki campus, which after the Second World War was allowed to expand over the grounds of the old Jewish cemetery of the city.

When Mercouri failed to respond in any manner to the letter, the folklorist sent off a second appeal in April, 1982. "My appeal for a commemoration of the 40th anniversary of the Holocaust of the Jews of Salonica is not an entreaty but rather a demand," he wrote. "The Jews of Salonica were Greek citizens who paid taxes and who were regularly called up to serve in our Armed Forces. The Jews of Salonica left some 500 dead on the Albanian front. Not to mention their participation in the Greek Resistance."

Mercouri neglected to answer Petropoulos's second letter as well. By no means discouraged by this indifference, Petropoulos organized, in collaboration with Jewish groups, his own memorial service in Paris. It took place at the Centre Rachi on 13 March 1983 and was attended by a major part of the Jewish population of the city. The erstwhile ambassadors of Israel and Greece, Meïr Rosen and Christos Rokofyllos, were present, as well as Elie Nahmias and Nessim Gaon, respectively the former and then-acting president of the World Sepharadi Federation. (The irony of Petropoulos's entanglements with Mercouri and the Greek Socialist government during 1982-1983 is that he remained close to Rokofyllos, who had been a founding member of the "Democratic Defense" resistance movement during the Dictatorship and was subsequently an important PA.SO.K personality. Rokofyllos often invited him to receptions at the Greek Embassy and was an enthusiastic member of the audience—I remember distinctly—at the writer's lecture on rebetic songs, which took place on 3 March 1987 at the Maison de la Grèce, in the sixteenth arrondissement.)

At the memorial service, Petropoulos displayed *The Jews of Salonica / In Memoriam / Les Juifs de Salonique*, his own commemorative album of 140 old photographs, rare postcards, and drawings, some of which came from his own archives, others from that of his friend, the Judeo-Hispanic writer Enrique Saporta y Beja, who was born and raised in Salonica at the beginning of the twentieth century. The cover was illustrated by the French artist Roland Topor: it depicts a skull, whose mouth is replaced by the year "1943," which hovers ghostlike over a sort of wasteland spiked with pickets or perhaps tombstones. Inside the album is a second, much larger, drawing, showing the same skull hovering over a desert on which a crowd of people, alongside a Star of David, stands in a hole. Another friend, the linguist Haïm Vidal Sephiha, who taught Judeo-Spanish at the Sorbonne and whom the writer often consulted about Judeo-Spanish words, also spoke that day.

The album is no traditional production. Petropoulos had the old black-and-white photographs and postcards re-photographed in a special way that the French call a "tirage au trait." The darker grays in each old photograph became black in the new photograph, while the lighter grays became white. The professional photographer whom Petropoulos had commissioned to perform this task had tried to talk the folklorist out of it, insisting that the new photographs would be incomprehensible. Petropoulos persisted with his characteristic stubbornness and resolution. That he knew what he was doing is evident from the very first pages of this extremely moving album. The *tirage au trait* technique creates a particularly graphic and haunting effect accompanying these remembrances of the Jewish life that was once so present in Salonica, up until the arrival of the Germans in 1941, and that vanished brutally in 1943: there are many pictures of Jewish tradesmen, sidewalk barbers, peddlers, bootblacks, tinsmiths; of *hamals* (porters) bearing their burdens; of indigent Jews fishing rotten lemons out of the sea; of merchants posing with their families. There are several photographs of the synagogues destroyed during the war; others taken during the Great Fire of 1917. A few photographs portray the Jewish working-class quarters of Campbell and 151. A collage of newspaper clippings and a political cartoon showing a Turk spitting in the face of a Jewish bourgeois recall the Pogrom of 1931. The last pages of the album exhibit clandestine snapshots taken while 9000 Jews were being tortured in Liberty Square on 11 July 1942: the Germans forced them to perform gymnastic exercises from dawn until nightfall in the scorching heat of the Greek sun.

Apart from the captions and a brief historical summary, printed in both French and English, the album contains no text: the photographs, postcards, and other memorabilia speak for themselves. A community is born, grows, flourishes; is suddenly annihilated. In the case of the Jewish community of Salonica, nearly all traces of its existence were erased from memory. When Petropoulos launched his project, how many Greeks (not to mention the rest of us) knew that Thessaloniki, which according to chauvinistic legend was founded by Cassander, brother-in-law of Alexander the Great, was in fact until 1943 a Jewish city?

LIV

As to Petropoulos's special relationship to Jews and Judaism, a revealing indicator is this short text that I translated for the *Newsletter* of the Jewish Museum of Greece in December, 1985:

> As a child I had the habit of sneaking into Jewish homes. Among the objects that impressed me back then were *Jewish* wooden chests. I emphasize the word "Jewish" because our own Greek chests were shaped and decorated in an entirely different way. Traditional Greek chests were low and narrow, like oblong boxes, and often reminiscent of coffins. The lids of Greek chests were usually flat and thus Greeks could use their wooden chests as makeshift sofas.
>
> The Greeks of Salonica said that Jewish wooden chests looked like "camels." Indeed Jewish chests typically stood high, were made of light-colored wood, and had humped lids and lavishly carved front sides. Naturally it was impossible to sit on a Jewish chest. We Greeks found that strange. Equally strange to us were the Jewish decorations: the star of David, the incomprehensible Hebrew letters which "looked" to the left, and so on.
>
> Later, in the spring of the fateful year 1943, I came across many pieces of Jewish furniture lined up for sale on the sidewalks and public squares. Once again I had the "opportunity" to compare the stylistic traditions lying behind Greek and Jewish wooden chests. At that time the Jews already knew that they would be rounded up by the Germans and sent to the mythical (and of course nonexistent) Kingdom of Krakow. For that reason, the Jewish families all hurriedly sold off their possessions. I remember well how they bartered their furniture, especially for pants, for canteens, and for knapsacks. Nearly all the Jewish women left Salonica wearing pants—which was a sight never seen in those days—so as to get through more readily the ordeal of the long journey by train.
>
> I unfortunately do not possess any photographs of Jewish wooden chests and thus have been obliged to sketch from memory a few examples of them. I think now that it must have been from Spain that the Jews of Salonica brought this particular style of high wooden chest.

One last thing. With typical German methodicalness, the Kommandantur of Salonica gathered up all the pieces of furniture belonging to the Jews of Salonica and then scrupulously distributed them (using special allotment orders) to the officers of the Greek Gendarmery, beginning with the notorious elite division, the Ekatontarkhia....

LV

Petropoulos and I sometimes lunched together, on Thursdays, in a Chinese restaurant located near the office of the art and literary magazine, *Le Fou Parle*, to which we both contributed: me, originally, thanks to him. The magazine office was located at 10, rue de la Félicité, in the seventeenth arrondissement. Jacques Vallet, the editor-in-chief, would have opened the door to the office at about 11:30 a.m. By noon, three or four lunchtime habitués would have arrived: the literary critic André Rollin from the satirical newspaper *Le Canard Enchaîné*; the political cartoonist Jean Kerleroux, who worked at the same newspaper and who had illustrated *The Good Thief's Manual* and prepared many more drawings for a new edition; the artist Christian Zeimert; and Petropoulos who, if he had not come with me on the métro, would have taken a taxi all the way across Paris to join us. I remember that my close friend, the artist Denis Pouppeville, was there at least once, as was also sometimes the artist Jacques Poli, whose artist's studio was on the floor just above the magazine office. I attended those weekly lunches, off and on, for about two years. My first article in *Le Fou Parle* had been published in the twentieth issue (April, 1982). I contributed book reviews to all the subsequent issues, including the thirtieth and last one, a double issue that appeared in November, 1984.

Long after Vallet had stopped publishing the magazine, I ran into him at the Salon du Livre in Paris in the late-1990s. I had always felt grateful to him because of the encouragement that he had given to me as an unknown American debuting as a literary critic—in French. "I made my first weapons," as the French say, as a critic for *Le Fou Parle* and, of course, as Petropoulos's apprentice. Vallet urged me to write about books that came my way and perked my interest, little matter whether they had been published recently or not. The books that I reviewed for the magazine ranged from a translation of poems written by the I.R.A. activist Bobby Sand and a reissue of Charles Nisard's 1872 lexicon of "Parisian patois" to Apicius's Latin recipes, Paul Verlaine's erotic poetry (that had been excluded from the Gallimard-Pléiade edition of his collected poems), and Yambo Ouologuem's novel *Le Devoir de violence*, which had been unjustly withdrawn from sale by its publisher, Les Éditions du Seuil, because of a dubious plagiary accusation. As Vallet and I were chatting amidst the publishing world brouhaha in the vast hall of the Porte de Versailles Palais-Expo, one memory led to another until the name of Petropoulos came up. Vallet remarked that he had always marveled that Petropoulos would take a taxi all the way from the fifth arrondissement to the seventeenth, just to have lunch. He thought that Petropoulos's effort showed that he sometimes felt isolated as a Greek writer in Paris.

This being said, Greek and even foreign writers, artists, editors, or journalists who were in Paris for short stays often paid Petropoulos a visit. Sometimes Petropoulos called and told me to drop by immediately so that I could meet them as well. Whenever I was working on a translation with him in his apartment, the telephone would invariably ring once or twice or thrice. Yet what Vallet had observed is also true. Although Petropoulos would never have admitted it, he craved attention, as a writer, from the French, and remained embittered that he received relatively little. Few of his books were available in French translation, and even they were little known outside of his personal circle. Except for his poems that were published by the Éditions du Griot in 1991, he had himself arranged for the publication of his other French books, printing them himself. It was Mary Koukoules who paid for these magnificent *auto-éditions*.

It must be conceded that many of his books were so specifically Greek in their subject matter and polemical focus that there was little chance of interesting a standard French publisher or even a small press in them. Although I managed to publish excerpts of *The Greek Kiosk* and *Turkish Coffee in Greece* in journals, I, too, failed to find an American publisher back then for my translation of *The Good Thief's Manual* (which was also originally supposed to be published by Nefeli, reached the proof stage, but never appeared). Because Petropoulos was living in Paris, if he had been more diplomatic and flexible in his relationships with certain French writers, editors, and publishers, perhaps arrangements could have been made: books like *The Brothel, Lousology,* or *The Good Thief's Manual* might have appeared in some form, perhaps abridged. A fine selection of rebetic songs was later produced by Jacques Lacarrière and Michel Volkovitch (*La Grèce de l'ombre*, 1999), but this did not involve translating Petropoulos's own writings. When he arrived in France in 1975, he was a notoriously famous Greek writer; he necessarily ran into all kinds of superficial, yet influential, French literati who had little, if any, idea of what he had accomplished. Often "the current did not go through [the electric wire]," as the French say.

The Jews of Salonica / In Memoriam / Les Juifs de Salonique was conceived of as a bilingual album. Françoise translated the French pages. But after a certain point in time, Petropoulos prided himself on printing my English versions of his work in Paris. This was true of another text on Salonica and the Shoah, *A Macabre Song* (1985), his text on Costas Tscolis's art (*Tsoclis's Tree*, 1982), his poem sequence *In Berlin* (1987), and his long four-part poem *Mirror for You* (1983), which was illustrated by Fassianos. It was also true of Mary Koukoules's *Loose-Tongued Greeks: An Anthology of Neo-Hellenic Erotic Folklore* (1983), which I translated. Petropoulos would declare: "Printing texts in English in Paris gives the French a good slap in the face!"

LVI

"Maître," I said, "May I ask you a delicate question? Have you been paid?"

"The question is not delicate at all!" Petropoulos retorted. "I asked him for my money immediately, as soon as we came to an agreement. Hasn't he paid you?"

"No, he hasn't."

"As I said, I asked him immediately. He's a nice young man and we get along well. But until I'm paid, I'm not afraid to act like a pig. You have to, if you're a writer." "Moi, je suis un cochon!" he bellowed in French, raising his eyebrows and opening his eyes wide.

LVII

On another occasion, Petropoulos called one of his publishers in Athens and reminded him that I needed to be paid correctly and on time. They argued. Petropoulos kept insisting on a certain sum. He eventually banged the phone down on the hook, yet turned to me calmly and confirmed that everything was perfectly fine. Not long afterwards, a check in dollars arrived via a bank account held by his American friend, Katharine Butterworth. She had carried out a transaction with the publisher. Back then, Greek drachmas could not be sent out of the country.

LVIII

In countless ways, he was generous. One afternoon, he insisted on walking with me down the rue Mouffetard, then continuing to the intersection of the avenue des Gobelins, the boulevard Saint-Marcel, the boulevard Arago, and the boulevard du Port-Royal. At first, I thought that he was accompanying me part of the way home, since I walked that way whenever leaving his apartment and heading for the place d'Italie.

However, at the corner of the boulevard du Port-Royal and the avenue des Gobelins, Petropoulos instructed me to wait outside the Crédit Lyonnais bank. He went inside. There was a long line of customers. When he finally emerged, he handed me a sealed envelope, telling me that it contained payment for a translation that I had recently done for him. Whenever I translated something for him, we never agreed beforehand on a fee: he simply paid me, always on time, and it was always more than what I had expected. Sometimes he included a gift along with the payment, such as a book or even two engravings by Fassianos, both of which hang on a wall, in the adjoining room, as I write this. When I returned home, I found two thousand francs in the envelope, a large sum for Françoise and me. We took the métro to the Bazar de l'Hôtel de Ville department store, near the Hôtel de Ville, and bought a kitchen table.

This morning I am sitting at that same round wooden kitchen table, far from Paris, and correcting these pages. More than twenty years have gone by. It is 6:10 a.m.

LIX

Whenever I tried to pay for lunch, even for a cup of coffee, Petropoulos refused. "An older writer always pays for a younger writer," he would declare.

He would tell me the story about an older Greek author who had helped him out for a while when he was an impoverished writer and journalist in Athens. Petropoulos had been instructed to take his seat in such and such a restaurant, and the writer would pay for his lunch.

LX

Whenever we worked together on a bibliophilic project at the Mérat brothers' printing shop, Petropoulos would take a break and go to a nearby pastry shop, on the rue de Rennes, and buy a large box full of small sugar cookies for the children of the two Mérat brothers. Such sugar cookies were actually *petits fours*, in other words the kind of cookie that is served in France at buffets and receptions but not eaten as a dessert and only rarely as snacks. Once or twice, in the pastry shop, I suggested that he instead get an éclair or a *religieuse* for each of the children, but he always instructed the woman behind the counter to fill up a large box with *petits fours*. It occurs to me that his systematic choice of these particular cookies—albeit somewhat resembling Greco-Turkish *koulouria*—for a gift reveals his lack of integration into French life, despite his vast culinary knowledge and irrepressible love of sweets. In any event, it once again reveals his generosity. Whenever we were going to finish one of our bibliophilic projects, Petropoulos would buy a bottle of champagne and bring it to the printing shop, even though he would not drink from the glass that he had poured for himself.

LXI

He would say: "Once you start working regularly with a person, you stick with him." I was hardly the only person to benefit from this faithfulness.

LXII

He was an adamant individualist, a hardheaded man, "une tête dure" (as he liked to say in French). I am making an understatement. He could be notoriously difficult to get along with. He sometimes made brash statements that provoked or even aggressed his interlocutor, not personally, but in the sense that the interlocutor belonged to a social, religious, or national group. Sometimes Petropoulos wrongly insisted on the pertinence of this group to the individual's deepest values; or miscalculated the degree or extent of the pertinence. He himself told me that when he first asked Roland Topor to illustrate the cover of *The Jews of Salonica / In Memoriam / Les Juifs de Salonique*, the artist hesitated, explaining that he was first and foremost an artist, not a "Jewish artist." Topor and Petropoulos gradually became good friends. Petropoulos valued the Frenchman's artistic work highly and eventually wrote a sequence of four long poems, *Topor: Four Seasons* (1991). In "Topor Spring," he observes that "through Topor's texts and drawings emerges Joy / the Joy of Living, and this strikes me as being his most significant character trait. / I would like to show, simply, that Topor is a Good Human Being." When Topor was dying in mid-April, 1997, Petropoulos sat for hours at the hospital, waiting. He called me on April 17th, the day after the artist's death, and told me that it was one of the worst shocks of his life.

LXIII

Long before then, beginning with his 1982-1983 campaign to get the PA.SO.K. government to commemorate the Holocaust of the Jews of Salonica, and continuing well beyond the year 1985, when he made an official appeal to the erstwhile West German Minister of Justice to prosecute the family and former assistants of the Nazi medical doctor Josef Mengele, Petropoulos became fascinated with Jewish identity in ways that sometimes made me uncomfortable. By this, I mean he became fascinated beyond the legitimacy of the questions raised in his article

"Was El Greco Jewish?", published in the July-September 1983 issue of *Tomes*. He wanted to know who was Jewish and who was not, and sought out indicators of Jewishness.

I have a calling card that I received from him, probably around this time and surely attached to photocopies. On it he writes: "Françoise + John, BONNE ANNÉE!" But he has blackened out his last name and written "GOY." Similarly, I have a greeting card that he designed and sent to me: it is a folded photocopy of a photo on which Françoise, Elias, Mary, the bouzouki player Nikolas Syros, and I are standing and laughing at a party. (I think that this photo was taken at a rebetic concert that took place in the Greek restaurant that used to be located across the street from the Greek bookshop on the rue Vandamme, near Montparnasse train station.) Petropoulos has highlighted our clothes, faces, and hands in green, pink, and yellow—a technique that he often used because it reminded him of how, before the invention of color photography, black-and-white photographs would be touched up with color. With his red pen, he has written "goy" above Françoise's, Mary's, and Nikolas's heads, and "juif" above ours. In very small handwriting at the top of the card, he has noted in Greek: "To John Taylor! Dinos Christianopoulos." He perfectly imitates the Greek poet's legible, but minuscule, writing. Included with the same mock greeting card, however, is a photocopy of the same photo, this one untouched. Petropoulos loved commemorating events with photos, especially when other writers and artists were involved. Many of these photos were taken by Vassilis Liappas, a young Greek photographer who was living in Paris and to whose talent and efficiency Petropoulos often appealed.

After a while, whenever Petropoulos mentioned that such and such a politician, artist, or writer was Jewish, I protested: "But Elias, who cares?" He could not always perceive the analogy between his own oft-proclaimed atheism (with respect to his origins, which were necessarily Greek Orthodox) and the desire of some Jewish-born artists or writers (especially those belonging to the atheistic and anarchistic circles of *Le Fou Parle*, the magazine that had enabled many of us to meet for the first time) to be viewed as artists and writers exclusively. Understandably, such artists and writers were reluctant to be identified systematically with a religion in which they (and perhaps their parents and grandparents as well) did not believe. The question of Jewish identity for each given Jew can of course be more complicated than what I have outlined here, but Petropoulos would insist on its pertinence in a manner that, paradoxically, recalled the vigor with which he highlighted the multiethnic origins of "typically Greek" phenomena.

Similarly, I received through the mail a mock certificate, dated 25 March 5982 (*sic*), stating that I—"Ioannis Raptis"—was a freemason. ("Raptis" means "tailor.")

If you belonged to his inner circle and knew how to laugh, you could chide him about his exaggerations. You would meet with little success perhaps, but it was possible to chide, even argue; he relished arguments.

LXIV

Yet with respect to his especial fascination for Jews, this candid passage from *A Macabre Song*:

> Greeks today nourish many illusions. One of them is that they helped the Jews, a point that they like to emphasize. It is true that the Greeks did not rejoice in the tragic suffering of the Jews. But it is also true that most Greeks, on the slightest pretext, bantered Jews sarcastically. In 1943, while living in Salonica, I heard my compatriots saying to their Jewish fellow townsmen: "The Germans are going to make soap out of you!" This injurious phrase raises the following important question: How did the Greeks know, as early as 1942, of the fate awaiting the Jews?
>
> Today it is a certainty that the Americans knew, as did the German people, of the existence of the Hitlerian concentration camps. But it has apparently never been learned by what invisible channels the related rumors reached Salonica. In any case, I remember well all that was said back then about the imaginary Jewish Kingdom of Krakow, about how the Germans were going to chop up the Jews and fill tin cans with human flesh, and about other similarly horrible, dreadful things.
>
> All of this, I maintain, was clearly asserted in a little song in fashion back then. We used to sing it aloud, we Greeks, especially when teasing Jewish kids. It was a simple march, which in 1942 spread

like wildfire throughout Salonica. Neither the versifier nor the composer are known. We sang the song up to the end of the war, but when the tragedy of the Jews became known we stopped singing it, out of shame. The song probably had three or four couplets. I remember only the following lines:

Damn the Germans
Who killed all the Kikes
And sent them to Krakow
To die of hunger.
. . . .
. . . .
and sent them to Poland
to die all alone.

(...) I also sang this macabre song, trying, as we all did, to imitate the pronunciation and the solecisms typically employed by Spanish-speaking Jews when speaking Greek. And with indescribable sorrow, I remember how whenever I got into a tussle with my friend Samico Howell, I would sing that ignominious song right to his face. Samico never returned...

The song has been forgotten by the Thessalonians: I will force them to recall it.

LXV

Petropoulos evolved during the next decade; he acquired nuance, even if as late as 2000, he speculated about the possible Jewish origins of the famous "national poet" of Greece, Dionysios Solomos (who, in any event, had intimate connections to Italy and to the Italian language). I do not remember him talking about Jews when he phoned during the 1990s, nor when we saw each other in Paris. In any event, in 1992, he published one of his most touching and self-revealing texts, "Ah, Allegra..." in a special "Salonique 1850-1918" issue of the French magazine *Autrement*:

> As the suffix *–poulos* of my name indicates, my family originally came from southern Greece. Around 1930, my father, who was a minor civil servant, was transferred to Salonica; at the time, this was a synonym

of exile. Nonetheless, because we were obliged to leave Athens, we settled in Salonica. In 1934, my father was able to buy a very beautiful house that had originally belonged to a *bey* who had left for Turkey a few years beforehand and about whom our neighbors had retained very precise memories. Our house was located near the Rotunda. This was important because, although we did not live in a Jewish quarter, I had come across some Jewish kids who lived here and there in our street and I had rapidly become friends with them. (...) Near us was a patriarchal Jewish family. I began to pay them visits. They accepted me affectionately because I was a close friend of their youngest boy, Samico.

Now that I have become old, I often ask myself why I feel such love for the Jews. When I analyze myself, I remember that, from my earliest years, I would play with little Jewish kids because my parents showed great sympathy to the Jews of Salonica. And this was strange because, for Athenians, Jews were unknown people: exotic human beings, as it were. In any event, my father had ordered us to do all our shopping at the Jewish grocery store in the neighborhood, not at the Greek grocery stores. Similarly, my mother never scolded me (as other Greek mothers would) because I went to play in a Jewish house. (...)

There is another reason why I liked Jews. In Salonica, many Jews had light reddish hair. As for me, I was a blond child with blue eyes, and I had freckles on my face. I looked like a Jew. And because I did not know how to speak Greek with a Salonican accent (at home, we spoke Greek as it is spoken in the south), many young Greeks thought that I was a Jew; for this reason, when I walked through certain quarters, I would be slapped, or hit with thrown stones. All this made me empathize, even when I was a little boy, with how the poor Jews suffered. I learned to identify with them.

My mother naturally had a Jewish seamstress. Her name was Allegra. (...) Often, whenever my mother had an appointment with Allegra, she would take me along. Allegra had light reddish hair and green eyes. She must have been twenty-six or twenty-seven. I fell in love with her instantly. I was only eight. Actually, I don't know if I fell in love with her or her house. (...) In the parlor, I would become giddy with the special smell that Jewish houses in Salonica had, that is a blend of rosewater, sautéed onions, and ripe melons—a smell that always makes me nostalgic. Along with my mother, other customers would be trying on dresses. The women would undress in front of me without the slightest shame, giving me glimpses of female anatomy in the process. On her knees in front of a customer, her mouth full of needles, Allegra would correct a hem. I watched her. I admired her.

The young Greeks of Salonica never went into Jewish houses. For me, every Jewish house was like a fairy tale. (...) To use a metaphor, let me say that Greek houses had a green atmosphere and Jewish houses a red atmosphere. Allegra's parlor had large windows with colored windowpanes. Of course, I had already seen Turkish windows with yellow, mauve, red, green, and blue windowpanes in many other Salonican houses. But in Allegra's parlor, I had the impression of flying through a rainbow along with my red-haired witch.

In 1939, I started junior high school. I had grown, and my mother no longer took me to Allegra's seamstress shop. In the fall of 1940, war knocked on our door. In April 1941, the Wehrmacht occupied Salonica. The terrible famine of 1941-1942 followed, and soon thereafter the Holocaust. In 1944, my father was murdered. (...) I have never been able to learn in what Auschwitz, in what Buchenwald, my beloved Allegra was killed.

LXVI

Although Petropoulos was considered by his enemies to be a provocateur and a sociopath, he could be animated by a gregarious spirit. He liked to get out, to meet people (including younger artists and writers), and he was present at countless gallery openings and literary evenings. He was often amused by the idiosyncrasies of his writer- and artist-friends. Capable of accepting and respecting them on their own terms, he demanded the same treatment.

He was no solitary writer exclusively imbued with himself and his creativity, however simultaneously egocentric or egomaniacal he could also be. He believed in—knew that he belonged to—an international fraternity of writers and artists. Simply, the literary and artistic Republic that he envisioned was no democracy based on egalitarian principles. It implied an aristocratic hierarchy in which certain writers (or artists) were superior to others, not by birth or success, but rather by talent. He had an utter contempt for mediocre writers. "Les minables," he called them in French.

One evening at a meeting of the French Union des Écrivains (to which he belonged, essentially because of his constant fears of being deported from France), a young writer named M. took the floor. He was campaigning. Elections were going to be held: the positions of president, vice-president, treasurer, and the like, were open. The writer M. expatiated on all sorts of potential projects. His way of speaking made him seem both pretentious and ridiculous. Rather loudly, Petropoulos whispered in my ear: "He doesn't want to be a writer. He wants to have "sardines"—as one says in Greek—on his shoulder, like in the army!"

LXVII

Leafing through my tattered blue Paris address book from the 1980s. At the top of the "P" page: Elias Petropoulos's name, addresses, telephone numbers. Just names and numbers, but...

— 34, rue Mouffetard, 75005 Paris. This home address was eventually replaced by B.P. 36, 75221 Paris Cedex 05. Petropoulos rented the post-office box when he initiated his Pornographia Maxima project. He asked his writer- and artist-friends to give him copies of the most extreme pornographic images or descriptions that they could find or produce. I am not sure how much success he had. Françoise and I were readying to leave Paris, then we did leave: in August 1987. Several images later reproduced in *A History of the Condom* may well have come from this appeal. He regularly asked friends for images, documents or information about the topics that impassioned him, including even mustaches (*The Mustache*, 1990) and chairs (*Chairs and Stools*, 1995). The post office address offered discretion. Moreover, he was always worried about someone stealing his mail, and for a while the lock on his rue Mouffetard mailbox was defective. Sometimes I accompanied him to the post office on the rue de L'Épée-de-Bois.

— the country home at 10, rue du Roncier, Coye-la-Forêt, 60580 Oise. The telephone number was 458-68-33. Back then, you dialed the prefix 16 when you were calling from Paris to a locality outside of Paris. I remember a late-summer afternoon when Petropoulos and I had a cup of coffee in the PMU horserace-betting bar on the boulevard Vincent-Auriol. He had dropped by our apartment to give me a letter to translate, then had suggested that we go elsewhere so as not to disturb Françoise, who was putting the finishing touches on her doctoral thesis about "sein" and "haben" in the German verb system. Because of her competence in German, Petropoulos would ask her questions about the language. Once, he phoned and wanted to know the etymology of "nazi," why there was a "z," and why different pronunciations existed. In such cases, Françoise would get out her books and dictionaries to verify and double-check, and these conversations could go on for a long time.

In the horserace-betting bar, Petropoulos studied the men sitting at small tables and watching the race results on a television screen. He commented on their gestures. He explained how, as a boy, he would listen to, as much as watch, his father playing cards, especially paying attention to how bids were slapped down hard on the table. He accompanied every memory of these remote fatherly card games with the appropriate gestures. After our chat, we left to find a taxi that would take him to the Gare du Nord. He needed to take the train to Coye-la-Forêt, water the lawn and flowers, then return to Paris that evening. Apropos of gestures, Petropoulos sometimes watched television with the sound off in order to "study gestures," as he put it.

— the Berlin address at the Künstlerhaus Bethanien, Mariannenplatz 2, 1000 Berlin 36. Elias Petropoulos and Mary Koukoules left for Berlin in the fall of 1983. He had been invited to spend a year at the Byzantinisches Seminar at the Freie Universität and they were going to live in the Künstlerhaus Bethanien, alongside other writers, artists, and film directors (including Andrei Tarkovski, whose films he admired). Petropoulos was, to all appearances, relatively happy in Berlin, even if he did not speak German. He was respected and admired by the professors in the Greek department at the Freie Universität, who had awarded him a scholarship. He could have stayed on in Berlin, teaching and lecturing. Some of his books might have been translated into German, adding to the versions of *In Berlin, Suicide, Mirror for You*, and *Rebetology* that had been published in German reviews. He had hopes for a German translation of *The Good Thief's Manual*, as his Berlin letters to me reveal. (A selection from the *Rebetic Songs* anthology was eventually published as *Rebetiko: Die Musik der städtischen Subkultur Griechenlands* in 2002.) But he declined to remain in Berlin. He returned to Paris, the city in which he maintained such a difficult and defiant relationship with the French, and in which next to no publishers showed interest in his work.

— and the address of the small apartment that he rented to work in, for a few months, at 32, rue Boussingault, 75013 Paris. The telephone number was 588-59-70. For this last telephone number (for instance), a French person customarily said the equivalent in French of "five hundred eighty eight, fifty nine, seventy" ("cinq-cent-quatre-vingt-huit, cinquante-neuf, soixante-dix"). If pronounced rapidly, this way of reciting a number was difficult to understand even for a foreigner who could otherwise speak and understand French well. Numbers like "quatre-vingt-huit," literally "four-twenty-eight" for 88, or "soixante-dix," literally sixty-ten" for 70, confused the ear and the mind, even when one had heard them often. Petropoulos hated this lexical rule and sociological habit. When speaking French, Petropoulos would say: "cinq, huit, huit, cinq, neuf, sept, zéro." He was always precise when pronouncing addresses and telephone numbers. When he wrote an address on an envelope, it was always perfectly legible. He often ordered me to write more legibly.

The rue Boussingault apartment was about a twenty-minute walk from our apartment on the rue Albert-Bayet, which was located on the other side of the same arrondissement, the thirteenth. Whenever I went to the rue Boussingault apartment to work with Petropoulos, he asked me to pick up an entire carton of cigarettes (or cigarillos) on my way, at a tobacco shop on the rue Bobillot. There were no tobacco shops on or near the rue Boussingault.

The day he moved his books into that apartment, I helped him. We carried boxes of them down to a taxi waiting at the place de Contrescarpe, near the rue Mouffetard, and we made several subsequent taxi trips between the two apartments. After we had arranged his desk and shelved his books, Petropoulos hung paintings and drawings on the walls. He had a talent for interior decorating. Today, whenever I hang a painting or drawing on one of our own walls, I think of him. He once told me: "Make your writing space personal. You can even put a vase of flowers on your desk." I tried that for a few days, then threw the anemones out.

The rue Boussingault apartment was burgled twice. The first time, it was a mere reconnaissance run. The second time, a week or two later, a folding screen made out of glass and designed by a young German woman artist whom he knew was stolen. Petropoulos would tease Alekos Fassianos because another folding screen, this one wooden and decorated by Fassianos, had been left behind by the burglars. Petropoulos reported neither burglary to the police. When I offered my condolences to him about the robbery, the author of *The Good Thief's Manual* replied with a slight smile: "C'est normal. Stealing is normal."

LXVIII

Other names and addresses from my life back then:

— that of Anna and Christos, the young Greek couple who lived on the rue de Milan in the ninth arrondissement and gave me conversation lessons. Sometimes Anna verifed my translations of words or expressions before I went over the fine details with Petropoulos. Sometimes Anna could not help, however. Many words and expressions noted in Petropoulos's books were appearing in print for the first time. Petropoulos was teaching his readers what the words or expressions meant. While speaking with one of his compatriots, he sometimes whipped a small steno pad from his pocket and noted down an expression that he had never heard before; the expression inevitably ended up in one of his books.

— that of a high-ranking French civil servant who had been married and had fathered children before deciding that he was gay; he moonlighted as a journalist for the homosexual magazine, *Le Gai Pied*. One afternoon he interviewed Petropoulos for an article. I was present, as was Alekos Fassianos, when Petropoulos declared: "Je suis un sodomiste!" The journalist-civil servant laughed, remarking: "Don't worry, I won't quote that." Whereupon Petropoulos retorted: "By all means quote that!"

These musings, digressions, and still others, because of my tattered Paris address book from the 1980s....

I began noting the graffiti that I came across in Paris, re-sketching whatever images accompanied the phrases, and copying them both in a small notebook. This habit, which lasted for a few months, was inspired by Petropoulos's album *From the Jails*, a collection of ten essays on such topics as prison graffiti, tattoos, embroidery work, and handicrafts. Most items displayed in the book were sketched (because cameras were prohibited) while Petropoulos was in prison. This book contains the tattoo that is often mentioned in reviews of his work: the convict who had had "A. P.," the Greek initials for "City Police," tattooed on his penis. The same convict also had a fish tattoo on his tongue in order to show that he could keep quiet.

LXIX

So many unforgettable details! In *The Good Thief's Manual*, Petropoulos shows step by step how pickpockets, picklocks, safecrackers, and other underworld figures live, work, are arrested, tortured, tried, sent to prison. He devotes an entire chapter, then a "supplement," to burglars:

> *A Burglar is a Thief who Forces.*
> A Burglar forces doors, windows, locks, drawers, dressers, strongboxes. A Burglar works at night. Usually alone. For big jobs, two

or three Burglars work together. A Burglar's most important tool is the *jimmy*, a small crowbar.

Burglars can be recognized by their methodical techniques.

Burglars leave nothing to chance. They work deftly, discreetly, quickly, reliably. They are completely aware that their profession is dangerous and almost artistic. (...)

Before breaking into the house, the Burglar takes a little stroll around the neighborhood, looking over the neighboring houses. He progresses, slightly in a hurry, feigning indifference. He neither raises his eyes nor turns his head. But he naturally takes in everything, just by shifting his eyes. Once he is sure that no one is watching him with curiosity, he *hits* the target *at its weakest point*. He enters through a basement window or forces the backdoor of the kitchen.

During work hours, a Burglar is decently dressed, and *always* wears a suit. He carries an ordinary bag or small travel bag. In it he totes his tools: shears, a jimmy, a betty, a screwdriver, a flashlight, gloves. *Shears* are a sort of scissors with which he cuts locks and chains. A *jimmy* is a short, solid crowbar with a flat, slightly convex and forked end: it is used to force doors. A *betty* is a Burglar's tool that looks like an "S"; its two ends are inversely convex; one of its ends is forked. The large *screwdriver* is made of an experience-tested, highly resistant, metal: it is used to force drawers. The *flashlight* is indispensable, but the lens is covered with adhesive tape, except for a little hole from which a tiny ray of light can shine. During the Theft, the Burglar never turns on a light (*never!*). Even the flashlight is used *rarely and, even at that, only for a second*. (...)

The Burglar leaves his tool bag near the *getaway*; he takes the large screwdriver and the flashlight with him. Naturally, he is already wearing gloves. The Burglar's gloves are black so that they will be invisible in the darkness. The gloves are either silk or light cotton women's gloves. Burglars have small delicate hands. They *never* use rubber, nylon, or leather gloves because such might be ripped open without their realizing it, and fingerprints left everywhere. Many Burglars use dark cotton men's socks instead of gloves. Some Burglars go barehanded, carefully wiping off anything that they have touched with a handkerchief. Again, if danger arises, the Burglar takes his bag with all the tools and vanishes.

During work hours, a Burglar takes care not to bump into a piece of furniture or knock over a vase. The soles of his shoes must be spotlessly clean; he wipes his feet before entering the house. A Burglar does not wear a hat because it might fall off and be left behind (a mortal danger) should he have to run.

A Burglar does not carry *personal* objects like a passport, a watch, bills, etc. *No Burglar wears a mask.* The idea that Burglars wear masks comes from idiotic Crime Reporters. From these same idiots comes the idea that a Burglar carries hundreds of keys on him, and a case of high-precision tools, like a surgeon.

LXX

Details, more details, ever more details—many of them extraordinarily rich, revealing, or poignant. An original contribution of *The Good Thief's Manual* is its precise evidence on how the space defined by the very architecture of the prison tortures the prisoner: not merely the exiguousness of solitary confinement cells but also supposedly minor details such as the placement of windows (requiring convicts to hoist themselves up so that they can see what is going on in the courtyard) or the height of walls with respect to the size of the inner courtyard (the vision of longtime prisoners is permanently impaired because their eyes become accustomed to only short distances). For the latter dilemma, Petropoulos recommends studying clouds.

The critic should never underestimate Petropoulos's scrutiny of architecture, specifically of what he called "popular architecture."

The reader also descends into the inferno of a convict's everyday life: the toilets without stools, the concrete beds, the absence of heaters, the prohibition of forks, knives, matches, and mirrors. Petropoulos once told me about his own humiliation whenever he had to defecate in front of the other convicts. As has been seen, in some Greek prisons there were neither stools nor stall doors. The prisoner defecated into a hole that in French is called a *toilette à la turque*, a "Turkish toilet." "I know that this detail is not particularly interesting," he told me on that occasion, "but for the prisoner it is his everyday reality, and a torture."

LXXI

When you entered the rue Mouffetard apartment, you saw, to the right, a very large painting by Costas Tsoclis, another of Petropoulos's close artist-friends. It hung on the wall near the kitchen door. The painting belonged to a series that Tsoclis was putting together at the time: he would paint a pale blue background on a canvas, then affix to it, at an unsettling angle, a long wooden board whose edges had been sanded down. Petropoulos wrote his long prose text *Tsoclis's Tree* about the paintings and lithographs that the artist was producing back then:

> I bought one of Tsoclis's paintings. I hung it up across the room from my desk. (...) I focus my eyes on Tsoclis's large white painting with the Tree, the Tree, the Tree. The perspective gives an illusion of the Renaissance. Tsoclis's board gives an illusion of a tree. But the tree isn't taken captive within the border of the painting. In Tsoclis's painting, typically only one object is present, floating in a generally chromatic composition. A real tree is the motive behind the painted tree. But a motive is not an explanation. I approach the real tree in the real forest. Tsoclis's tree has another code. Tsoclis refuses to bear the Past like a hamal who...
>
> (...) Suddenly Tsoclis puts it to him: So why did you want to see my paintings? Take a look at this one. I finally ended up being a journalist. My objectivity is imaginary. It's a leap I take inside the description of the object. Taking the tree's hard shell in hand, I ossify Time. I employ only a handful of words and a simple syntax. Out of spite I repudiate various colors. That whitish background dismantles our censorship of the painted object. (...) Since I am able to perceive a human being (-in-himself) both as a divine creature and a future corpse, I am also able to perceive a tree (-in-itself) both as thick foliage and a wooden beam. Hey, don't touch that picture! I said I was depicting the Tree-Idea, the Tree-Image.

Because of the boards, Tsoclis's canvas-sculptures were heavy. One afternoon, I helped Petropoulos, Tsoclis, and Mary Koukoules hoist the painting from the inner courtyard up to their courtyard window. It was not easy. The cumbersome painting had been secured with a thick rope, which Petropoulos, Tsoclis and I were tugging on; but the canvas swung against the wall as we hoisted it. We struggled ever so slowly, following Petropoulos's orders to hoist, then wait, then hoist again. Once we finally got the painting into the apartment, at an angle (the canvas fit through the window only diagonally), we all took a rest. We were sweating profusely. Then I saw that someone's fingernail had dented the canvas, on the left-hand corner toward the bottom, during our struggles to bring it through the open window.

Tsoclis took a look. He asked Mary for a blow-drier. She went upstairs, then returned.

Tsoclis gave the blow-drier to Petropoulos, and had him hold it at just the right distance and angle. As the canvas was heating, Tsoclis gently rubbed the canvas with his finger, smoothing out the dent.

Petropoulos liked to recall Tsoclis's technique for repairing the painted canvas. It was exactly the kind of practical knowledge that he relished: the fruit of long experience and attentive care.

LXXII

Practical knowledge, long experience, the art of paying attention: he cited examples time and again. In *The Greek Kiosk*, he relates how a kiosk owner will secretly slip a condom into his customer's hand or fold a leftist newspaper in two so that the police will not see its name. In *Birdcages in Greece*, he explains how a depressed canary can be cheered back into singing. In *Turkish Coffee in Greece*, he expatiates on the "secret" of making a good Turkish coffee, to wit the "slowness" of the cooking:

> A good coffee maker must necessarily be a patient coffee maker. In order to make a connoisseur's coffee, it is necessary to heat it over a gentle fire for nearly twenty minutes. At the same time, the coffee maker must mix his coffee ever so slowly, sometimes stirring with the "swizzle stick," sometimes tapping it lightly on the bottom of the *briki*. Only in this manner will the coffee take shape. For it must never be forgotten that making coffee is as difficult as cooking *saleps*.

In *The Good Thief's Manual*, Petropoulos gives instructions for making a kind of primitive cigarette lighter that is fashioned in reform schools: the explanation is sufficient for fashioning a *tiritrompa* yourself. Posing in the same book as an eminent professor at the Royal Institute for the Art and Practice of Burglary, Petropoulos provides the step-by-step techniques for snatching purses:

> The *Purse Snatcher* is always young. He has to be young. He has to be nimble and fast on his feet.
> The Purse Snatcher lies in wait > snatches > runs.
> Often the Purse Snatcher owns a moped, which he parks near his theater of action. Sometimes he snatches a woman's purse while astride his machine. Otherwise, Purse Snatchers work in pairs. One Purse Snatcher waits on the moped, with its motor running, while the other one, walking *up against* the victim, snatches the purse, tosses it to the driver, and then runs off in the other direction. After running a block or so, he slows down and begins to walk normally. The other one disappears with the moped (and the purse). This method is psychologically effective: the victim follows her purse with her eyes. Hence both Purse Snatchers escape.
> Purse Snatchers mainly snatch women's purses. Sometimes, however, they steal briefcases held by old men.
> Purse Snatchers act ruthlessly in bourgeois or upper-class neighborhoods, where women carry a lot of dough on them, few pedestrians are about, and streets are never busy: as everyone knows, well-heeled neighborhoods have no shops. Moreover, what proud bourgeois gentleman would cry out even if a Purse Snatcher ripped off his neck chain?

Here is another characteristic passage from *Turkish Coffee in Greece*:

> Women were tacitly prohibited in coffeehouses. As for young boys, fathers would often take their sons to the coffeehouse, especially on Sundays. The boys would be served a *loukoum* (a piece of Turkish delight) or a spoonful of vanilla cream, better known as a "submarine" because it would be dunked in the glass of water. Old men like loukoums because they are soft. Before eating one, however, an old man typically shakes the powdered sugar off onto the saucer, then dunks the loukoum into his glass of water: a moistened loukoum will

not stick to his dentures and yank them out. The powdered sugar that covers loukoums (so that they will not stick to each other) is called *loukoumoskoni* ("loukoum powder"). From the coffeehouse, old chaps insult passing homosexuals with the cry: "Smother her with loukoum powder!" In Greek shadow theater, Karagiozis's elusive dream is the "loukoum death," the *loukoumothanatos*.

LXXIII

Every time I write a book review, I hear Petropoulos exhorting me to write books: "You waste your time otherwise! Articles vanish into oblivion!"

Whenever he spoke about his own critical writings in literature and especially art, he summed them up, not as "criticism," but rather as "impressions" or "appreciations." Much of his early work was of this kind: *Nikos Gabriel Pentzikis* (1958), *Pavlos Moskhihdis* (1959), *Yiorgos Paralis* (1959), *Karolos Tsizek* (1959), *Bost* (1959), *Kharaktiti / P. Tetsis* (1960), *Stam. Stam.* (1963), *Georgios Derpapas* (1965), as well as the aforementioned first essay ever written about Odysseus Elytis, which was included in *Elytis Moralis Tsaroukhis*, an album reproducing the poet's erotic collages alongside the work of the two artists. (Petropoulos's own erotic collages, which resemble Elytis's, are gathered in *Mainly That*, 1994.) As late as 2002, Petropoulos wrote ten poems inspired by the paintings of the sensitive and thoughtful young Greek artist, Dimitris Souliotis, who became close to Petropoulos in the 1990s; these poems were published in Souliotis's catalogue of February 2002 (Yiayiannos Gallery) and, beforehand, in Petropoulos's *Four Artists: Anton, Vitastali, Dourali, Souliotis* (1999). Petropoulos often remarked: "I always listen attentively to what my artist-friends say. I try to grasp each of their so very different perceptions of the world."

LXXIV

Souliotis did some fine drawings of Petropoulos. He also painted a large canvas that movingly, even hauntingly, evokes the poet-folklorist. In the painting, Petropoulos walks across a rose-hued desert or perhaps a concrete surface of some sort. He is groping for something with his hands or possibly holding onto an invisible object—call it his own life-long literary quest for goals that were necessarily escaping from him at the end of his life. There is a determined look in his eye, as there always was in real life when he was not laughing or playing a practical joke. Characteristically, he is wearing a hat, which he himself associated with the Jewish custom. He is about to pass by a tree, ostensibly the most important element in the painting, for it is placed conspicuously in the foreground; the tree is casting a long shadow parallel to Petropoulos's relatively much shorter one. Incidentally, this is another instance where Souliotis has skewed the perspective in his painting, for in the foreground Petropoulos is not as dwarfed by the nearby tree as the respective shadows would make one expect. In any event, it can be deduced that the sun is low in the sky, whereas our own vantage point as observers is relatively high. Is this tree the Tree of Life, the Tree of Death, a "real" tree to which Petropoulos—who loved natural things—attended in the back yard of his country home, or somehow all of these? Small smokestacks have sprouted from the ground, as if foretelling Petropoulos's own cremation or, alternatively—given his hat—evoking the Shoah. The painting was made well before Petropoulos's death and any observer not recognizing the full-bearded author will, I am sure, think of Auschwitz. This finely detailed portrait is an extreme case of the figurative, human-oriented references that crop up even in Souliotis's most abstract paintings. A final observation needs to be made: despite the size of the tree and the details of the portrait of Petropoulos, the central focal point is actually located in the slightly darker empty space just behind the tree, an optical effect created by the geometric arrangement of the smokestacks. That empty space is, of course, open to various interpretations, some of them inevitably metaphysical.

LXXV

Petropoulos claimed to have written over a thousand articles. This is probably true; the researcher looking into the question needs to know that he used pen names, for newspaper articles, during the years of the Junta and perhaps before this period as well.

He wrote the articles out in one draft and, like all writers, was delighted when they were published quickly. I think that they gave him the impression, even more than did his books, that he was back in Greece after so many years of exile, participating in heated day-to-day debates.

He would imagine readers sitting in houses, coffeehouses, bookshops, and reading the newspaper, the magazine—and disagreeing with him. Agreeing! Disagreeing!

Many of these articles, gathered alongside other articles, would grow into a thick book after they were published in magazines. Petropoulos's book about mud and shoescrapers (1994), for example, grew from an article (1986) that had in turn grown from a paragraph in the concluding essay of *Wooden Doors Iron Doors in Greece* (1981):

> On a sidewalk, just to the right and left of an outer door, are a pair of shoescrapers. Shoescrapers came to Greece from Europe. There is, consequently, no Greek word for "shoescraper." In 1980, however, I launched the neologism *laspokatharistiras* (= "mud cleaners"). If a shoescraper is not in sight, muddy shoes may be cleaned on a *skhara* (=a latticed metal doormat < Ancient Greek *eschara*), or on a good hard *psatha* (= doormat). These three objects were unknown in Greece before 1850. Back in those days, Greek peasants used to face up to the mud problem in a most ancient Anatolian way: they would leave their muddy shoes outside the door and enter the house in their socks. Most of the time, however, their "shoes" were not what we now call "shoes." They were *ghourounotsaroukha* (= "Spartan" pigskin-thonged sandals) or *tsaroukhia* (= a clog-like shoe of hardened leather) with *phountes* (= pompons) at the shoes' tips and with *prokes* (= tacks whose slightly knobbed heads made cleats). Greek peasants also wore *pantofles* (= pantofles), slippers which were worn *inside* hard, heavy-duty overshoes called *kountouria*. The muddy overshoes would be left outside on the doorsill and the peasant would enter the house in his pair of clean pantofles. To remove these overshoes easily, one made use of a small leather tab just above the heel on the back of the shoe. I haven't seen any of these overshoes and pantofles around since 1941.

At the same time, Petropoulos, who had himself worked as an art critic, literary critic, film critic and political journalist in both Thessaloniki and

Athens, despised some journalists, especially literary journalists. For a while, he refused to buy either *Libération* or *Le Monde*, insisting that *Le Matin* was the most serious newspaper. This attitude lasted for a while after the Socialists had come into power, in France, in 1981-1982. *Le Matin* was considered to have a Socialist Party orientation, though this was not the reason why Petropoulos bought the paper: he found the other two dailies and their journalists "pretentious." I followed his example for a few weeks, then went back to buying both *Libération* and *Le Monde* for their literary supplements. They were definitely much better. This was not a subject that could easily be discussed with him.

Petropoulos wrote over a thousand articles, but he also wrote some seventy or eighty books. (How to count them accurately, since several were expanded or were absorbed into new, overarching volumes when they were republished?) He collected notes, illustrations, photographs, engravings, documents, and (sometimes rare) books on all sorts of topics, but above all his goal was, as he said, tapping his forehead, "to get everything in his memory down on paper."

He succeeded almost entirely. Reflect on those twenty-eight years of French exile during which he so intently continued to get down on paper some forty-seven years of experience in Greece. His folkloristic projects about France notwithstanding (and most were not finalized), Greece remained his obsession. Perhaps tellingly, perhaps simply because opportunities arose at the right time, he published several articles and two books, *In Berlin* and *The Mythology of Berlin* (1991), based on the research that he undertook, and on his personal experiences, during his one-year sojourn in Berlin. This body of work is comparatively more copious than what he wrote in regard to France.

Yet because of the Nazi Occupation of Greece and, in particular, of Thessaloniki, a period and a town in which he had suffered and taken up arms, and of course because of his father's mysterious disappearance, which was hypothetically caused by the Germans in one way or the other, he had an especially intense relationship with Germany.

In any event, did his French remove perhaps stimulate him more than he knew or let on?

And is the following declaration, in *Suicide*, ironic? "I was born in Greece—this is the only favor that the goddess Chance has granted me."

LXXVI

May it always be remembered how hard he worked. His insatiable curiosity led him into an extraordinary number of fields, in our age of specialization, and in these fields he not only compiled enormous, monumental, annotated anthologies, dictionaries, and photo albums, but also became an authority on these subjects. He became the authority, or one of the authorities, on Greek slang, the Greek underworld, rebetic songs, shadow theater, the history and topography of Thessaloniki, countless aspects of urban folklore and architecture, and several popular art forms. Someday all Greeks, both those who are "for" and "against" Petropoulos, will be grateful to him for having preserved such an extensive and precise visual and written record of a Greece that has vanished. Add this concern for safeguarding to the many other examples of his generosity: he was a troublemaker indeed, but a generous one.

An indication: there are some 820 photos in *Ironwork in Greece*, 300 in *La Kiosque grec*, 300 in *Balconies in Greece*, 180 in *Windows in Greece*, 70 in *Cages à oiseaux en Grèce*, 60 in *La Voiture grecque*, 400 in *Wooden Doors Iron Doors in Greece*, 100 photos and sketches in *Turkish Coffee in Greece*, 60 in *The Brothel*, 50 in the first edition of *Lousology*, and 100 pages of photo-documents in the first edition of *The Underworld and Shadow Theater* (and even more illustrations in subsequent editions). In *Old Salonica* and *La Présence ottomane à Salonique*, there are respectively 440 and 270 photographs and postcards. I am not going to count all the illustrations in *A History of the Condom, Hats and Caps, Knives and Pistols*, and the other big books from his last decade.

Petropoulos began compiling his photographic archives in the 1950s, long before publishers became interested in his album-projects, and he never received the slightest drachma of academic, governmental, or institutional aid during this time. In the early stages of his career, the gathering of material for these albums, which Petropoulos considered to be more important than his bestsellers, *The Brothel* and *Lousology*, "nearly brought on [his] financial ruin," he avowed.

When he started living with Mary Koukoules, her personal wealth enabled him to increase his archives many times over and to self-publish some of his work, especially his poetry, in exquisitely printed volumes illustrated by his artist-friends. Her own generosity enabled his subsequent oeuvre to blossom prolifically.

LXXVII

Petropoulos usually photographs the entire object instead of focusing on decorative motifs or systematically evoking the nostalgia associated with objects from bygone days. There is nonetheless an undeniable charm in some of the photographs that is equivalent to a minimalist poetry of everyday life. Sometimes his photographs were criticized because of their subject matter or technical drawbacks, notably their lack of contrast. But the originality of his photographs lies in the recording of objects that are neither too far away, nor too close; the accumulation of the same object—doors, windows, balconies, wrought ironwork, "etc. etc. etc."—educates one's way of looking. One learns how to see what Petropoulos called "popular architecture." Apropos, in *The Oeil-de-Boeuf Window* (1980):

> I am publishing here a few pertinent photographs [of oeil-de-boeuf windows] from my archives. Be assured that I do not consider our popular architecture to be a uniform, indivisible, entity. A *Greek house* does not exist. There are all kinds of popular architecture on Greek soil. For the time being, we need to collect and preserve examples. Let's leave the chatter for later...

He expatiates on this question in *Windows in Greece*:

> One cannot speak about a window without speaking about the facade. Likewise, one cannot speak about a facade without speaking about the entire volume of the house, its size and shape. In my short study *The Oeil-de-Boeuf Window*, I maintained that what one would like to call a *Greek house* does not, in fact, exist; instead, that all kinds of architectural styles exist within the borders of Greece. I am still of this opinion and would like to insist upon it. The nebulous *Greek house* concept / theory is, in fact, a concoction of Modern Greek folklorists. It should furthermore be noted that the traditional architectures of modern Greece were first researched, not by architects, but by

folklorists. During the first half of this century, the chauvinistic theories of the so-called *National Schools* reigned not only in Greece, but throughout the entire Balkan region. Their very memory is revolting. Greek folklorists were so preoccupied with fashioning and launching their *Greek house* theory that they neglected more important duties: those of collecting / preserving their material by means of drawings or photographs. (...)

During the 1960s, the first loopholes in the illustrious, brilliant *Greek house* concept / theory began to appear. I do hope, indeed, that others will soon come to light as well. Professor N. Moutsopoulos, who has been teaching at the Polytechnical School of Thessaloniki ever since 1957, is the person responsible for discovering the first loopholes. It was relatively easy for him to begin a systematic study of the traditional architectures of northern Greece: the task of collecting material was naturally carried out by his students. Indeed, Professor N. Moutsopoulos proved himself to be an excellent general. And the fruits of this systematic endeavor did not tarry long to appear. Through a series of books, Professor N. Moutsopoulos has brought forth many important examples of the traditional architectures of Greek Macedonia. Professor N. Moutsopoulos's industriousness is truly admirable. His courage less so. While completely avoiding the problem of the nonexistence of the renowned *Greek house*, Professor N. Moutsopoulos came up with his own theory of a so-called *Macedonian house*. According to Professor N. Moutsopoulos, *Macedonian houses* only exist within the borders of Greek Macedonia. But elsewhere in the world, Macedonia / Macedonian do not quite mean what chauvinistic Greeks think they do.

As of today, I am still not ready to speak in more general terms about the traditional architectures found in Greece. For the moment, I have been busy publishing a series of books in which I examine several specific technical / folkloric matters concerning what we could call the "popular architectures" of modern Greece: wrought ironwork, doors, windows, balconies, and so on. Only when these books are finished and published will I be able—and have the right—to speak in more general terms about the traditional popular architectures of Greece.

Today, in Greece, everything now tends towards a sort of chaotic monotony. But before the beginning of the twentieth century, Greece was an exceptionally multifarious country in terms of its geography, economy, and social life. The traditional popular architectures of the country were equally multifarious and diversified. But today's means of communication—from the automobile to the television set—have radically overthrown the former civilizational setting of Greece once and for all.

LXVIII

A postcard in Greek from Berlin, dated 28 April 1984:

John, thank you for the photocopies. I have indeed been working like crazy. Every day I have been walking some 40 kilometers in order to look carefully at and take pictures of the 400 (!!) cemeteries of Berlin.

Happy May Day,
    * Elias

The star preceding Petropoulos's name is not an asterisk, but rather the Star of David. The postcard, featuring a sculpture of a small man and a tall woman, announces an exhibit by Hartmut Bonk in the Künstlerhaus Bethanien. Petropoulos has penned in names on the reproduction so as to poke fun at one of his Greek artist-friends. Guess which one!

At another exhibit in the same institution, Petropoulos displayed a collage bringing together a flag with a skull emblem and a naked Jewish woman with a star of David visible on her upper chest; she has been mutilated by the Nazis. On the photocopy of the collage, which similarly dates to 19-29 April 1984, Petropoulos notes that the group exhibit has been organized to protest against the deportation of the Tunisian artist Messaoud Chebbi, from Berlin, by the German police. Later, back in Paris, Petropoulos had the Mérat brothers print up some calling cards showing the collage on one side and a caption about the deportation on the other. The collage also appears at the beginning of *A Macabre Song*.

LXXIX

Besides the dozens of Greece-oriented books that were growing in his archives for ten, twenty, thirty, even forty years before they were finalized and published, a French project that Petropoulos sometimes mentioned (though unfortunately never completed) was a study of Coye-la-Forêt. He collected facts and anecdotes in the hopes of producing a short study of the "urbanism" (as he always put it) and sociology of the village. Weathervanes attracted him, as did French sundials, public clocks, cemeteries, and gravestones. One day he said to me: "You know those painted, plaster-cast dwarves that the French stick in their gardens? Well, as kitsch, *nains de jardin* aren't bad at all!" Petropoulos was attracted to kitsch and wrote about it often, even in *Mirror for You*:

> My heart is like a shattered mirror!
> I've just written down this run-of-the-mill expression and
> Let me assure you that I think highly of kitsch.

In *Balconies in Greece*, Petropoulos's highly technical analysis of the asymmetrical, disproportional, and non-superpositional arrangement of windows on the facades of traditional Cycladic and Aegean houses induces an insight into the "kitsch" that had been ascribed to this kind of architecture by Greek specialists influenced by the "European" aesthetics of classical architectural harmony. On the contrary, notes Petropoulos, such arrangements "make all the more evident the *interiority*, the *interior* function of this type of house. Common folk have no trouble whatsoever with this truth, which is by no means inconsistent with beauty. So much so that today it indeed behooves us not to underestimate the enormous significance / value of *kitsch*."

After Françoise and I had moved to Angers, Petropoulos would tell me on the phone that he would come by train to visit us one day and that we would "tour the cemeteries there." Thinking once again of kitsch, I wanted to show him the family vault, in the Cimetière de l'Est, where the eccentric French novelist, Maurice Fourré, was buried. I knew that anecdotes about Fourré would interest him. This visit never came about, and Petropoulos's collection of photographs of French graves has never been published. In the June 1981 issue of *Le Fou Parle*, he published three of his several photographs of French "atheist grave markers." He may well have been the first person, French or otherwise, to discover them.

LXXX

The old man has long lived in Coye.
I have run into him ever since 1976.
Today, Saturday, he's wandering around
the village fruit market.
I greet him, saying "Bonjour, Monsieur!",
all the while marveling: "He's still alive!"
And I suppose the old geezer
Has the same secret thoughts about me.

(From *After*)

LXXXI

Leafing through the photocopies that I received from Petropoulos, I confirm my impression that he was sending fewer by the early 1990s. But during our first years in Angers, they kept coming and coming. I have one in hand now: the first publication of "The Mustache" in *Ikhneftis* (No. 40, January 1989), a literary review (directed by Kostas Voukelatos) that brought out numerous studies by Petropoulos as well as some of my own work, thanks to him. An inveterate bookbinder, Petropoulos has characteristically made a small booklet out of the photocopies. On the inside flap, he writes: "M^e [the French abbreviation for Maître], we are leaving for Italy..." As I continue to leaf through my files, I find a photocopy dated 21 March 1989 and accompanied by a note stating that he and Mary Koukoules have returned from Italy: it is an article about him that was published in a Turkish periodical. On 4 December 1989, I see that he participated in a colloquium at the Sorbonne...Think of the number of times that he had held up that institution to contempt! It was a three-day conference on

"Death and its Representations in Judaism," and Petropoulos gave his talk on "Le grand cimetière juif de Salonique." On an enormous A-3-format photocopy featuring two of his articles on the artist Bost (Mentis Bostantzoglou) and dated 12 February 1990, he writes that he has been in Brussels to give a lecture. (Etc. Etc. Etc.)

LXXXII

You wanted to go to Rome
because I wanted to go there,
because you knew of my passion for the Italians,
for their magical language,
because I speak to you all the time about Italy.
At the end,
you understood that I am no archeologist.
As much as I adore the Villa Julia,
I love that clam casserole dish
that we ate near the Piazza di Spagna.
And I want to return to Rome.

(from *Never and Nothing*)

LXXXIII

It was Mary Koukoules and Elias Petropoulos who suggested to Jacques Vallet that *Le Fou Parle* ought to publish a piece on Gershon Legman, the American folklorist who had been living in France since the 1950s and whose work on erotic folklore Petropoulos deeply admired. (In 1979, Mary collaborated on Legman's translation, for the review *Maledicta*, of the first original article written by Petropoulos for an English-language publication: "Fist-Phallus.") When Vallet agreed, Petropoulos mentioned me, declaring that I could write the article in French. I had never written anything in French, let alone published a text in that language. At the time, I had published only a few scattered poems in ephemeral American small-press magazines. My article appeared in March, 1982. It was my first article written in French (and was duly corrected by Françoise, of course, before publication); it was one of my first articles *tout court*.

Petropoulos rarely commented on the other articles that I published in *Le Fou Parle* or elsewhere. I doubt that he realized how extensively, by the early 1990s, I was covering contemporary French literature for the *Times Literary Supplement*, the *San Francisco Chronicle*, *France Magazine*, and other publications. I was touched, however, that he especially liked my piece on Henry David Thoreau, bought out in *Le Fou Parle* of March, 1984. Thoreau was one of his favorite authors, as he declares in this short piece from *In Berlin*:

> Dammit!
> I came to Berlin without
> my beautiful edition of Casanova's *Memoirs*.
> Luckily I didn't forget Thoreau's *Walden*
> and *The Iliad*.
> My three favorite books.

Was Thoreau really one of the favorite authors of the man who had written *La Voiture grecque* and who emphasized his love of cities? Petropoulos was much more of a nature lover than his immersion in and advocacy of urban folklore might suggest. He not only liked to stroll in the woods near Coye-la-Forêt, but also sometimes watched documentary films about animals on television. According to Mary Koukoules, he began to write, but never finished, a play involving animals as characters; she found the manuscript among his papers after his death. He once told me that, although he was a Greek writer living in exile in France, he was happy to have planted a few trees in the garden of the Coye-la-Forêt country home. I often think of Petropoulos watering saplings and flowers, even as I chose to begin this book with a depiction of him laying a stone path in his garden. Should we be calling him the "groundbreaker," the "path-layer" of Greek cultural studies? Of course! Much breaking occurred, and paths resulted.

He wrote to me from Berlin, on 19 March 1984, that he liked the "aggressiveness" of my article on Thoreau. What he meant by "aggressiveness" was that I had written about a famous American author who was, strangely, still little known in France. This type of "aggressiveness"—showing readers that they knew less than they thought they did—was an important lesson that I learned from him. He believed that the noblest task of the critic is to shake up literary history, to highlight writers who have been neglected, underrated, or slighted by academics. (Analogously, in his study of lice, he notes: "What I am writing here is not intended to be a joke. Our academic folklorists will find it meaningless and unserious. But I find it extremely serious and significant.") His own articles and books rehabilitate forgotten figures, not only in folklore studies, but also in Modern Greek literature. Whenever Petropoulos met a well-read foreigner for the first time, he invariably asked for a list of the "real writers" of the country in question, with an emphasis on the unheralded. He and Elias Papadimitrakopoulos defended Nikos Kachtitsis long before the novelist was "discovered" by others and became better known in the mid-1980s. I am referring here to Papadimitrakopoulos's phamplet, *Notes on the Work of the Prose Writer Nikos Kachtitsis* (1974), which was printed "under Elias Petropoulos's supervision" and dedicated to Nikos Gabriel Pentzikis. And of course to their aforementioned tribute, *Nikos Kachtitsis in Memoriam* (1972).

Literary references abound in Petropoulos's folkloristic work, and he uses information gleaned from descriptions made by realist writers to cast light on modern Greek mores. Always a skeptic about hearsay, rumor, and commonplace facts, he also knew when it was possible to take a poet or a fiction writer seriously, as when he links (in *Turkish Coffee in Greece*) the strange-sounding adverb *polla* (instead of *poly* for "very"), used by customers ordering a Turkish coffee, to the short-story writer Georgios Vizyenos's term *pollakameno* ("very, very poor"). He likewise knew when even a writer whom he admired, like Papadiamantis, erred or exaggerated: Petropoulos wrote a study called "Papadiamantis's Mistakes" (published in the journal *Ikhneftis* in November-December 1994), which he intended, but ultimately failed, to expand into a book. He also knew when a mentor should be taken ironically:

> The monastic tradition at Mt. Athos has developed its own coffee: there, the monks will put two or three drops of ouzo into their *brikia*. What Greek does not know that one? But N. G. Pentzikis coolly mentions it twice, as if he had first discovered it. Papadiamantis, in his story *I Pepoikilmeni* (1909), writes: "large cups of coffee, monastic

miracle." This monastic coffee (with the aroma of ouzo) reminds me, in turn, of those delightful little Smyrnean meatballs into whose dough a little raki is mixed, along with abundant spices and aromatic herbs. (from *Turkish Coffee in Greece*)

In the same book, Pentzikis is favorably quoted with respect to a sentence, in his *Pragmatognosia* (Knowledge of Things), about reading fortunes in the dregs "settled in the coffee cup—open road, great gate, news of someone, two or three periods, distress or money, connection, wreath, and all of this mysteriously unveiled."

LXXXIV

For a writer intent on determining what our day and age was like, especially in its harshest aspects, Petropoulos was not always in step with his times. Though he was a stickler for typographic perfection and much used his desk telephone, he never owned a computer or a cell phone. He wrote out his texts by hand, with a felt pen. In addition, this first draft would be almost perfect, with very few words crossed out and changed. He would then type up these manuscripts on a small manual typewriter. The manuscripts would be stapled several times down the side—like a book—so that pages would not be "lost" (as Petropoulos would repeat sternly) in the printer's shop. The words to be italicized were typed in red or underlined by hand. Other annotations would be found in the margins. A few "personal spellings" would be specified. Sometimes the instructions were eccentric, such as when Petropoulos started insisting that a period should be placed after a title or a chapter title. (See the lessons of *The Good Thief's Manual* and the book *Irons. Mud. Canes.* for examples.) We argued about whether the first letter of the first word of the phrase following a colon, in both Greek and English, should be capitalized or not. We came to agreements, not always easily, about commas, semi-colons, exclamation marks, apostrophes, and the kind of quotation marks that should be used. Pointing out typographic norms and traditions in a given language was not always a sufficient condition for convincing him to adopt such or such a solution, for he also intended to innovate. Woe to the translator, publisher, editor, or typographer who ignored the master's orders!

There are next to no typos in Petropoulos's books, for he usually insisted upon receiving two or three successive proofs. He also demanded proofs from his magazine editors. He could correct a page of proofs for an article quickly, in one nevertheless meticulous pass, as I sometimes noticed while we were waiting to be served lunch in a café (on the rue de Rennes) to which we went whenever we were working at the Mérat brothers' printing shop for the day. His eye was as sharp as a hawk's, and this is an understatement.

One day, while I was translating a passage of *The Brothel*, I found a typo on page 32. Actually, suspecting that there was no typo, I did not understand who "Ali Para" was in a demotic song cited by Petropoulos. Taking a look, he shouted: "But that's Ali Pasha! They were supposed to change that!" He immediately called his publisher to protest; their conversation finished with laughter.

(Maître, I am revising my old translation of *The Good Thief's Manual*, and I notice that you place a comma after every entry of the lists on pages 33-34 and page 57, but that you place a period after each entry of the similar list on pages 70-71....)

In any event, some of Petropoulos's lists are sometimes funny, macabre, or grim objectivist poems:

> A Man wearing handcuffs obviously breathes, but he breathes as if he were a wolf snared in a trap. A Man wearing handcuffs has a *special* psychology. I am already working on a psychological study in which chapters will respectively examine the following situations:
> A Man wearing handcuffs,
> A Man whose hands are bound behind his back,
> A Man whose feet and wrists are bound together,
> A bound naked Man,
> A Man with ball and chain,
> A Man chained to a wall,
> Two Men handcuffed together,
> One Man and one Policeman handcuffed together,
> A bound Man who is tortured,
> A bound Man in total darkness,
> A bound Man who is starving,
> A bound Man who is fucked,

A bound Man who is examined.

LXXXV

Petropoulos sometimes told me, while making flowery gestures in the air, that an elegant prose style did not interest him at all. He would cite with disgust the French style of Chateaubriand as an example not to follow. He detested Roland Barthes's cool stylistic elegance. He tended to believe that all French writers aspired to such stylistic norms. In this, he showed an incorrigible unfairness and revealed the limits of his knowledge and understanding of the multifarious history of style in French literature. He is perfectly explicit in *In Berlin*:

> My balls are swollen.
> The cause? *La littérature française*.
> I'm sitting in a café on the Kudamm
> and from a nearby table
> hear people talking about Chateaubriand, about La Fontaine,
> and about other little doodads
> that France has been slipping us for centuries.

There was nothing to be done. No cogent and amply illustrated argument could convince him. He did not have the time, even if he had the interest (which he did not), of reading widely and deeply in French literature. Whenever an objective appraisal of a notable French writer was called for, Petropoulos's difficult relationship with the French and his own exile from Greece clouded over his thinking. I regret now that I never asked him whether he had come across the writings of Louis Calaferte from the 1990s. It seems to me that Calaferte, who himself practiced several different prose styles (not to mention poetry), might have challenged Petropoulos's thinking in beneficial ways. (But Petropoulos would have pointed out that Calaferte was born in Turin and thus Italian!) I also wonder if Petropoulos ever ran into the unclassifiable French writer Michel Fardoulis-Lagrange, who was born and raised in Cairo and whose mother tongue was Greek. It seems not.

Petropoulos himself wielded an unmistakable prose style, based on vigorous declarative sentences, precise descriptions, etymological digressions, ironic allusions, rare words, and occasional idiosyncratic spellings. Most important of all, between two passages or even between two sentences, that is, in the midst of a discursive argument, odd transitions cropped up; or there were no transitions. Perspectives shifted abruptly. Petropoulos leapt to a related subject, back to the first one, then on to a third. What the reader was examining head on suddenly revealed other facets. Such stylistic and rhetorical leaps produced the particular emotion emanating from his writings. Such was their undeniable "poetry," but also their rigor. Petropoulos saw valid connections where others did not, as when he peered deeply into unexpected interrelationships between the underworld and folk traditions. He insisted, at once aggressively and humorously, on the profound pertinence of these surprising connections.

In the different context of *Suicide*, Petropoulos both insightfully and self-revealingly writes: "In every moment, everything has another definition. Long live contradictory definitions!"

LXXXVI

Wasn't Nikos Gabriel Pentzikis's faithful (if turbulent) pupil a poet at heart, even in his folkloristic work? Wasn't one of Elias Petropoulos's main goals as a folklorist that of recovering and preserving what can properly be called the "poetic" vestiges of a now nearly vanished popular culture? Wasn't his very methodology as literary as it was "scientific" or "empirical"? For although many prose writers (and even scientists) have versified on the side, Petropoulos's case was different. Writing poetry for him was no pastime, but rather participated fully in the vision underlying his entire oeuvre.

This unity between the folkloristic writings and the poems can best be discerned in the arresting melancholy informing them both. For even in his prose writings, he never hypocritically conceals his personality, or his subjectivity, behind the multitude of "objective" facts that he catalogues or describes. He wasn't Pentzikis's pupil for nothing! Petropoulos was too interested in language and perception to be deceived by naive notions of so-called "scientific" rigor and objectivity. And yet there is unquestionably an attempt on his part to objectively express the world—in his poetry as well—by means of an exposition of brute facts. This is no contradiction. Petropoulos knew all too well that observing entails selecting, the subjective act *par excellence*. Not only the poet, but also the urban folklorist must live "harmoniously," as he puts it in a poem in *Never and Nothing*, with his "innate melancholy."

Never and Nothing marked a new step in the continuing evolution of Petropoulos's poetry, notably from *Body* and *Suicide*, and even more strikingly from the lyricism of his earlier book, *Elytis Moralis Tsaroukhis*, the latter volume ostensibly a critical work. Rereading these works gives one the impression of a metamorphosing unity. "Deep inside me a battle wages," writes Petropoulos in *Body*, and his poetry, from his earliest efforts to *Never and Nothing*, chronicles that ongoing war. In this latest stage, which dates from *Mirror for You* and *In Berlin*, the war is reported on in a much more direct fashion than ever before. One is tempted to say, in the light of the wars in Iraq, that well-penned letters from the front have been replaced by the willfully fleeting images of CNN cable television.

War indeed. For the inner strife that Petropoulos evokes with increasing forthrightness in his poetry likewise originates in his memories of "all those friends who were shot by firing squads" (*Five Erotic Poems*) and, still more painfully, in the disappearance and probable murder of his father in 1944 (evoked in *In Berlin*). The latter event—surely a key to the writer's personality and oeuvre—was never elucidated: like Petropoulos, his father was in the Resistance movement; the corpse was never found. Much has already been written about the impact of the Second World War and the Civil War on the Greek writers of Petropoulos's generation (he was seventeen years old in 1945), and his poetry, as well as his entire folkloristic approach, can profitably be viewed in this light. Behind even his most brutal remarks nearly always lies moving remembrance. Petropoulos is brutal because of remembrance. As he avows in *Never and Nothing*, in a self-revealing notation, "But the women, the friends, whom I loved / are not phantoms. / And they know that I'm constantly thinking of them."

Before and after these meditative moments in *Never and Nothing*, Petropoulos characteristically rages against the Establishment, against Academe, against bourgeois values, sometimes even against countries or groups of nationals (especially the French, often the Greeks; in fact, nearly everyone). A genuine *poète révolté*, Petropoulos also relishes leveling his guns at pretentious, academic—one thinks of the term "cacademic" forged by his friend, *Maledicta* publisher Reinhold Aman—uses of language. Already in *Body*, *Suicide*, and *Five Erotic Poems*, a few lines end abruptly, with a period, in mid-sentence, creating the effect of an interrupted scream. Such stylistic provocations take on renewed vigor when the writer, starting with *Mirror for You* and *In Berlin*, begins incorporating "kitsch" into his poems. After experimenting (in those works) with intentionally ridiculous uses of traditional meter and rhyme, Petropoulos came to make blatant voluntary grammatical errors, as in his poem, included in *Never and Nothing*, beginning: "Ston leoforo to avtokinito." The poet concludes: "I fuck your grammar." "Obscenity" is indeed his "pride," as he declares in *Body*.

Yet the opening poem of *Never and Nothing* surprisingly claims that the poet is "harsh...out of tenderness." Given the violence of some of these verses, it is difficult to take him at his word. Or is it? For as is obvious in the folkloristic writings, an innate tenderness—a sympathy for the underdog—obliges Petropoulos to look closely, meticulously, at life; and often, in consequence, to speak out strongly. Petropoulos likewise knows how fragile artistic creativity is; unforgettable is his warning, in *Five Erotic Poems*, to a younger poet, Manolis Xexakis: "patience Manolis patience my soul / because the shabby bastards will crush you without shame." Moreover, concealed behind the writer's proverbial aggressiveness are ceaseless ruminations on mortality. Explicitly rendered in the drawings of *The Graves of Greece*, death is present in all of Petropoulos's writings, especially his poetry. And even more especially in the last period of his poetry.

For this very reason, Petropoulos's late poems unambiguously express what he already announces in *Mirror for You*: "I don't believe in so-called Great Poetry." "I'll have to write a Manifesto of Ugly Poetry," he likewise proclaims in *In Berlin*, adding: "Throw away the Poetry of Ideas and of Symbols and of Colors. / Prefer Everyday Images / and insignificant Snapshots, one after the other; / that is, Poor Poetry." Yet this ongoing "manifesto," set forth in *Never and Nothing* with still greater resolution, is based as securely on the author's unequivocal theories—a "non-poetry" or an "anti-poetry" representing an aesthetic position, after all—as on the irrepressible, haunting fact that he (and those whom he loves) are aging—yes, dying. Perhaps it is best to read his voluntarily un-poetic poems as expressions of what happens when grim observations of time's and death's ravages are allowed to overwhelm all the nuances, refinements, and restraint of classical poetics. "The closer you get to the coffin, / the more you abandon *fioriture*, / the beautiful hollow words," he writes in *Never and Nothing*.

Petropoulos is not the first poet for whom, with age, idealism veers to melancholy; and melancholy to disgust. Yet he is one of the very rare poets who, affected by extreme feelings, is willing to relinquish all ties to formal literary elegance. And although he has always taken great risks with his readers, never were the risks as great as in his late poems. For he shows that the very form of a poetry inspired by melancholy and disgust must necessarily be melancholic, even disgusting. The reading of *Never and Nothing* is disquieting, to say the least.

LXXXVII

In *Suicide*, he notes that he "has not lived in peace for a single minute." In *After*, he mentions "the unbearable melancholy / that has haunted me ever since '44," the year when his father vanished and was probably murdered; and in the third piece of the *Five Erotic Poems*, which recalls his friends who died in the resistance movement of the Second World War and in the Greek Civil War, he avows: "I feel disgust for myself because I have survived my friends (who were courageous)." "Melancholy" is probably the most self-revealing recurrent word in his oeuvre.

Listen to these self-revealing lines in *Body*, one of which has already been quoted:

Deep inside me a battle wages.
(...)
Life is mute indeed it is. I demand dreams.
My sorrow constitutes my happiness.
Body, it's you who are the soul.
O memorable vulva, O double-lipped slit with its silvery moisture.

LXXXVIII

A reading excursion through a book by Petropoulos is to experience an astonishing rigor, erudition, and candor, yet at the same time a humor and irony found only in the wisest novelists. He can spend a page examining the recondite etymology of a commonly used word not found in any Greek dictionary because it is of Turkish origin, and he can also spend a page recounting a comical anecdote about a pickpocket whom he once met. There is some resemblance between Petropoulos's style and that of H. L. Mencken, full of acerbic wit and know-it-all rigor. Mencken was not a "professional" philologist, as he himself admitted, but he did happen to be the first to examine "American" as a language in itself and not just as a dialect of English. Interestingly enough, Mencken makes this falsely modest confession in the preface to the fourth edition of *The American Language*: "My inquiries and surmises will probably be of small value to the first successor who is [a philologist], but until he appears I can only go on accumulating materials, and arranging them as plausibly as possible." One recalls similar statements made by Petropoulos who, like Mencken, often underscores the *obligation* to search for the truth and thus to venture well beyond more natural fields of enquiry: no one else is willing to do the job. This parallel or, rather, contrast can be extended: Whereas Mencken sought to distinguish American language and culture from British and, in general, European culture, Petropoulos endeavored to view Greek language and culture in a broader, much more realistic, cultural, sociological, and linguistic context. Both writers attempted, less through theory than through the accumulation of masses of firsthand data, to constitute a more accurate, non-ideological, image of their respective languages and cultures.

Other parallels can be drawn between Petropoulos's work and that of Gershon Legman in erotic folklore and Reinhold Aman in verbal aggression. These otherwise very individualistic writers who, along with Petropoulos, became acquainted with each other through Aman's journal *Maledicta*, shared a common passion for collecting and preserving as many materials and documents in their respective fields as possible before elaborating theories and conclusions. As with all smart-alecks constantly showing up their teachers, these three independent researchers had a rough go in the lofty pastures of Academia, and, at times, at the hands of the governmental authorities of their respective countries.

LXXXIX

Sometimes when I arrived, I found Petropoulos typing. He would have pushed books and papers to the side and created a small space, on his desk, for the typewriter. In the time that it had taken me to climb the spiral staircase leading up to his study, he would have returned to his desk (after answering the intercom buzzer) and typed a few more words.

However, although he eschewed the electronic facilities of our technological age, he loved photocopies. I have folders filled with photocopies that he gave or sent me. I was, by far, not the only recipient. Whenever articles appeared about him or one of his own articles was published, he sent out photocopies to friends and acquaintances. One Greek writer-friend, who also lived in Paris, found this overbearing, quipping gently in French: "Que veux-tu? C'est le père Petropoulos," by which he meant more or less, in paraphrase: "What do you expect? He's just playing the role of Petropoulos-the-Patriarch that he has assigned to himself."

Petropoulos was especially proud of the articles published about him outside of France and, naturally, outside of Greece. I gave him oral translations of the German articles. The Turkish articles delighted him more than any of the others. Like the issue of Petropoulos and Jewish culture, that of the folklorist and Turkish culture needs to be understood deeply. His writings provide the best guide to this question, of course, but, socially as well, he was always getting Greeks and Turks together. His Parisian friends numbered many Turks, including the artist Yüksel Arslan (at the time his neighbor, up two streets then round the corner on the rue Thouin), the political cartoonist Selçuk Demirel (about whose work Petropoulos wrote—see *The String* (2002)—and who illustrated the cover of Mary Koukoules's *Loose-Tongued Greeks*), the writer and painter Abidin Dino, and the younger journalist Sinan Fisek. Petropoulos often talked about Yaşar Kemal, whom he also knew well and saw every time the Turkish novelist came to Paris. (Mary

Koukoules and Kemal wanted to put together an anthology of Greek and Turkish songs of lamentation, but they did not get around to making progress on the project.) I am forgetting other Turks among his friends. Petropoulos attended the funeral of the Turkish film director, Yilmaz Güney, on 9 September 1984: I was supposed to accompany him, but could not do so at the last minute. He phoned these friends whenever he had a question about a Turkish word or an aspect of Turkish culture. He had questions all the time.

Ever a prankster, Petropoulos sometimes illustrated photocopies, penning a pair of glasses on his face if a photograph of him with glasses had appeared with the text. I received several false photocopies, some of them erotic (so as not to say pornographic), supposedly sent by someone else (usually Alekos Fassianos). At the top of some of them, Petropoulos would write "Happy New Year" and the like. They were his greeting cards. No one ever sent more holiday greetings to Françoise and me than Elias Petropoulos.

One day, for the German journalist Armin Kerker, Petropoulos and I photocopied nearly half of my translation of *The Good Thief's Manual*. Instead of going, as I had suggested, to one of the cheap student photocopy shops near the Sorbonne, Petropoulos shrugged this idea off and entered as usual the small newspaper shop on the rue Blainville.

The cost of making so many photocopies was prohibitive. The proprietor, making a gesture with the back of his hand, rounded the sum off to the already high figure of two hundred francs. Petropoulos paid in cash. Then the proprietor turned to me and confided, as if I were a Frenchman and Petropoulos a foreigner unable to follow our conversation: "Monsieur vient souvent ici," that is "the gentleman comes here often."

XC

One of the books that he gave me was Abraham Roback's *A Dictionary of International Slurs*, the 1979 reissue by Maledicta Press of the 1944 original edition. Petropoulos owned two copies and, if I remember correctly, both were heavily annotated. In any event, mine includes words highlighted in pink on many pages and otherwise comprises blue marginal remarks (and additional blue highlighting) in several other places. Typos are corrected here and there. The bibliography has been studied closely (corrected here or there, or amended), as was the case with all the books that he read. On the title page, Petropoulos characteristically stamped in red ink both his name (in capital letters) and a date (19 January 1980), the latter probably indicating the arrival of the book in his rue Mouffetard mailbox. (He had several rubber stamps, some of which were reserved for practical jokes.) On the cover of the book, my own first name is written in black and underlined. This indicates that Petropoulos had set the book aside for my next visit. Indeed, it was waiting for me on a corner of his desk when I arrived. The reasons why he was interested in this classic lexicon are obvious. He was fascinated by the slang of all languages, and collected lexicons and glossaries devoted to the topic; they helped him to elucidate the etymologies of Greek slang terms, especially those from the underworld.

Less known is that Petropoulos was a maniac with all stationary products. He despised Bic pens. He hesitated not an instant in informing me of this when I pulled one out of my briefcase before taking a few notes on a translation that we were working on. He wanted me to throw the pen away on the spot. He himself loved writing with high-quality felt pens; on his desk he kept several kinds, with different colors of ink. He was always testing new models, some of them quite expensive. Sometimes he gave me one that he found particularly pleasant in the hand and precise on the page. He especially liked red felt pens, even for writing letters. Many of the photocopies that he mailed to me have a message or a greeting at the top, in red.

Following suit, I have become a maniac with blue Pilot Ball No. 05 pens. I can write comfortably with no other kind.

Some books that Françoise and I own—books that have nothing to do with Greece or Elias Petropoulos—bear the mark of another habit that I picked up from him. Petropoulos would stick small colored circular stickers in the margins of his books, drawing attention to important passages. Above all, he used such stickers when correcting galley proofs. He would rectify the typo with the appropriate typesetter's marks (which I also learned from him), then place a sticker next to the correction so that it would have a better chance of catching the printer's eye. The first versions of my translations came back to me marked up with rectifications or questions and were covered with small circular stickers. Sometimes there were more stickers than words.

Petropoulos gave me sheets and sheets of these stickers; he gave me felt pens; he once gave me a magnifying glass, explaining that he had two. (My son Justin and I now use that magnifying glass, whose white plastic handle perfectly fits my hand, to examine the stamps in our collection.) During another work session, Petropoulos asked me if I had a letter opener. He would have given me one, had I not replied that I already had one. On another afternoon, he asked what kind of glue I used, ensuring that it was the more expensive brand that "did not drip."

In his view, a writer should never be a cheapskate about stationary products. He loved cutting out newspaper articles or photos and gluing them on white (or sometimes colored) sheets of paper. He always wanted to re-publish the article, as it were. A photocopy of my aforementioned article about Gershon Legman came to me through the mail one day, a year or so after it had been published; it had been pasted onto a piece of lavender construction paper. Because he designed all his books, Petropoulos was naturally an expert at manipulating a professional typesetter's ruler. Usually it was lying on one side of his desk. He liked stamps and envelopes for their own sake, as it were. As I have mentioned, he always wrote out the addressee's name and address on the envelope very legibly. I never received a note or letter from him with a word crossed out and another written above it.

XCI

My memories of Petropoulos often involve carrying heavy books. The *Rebetic Songs* anthology I lugged far and wide, often even to the language school on the boulevard Saint-Michel where I was teaching English to ambitious businessmen, bored housewives, and a few university students. It was impossible to get an efficient schedule there so that my classes would be lined up, one after the other, without breaks, giving me mornings or afternoons off to work on my writing and translating. I would leave the school during the hour- or two-hour gaps in my schedule, walk up the boulevard, and labor on my translations at the back of Le Luxembourg, a café facing Luxembourg Gardens. In the middle of the morning or the afternoon, only a few customers would be sitting near me, at the back of this café. Their chatter did not bother me.

Several times, when I dropped by the rue Mouffetard apartment on my way to the language school, Petropoulos gave me a book or two, which I put in my briefcase, thus adding to the weight of the folders and books that I needed for teaching.

Sometimes I took a sampling of his production (and inevitably the ponderous *Rebetic Songs* anthology) across Paris on the métro in order to show a French magazine editor what Petropoulos had accomplished. I would try to convince the editor that an in-depth article would be of interest. Once I presented Petropoulos's work to a Communist sociologist who published an academic review devoted to the various Mediterranean peoples. The sociologist had asked me to bring Petropoulos's books to his apartment, located in a stolid quarter of the seventh arrondissement. I filled two big briefcases. After climbing an elegantly carpeted flight of stairs and being shown into a large entryway, I found myself in the most impressive living room that I had ever seen. Its immense hardwood floor was covered with beautiful Middle-Eastern rugs. There were cushions lining two walls, but otherwise no furniture. It was like the inside of a mosque. The Communist sociologist and I sat down, side by side, on two large cushions. The sociologist set the *Rebetic Songs* anthology on the rug in front of him, opened it, began leafing through it. He kept muttering "hum, hum-hum" as I was telling him of Petropoulos's prison experiences. Then he asked me if Petropoulos were a member of the Greek Communist Party...

Petropoulos was not a member, nor was I; there was no article.

XCII

Another memory of carrying heavy books goes back to our summer vacation in Greece, in 1981. Just before Françoise and I returned to France, we dropped by the offices of the publisher Kedros, in Athens, and picked up ten author's copies of the album *Old Salonica*, which I had translated. Then we went to the publisher Hermes and picked up ten copies of *The Graves of Greece*. These were errands that we were running for Petropoulos who, to be truthful, had requested that we pick up only what we "could carry." Because we had also bought novels, poetry collections, grammar books, and dictionaries while we were in Athens, we realized, as we were packing in the Ideal Hotel for our return flight home, that our luggage would exceed the maximum weight permitted by Olympic Airways. Fortunately, we still had enough time to procure sturdy envelopes and mail back to Paris the dictionaries and some of the novels that we had acquired. As for the copies of *Old Salonica* and *The Graves of Greece*, they completely filled two medium-sized backpacks. At the airport, Françoise kept both backpacks at a distance as I was showing our tickets to the lady behind the Olympic Airways counter. Our two suitcases passed the weight check. Then, when we entered the Boeing, we kept our backs as straight as possible, as if the backpacks were light carry-on luggage. Somehow we managed to squeeze them into the overhead luggage compartments without damaging the books.

The next day, Françoise and I lugged the books from our apartment to the place d'Italie métro stop, went down several flights of stairs to the platform, and then, after a short ride and a welcome rest on a step of the escalator ascending to the place Monge, and after emerging on the shady square and trudging up the rue Ortolan, and after attaining the rue Mouffetard, No. 34, and after climbing two more flights of stairs, we finally pushed open the door to Petropoulos's study. Petropoulos was concerned about how much we had carried, but he was also delighted to have so many author's copies. Getting author's copies sent or carried to him from Athens was always one of his worries. That evening, he invited us to the Closerie des Lilas restaurant, where we were joined for dinner by the artist Takis and his wife. That coming winter (between 19 November 1981 and 1 March 1982), Takis was going to have a major exhibit—entitled 3 Totems—at the Pompidou Center, with an installation on the ground floor. It was an arrangement of enormous steel pipes that also formed a musical instrument. But he was not interested in talking about the preparations that were already underway. He and Petropoulos joyously swapped licentious jokes and stories all evening long.

After a long wait, we were served smoked haddock in a milky sauce flavored with parsley and shallots. Ever since that dinner, Françoise and I continue to prepare smoked haddock in exactly that way. (It's now one of our son Justin's favorite dishes.) The wine was red, probably a slightly cooled Saumur Champigny; that oenological fashion had arrived in Paris at about that time. Petropoulos left his glass untouched; he drank water. After dinner we strolled up the boulevard Montparnasse, stopping in at Le Select for a desert. Did we all order an *île flottante*, where a freshly beaten egg white meringue floats in a *crème anglaise*, a liquid custard base? Probably. Afterwards, Petropoulos, Françoise, and I climbed into the back of a taxi. Petropoulos had the driver drop us off on the rue Albert-Bayet.

On that same 1981 summer trip to Greece, Françoise and I photographed Petropoulos's books whenever we found them displayed in bookshop windows, both in Athens and in provincial towns. This was often the case because of the controversy surrounding *The Good Thief's Manual*. Copies had been seized by the police and the book was banned, but other copies were visible in the bookshop windows. Such was Greece that year, and long afterwards—a permanent exhibit of contradictions and perplexities. We had the film developed and gave him the photographs as a gift. Nothing could have made him happier.

Even after the PA.SO.K. Socialist government had long remained in power, Petropoulos never received an official amnesty for *The Good Thief's Manual*. After a while, it was generally considered that he would not be prosecuted if he returned to Greece; that the ban had been essentially lifted, or would be, because of a statute of limitations; but an ambiguity persisted, especially in Petropoulos's mind. Most importantly, he wrote a letter (on 2 November 1982) to the erstwhile Minister of Justice, Yiorgos Alexandros Mangakis, stipulating that he was asking not for a special favor in his own case, but rather for the repeal of the Greek Press Law and for the promulgation of a new law that would guarantee freedom of the press for all writers and journalists. Nothing came of this appeal.

XCIII

In order to expand this book, whose first draft did not quote at all from Petropoulos's writings, I carried two enormous cardboard moving boxes full of his books, and then two others full of my own files concerning him, up from the garage to my upstairs study.

When we moved into our house in the suburbs of Angers in 2002, there was not enough room on the shelves of my study for all my books. I had to make decisions. I boxed up Petropoulos's books and stored them in the garage. And I wrote a postcard to him, three weeks later, informing him of our new address. Soon thereafter we chatted on the phone. Such is how a relationship between an apprentice and his mentor necessarily evolves.

But I kept a photograph of him on one of my bookshelves.

Two years have gone by since I carried my mentor's books up to my study. They still lie in piles all over the floor. I have almost finished this book.

XCIV

Whenever Petropoulos signed a copy of one of his books for me, he usually penned only the most succinct message on the title page. At best, it was something like "me tin agapé mou," which is, arguably, more correctly translated into English as "with my affection" than "with my love." He often signed his name with the initial of his first name or with the two initials of his full name. However, he sometimes translated my own name into Greek and varied the spelling: "Yiani Raphti," "Yianni Rapti," "Ioanni Rapti," and so on, all the while amusing himself with the demotic and "purist" (*katharevousa*) levels of the language. This was one of our jokes, and I naturally had a rubber stamp with my name in Greek. Few of my signed copies of Petropoulos's books are dated. Compared to the notes, collages, and photocopies that he sent through the mail, there was little humor expressed in these dedications.

An exception to this rule is my copy of *Le Kiosque grec*. The dedication is dated 17 September 1987. Petropoulos actually signed this book several years before 1987, probably around 1979 or 1980. That afternoon, in his apartment, he handed it to me, declaring: "I'm giving you this book in the future." (Now, as I write this, that future is twenty years in the past.) Petropoulos wrote the dedication by using a mirror, à la Leonardo da Vinci. But such playfulness, so typical of Petropoulos in other ways, was rare with respect to the books that he gave me.

My copy of *Kaliarda*—the lexicon of Greek homosexual slang—is signed "apo ton kolo-syngraphea," "from the ass-writer," and dated 24 July 1983.

Another book, *Mikra rebetika*—a short paperback selection of rebetic songs—is dated 29 December 1982. Signed to both Françoise and me, the dedication commemorates the "French coffee" drunk in our rue Albert-Bayet apartment. We had next to no furniture back then. We had not yet acquired, from the departing Brazilian family next door, the dark-brown couch that later inspired one of my own stories. So Petropoulos sat on the three-piece fold-out mattress that we kept on the floor of the living room. Behind him, there was an Indian madras bedspread, which we had hung across the wall. The bedspread had been given to us by my mother. The other day (over a quarter-century later), while Françoise and I were searching for a large piece of cloth that could cover our new couch, we came across the madras bedspread at the bottom of a box. The colors had faded, though not the memories associated with the bedspread. One of these memories has Elias Petropoulos sitting there in front of the bedspread, on the floor, drinking coffee, and inspecting our several dictionaries, which we had piled next to him. He often boasted that he "read dictionaries." This was perfectly true. In his essay "Phallocratic Etymology" (1983), he observes:

> For linguists, dictionaries are a handy but dangerous tool. The academic method of consulting dictionaries leads to etymological gaffes. For many years, I have used a simple but effective method: I read every dictionary as a novel, that is from the first to the last page, and take notes at the same time. This method is tiring. In order to read a dictionary, I need two to six months of work. You need to read in a way enabling you to remember everything that you have read during all the previous days. I think that reading dictionaries is well worth the trouble, though I do not recommend this method very often....

He always wanted to know the average age of the readers who were buying his books. He attempted to glean this information from various sources. Above all, he hoped to be read by students. Sometimes he bragged: "The young people are buying up my books like *souvlakia!*"

No writer cared more for his manuscripts until they were published. Petropoulos saw each of his books through the entire publishing process, designing the book as a whole and in all its details: its size, the quality of the paper, the front and back covers. He established the page layout for every single page. He arranged for all the illustrations. In those years before the invention of scanners, he would make meticulous photocopies of drawings so that he would not have to send the originals to publishers and printing shops. ("They lose everything in printing shops!" he would bellow.) In regard to his active and extremely attentive participation in the book designing and printing process, he greatly irritated his publishers more than once. I was an eyewitness to, or rather an eavesdropper on, several thunderous telephone calls. In such matters, he was a redoubtable maniac. Every single detail counted; every millimeter was measured with his typographer's ruler. When a word was italicized on a galley proof, he would get out a magnifying glass to verify whether the comma or period following it was in italics or in roman. He also often envisioned second, augmented and corrected, editions for his books; and then third editions; and then fourth editions.

However, when Petropoulos took in hand one of his newly published books and showed it to me, I sometimes sensed that he felt pride and excitement, but also weariness—perhaps even disgust. And then, with sudden rage and resolution, a new project would begin.

XCV

A typical complaint, usually expressed orally but here on a postcard depicting the mills of Astipalaia: "I have tried to call you a hundred times." The card, originally brought to him from Greece by Mary Koukoules (who has a home on the island), was of course posted from Paris. Petropoulos never returned to Greece after his departure in 1975. The card is dated 12 December 1986. A small bearded face peers around the first and biggest mill in the foreground. It is Petropoulos who has drawn the face on the card. "I'm here," he has noted, using an arrow to point to his face.

Even more often, he declared: "I have tried to call you a thousand times!"

To a photocopy that he sent through the mail, he once attached—with a paperclip—a visiting card with these words: "I tried to reach you by phone. I will try again!"

We had no answering machine back then. Yet I worked at home, spent most of my time in the apartment. Petropoulos's exasperated claims sometimes surprised me.

I would retort: "A thousand times? But Maître, I was at home all afternoon yesterday. When did you call?"

"No, you must have gone out for a while!" he would reply sharply. "I called at least six times!"

We would drop the matter and get on with our business.

XCVI

As regards Petropoulos's long exile from Greece, I once received another false postcard from him, this one supposedly sent by Alekos Fassianos and dated 10 June 1985. The card shows Fassianos's painting "Dorades au soleil" (1984)—"Sea Breams in the Sun"—and on the reverse side is penned in Greek, in weakly disguised handwriting:

Yiani,
I am leaving for Athens on 15-6-85.

Yia sou,
A.F.

Messages like this would sometimes arrive in my mailbox, without further explanation.

XCVII

"Professor Taylor?"
"Yes," I answered, although I am no professor.
"This is the minister."
"The minister of what?" I asked him.

"The Minister of Justice. Me and those three other Communists."

This telephone conversation occurred on the evening after the French prime minister, Pierre Mauroy, announced that four Communists would participate as cabinet members in the new Socialist Party government. Although neither a Communist, nor a Socialist, nor even an anarchist, nor anyone but himself, Petropoulos never missed a chance to take a wisecracking potshot at authority or hypocrisy.

XCVIII

Imitating him, I concocted this "Translator's Preface" for *The Good Thief's Manual* and sent it to him on 2 July 1980:

> *The Good Thief's Manual* was translated during my sabbatical year (1979-1980) as Visiting Professor at the Royal Institute for the Art and Practice of Burglarly in Antiqua. At the time, I had been contracted to give a series of lectures on the theme "Taxation and Cost Accounting Methods in the Contemporary Massage Parlor," lectures that were, alas, cancelled due to the language barrier. Soon after my arrival in Antiqua and, more especially, during pre-registration counseling, I was forced to admit that my three-week Peace Corps Intensive Language Course had not sufficiently prepared me for the subtleties of Antiquan underworld slang. It was in these despairing moments that I met Distinguished Professor Petropoulos, who was so kind as to give me his *Manual* as a sort of *initiatio*. Subsequent conversations with Dr. Petropoulos concerning his fundamental research on criminological subjects convinced us that a translation of *The Good Thief's Manual* was to be urged.
>
> The John Dillinger Foundation was kind enough to provide us not only with a generous grant making this translation possible, but also to agree to sponsor my postponed lectures this coming year (Auditorium D, Monday and Thursday, 3:30-4:30 p.m.).
>
> The translator would like to thank Mary Koukoules for her perspicacious translations of certain technical Hypokosmos terms, and

especially the Old Professor himself, whose generosity, patience, and scientific insight were without bounds.

XCIX

Petropoulos was not interested in elaborating theories about the phenomena that he documented so rigorously, which is not to say that he did not forge or dismantle methodological concepts—as has already been seen. As for theory in general, he would sneer: "That's for university professors." He was extremely skeptical of professorial theories and practices. He demanded facts—very hard facts. (Interestingly, Petropoulos expressed ideas more consistently or explicitly in his poetry, which tended to be aphoristic in style, especially in the early and middle periods of his career.) Whence his insistence on photography and documentation. In nearly every book, he vents his spleen on professorial blunders, professorial pusillanimity. He never shied from taking on the big names in research. "The phenomenon of *argot* in the Greek underworld," he writes for instance in *The Underworld and Shadow Theater*,

> remains unexplored. Modern Greek linguists abhor the term *argot* and especially the term *underworld argot*. Professional jargons or *argots* have existed and still exist in Greece. Construction workers, charlatans, tailors, tinsmiths, gypsies, and so on each spoke their own separate *argot*. In Greece today, underworld hoodlums, sailors, homosexuals, prisoners, drug addicts, and soldiers each speak their own separate *argot*. For unknown reasons, Modern Greek linguists use the term *coded language* instead of the term argot. But a given *argot* is not a *coded language*; an *argot* is a language. The renowned linguist Manolis Triantafyllidhis (and all his students) worked on professional jargons no longer in use. Manolis Triantafyllidhis (and all his students) were well aware of the existence of *loubinistiki* (homosexual *argot*) and *tsaboukalidhiki* (underworld *argot*), but they preferred to keep their lips sealed....

Petropoulos had a penchant, to say the least, for studying subject matter that would be inconceivably daring for professors anxious about their social reputation and the evolution of their careers. Most of his books were the first books ever published on the topics in question, certainly in Greece and sometimes even internationally. And even if some of his topics are now fashionable in North American cultural studies departments, Petropoulos's methodology, his style, and especially his *tone* are hardly academic. He would simply declare: "They are anti-academic."

Somewhat similarly, Petropoulos was wary about articles describing life in the Soviet Union, but he often went to contemporary Russian films "because," as he once explained, "if you watch ever so carefully, little details slip through which reveal a lot about the true situation." Petropoulos made this statement in about 1985. While Michael Gorbachev was in power, he often declared: "Gorbachev, il est très sympathique."

C

Though I have never kept a diary, I can date one work session with Elias Petropoulos to the spring of 1986.

I usually dropped by his rue Mouffetard apartment in the afternoon or, at the earliest, at eleven in the morning. I never phoned him before ten, for he was a late riser.

Yet for some reason one day, he wanted me to come very early. As early as eight o'clock. I cannot remember what we were working on. Probably *In Berlin*, which was finally published in 1987.

I left our apartment on the rue Albert Bayet, crossed the boulevard Vincent-Auriol, circumambulated the place d'Italie, turned right and headed down the avenue des Gobelins. It was a brisk cool morning. Water was flowing vigorously down the gutter on my side of the avenue, disappearing down the sewer openings.

Suddenly, coming up the sidewalk was Jean Genet. He was wearing a worn leather coat; in his pocket was a rolled-up copy of the newspaper *Libération*. Genet had a day or two's growth of beard and was walking slowly. He glanced at me, then looked past me.

Though I had read all his books, I felt too shy to stop him, to express my admiration. I looked to the side, out of courtesy. Our paths crossed. I did not look back. I continued on my way to Petropoulos's apartment.

When I entered Petropoulos's study, he was busy at his desk. It seemed to me that it was not the time or the place to mention that I had just seen Jean Genet. What did Petropoulos think of Genet's prison writings? Even though I had now worked with him for some seven years, I did not know. He never spoke about Genet—which is probably evidence enough. He never commented on, nor did I ask him about, a footnote that I slipped into my second article on his work, published in the *Journal of the Hellenic Diaspora*: "One subject for a study of Petropoulos's writing would be to compare *The Good Thief's Manual* to Jean Genet's *Miracle de la Rose*. Genet, to mention just one similarity, was able to weave into a classical French style extremely colorful strands of underworld *argot* and thereby create a truly remarkable stylistic tapestry. The Greek critics have likewise been very enthusiastic about *The Good Thief's Manual*'s style." Moreover, in the list of questions that I had submitted to Petropoulos when I was preparing my ambitious critical study of his life and work in 1981 (as I mentioned in the Introduction), I reiterated the parallel: "In France, the best-known writer on prison life is most likely the novelist and playwright Jean Genet. When your *Good Thief's Manual* came out, several Greek reviewers evoked his work along with yours. Has Genet's work interested you? What about the image of prison life that he gives?"

I was as naïve back then as average French readers who, upon learning a little about *The Good Thief's Manual*, would automatically liken Petropoulos to Genet, even imagining that the Greek writer had been influenced by the Frenchman. After his death, Mary Koukoles confirmed that Petropoulos had no copies of Genet's books in his personal library in Athens—a collection of books that was also donated to the Gennadius Library when he left the country. He read some Genet in French, in Paris, long after writing *The Good Thief's Manual*. He absolutely hated being compared to Genet.

In his plea, in 2000, for the release of the imprisoned poet Kostas Samaras, Petropoulos mentions Genet.

About a month after that morning encounter, Genet died of cancer on 15 April 1986 in Jack's Hotel, located on the rue Stéphen-Pichon, not all that close to where I had crossed paths with him yet nonetheless in the same arrondissement.

CI

In *Never and Nothing*, Elias Petropoulos writes:

> I like Moravia because of his writings.
> But I also like him because he always wore
> very beautiful ties.

Replace "Moravia" with "Petropoulos." Even more striking than Petropoulos's elegant ties (as an object of apparel that would catch the onlooker's eye) was the overall impression that he created whenever he entered a crowded art gallery for an evening opening: his vigorous salt-and-pepper beard, his eyebrows (which tended to spring up at the ends), his striking tie of course, but also his refined three-piece suit and his perfectly ironed (perhaps even starched) shirt. I remember well his knit ties, for I myself hoped to find one at a time when they were no longer in fashion.

Petropoulos often expressed disgust at French clothing, especially French shirts. He considered French clothing to be "effeminate." He claimed to buy only Italian clothes. Dressing elegantly also resulted from his fear of being stopped by a policeman and asked for his *carte de séjour*.

In winter, he donned a dark wide-brimmed hat that I had (and still have) never seen on the head of anyone else: instead of pressed felt, it had a sort of short soft fur all over the top and the brim; the color was not entirely black, but rather a deep purplish black. Petropoulos liked to say that the hat made him look like a rabbi. He eventually wrote one of his biggest books about hats and caps, *The Cap* (2000).

When I began working with Petropoulos, I saw him only at his apartment; he was not necessarily wearing a tie. Later, after he had encouraged me to get out more and attend gallery openings or literary parties with him, I never found him dressed casually. Absolutely never. In public, he always wore a tie and a three-piece suit. Even at the

Mérat brothers' printing shop. Even when we would meet Jacques Vallet at the office of *Le Fou Parle*, then go out to lunch in that simple Chinese restaurant.

Once, at an evening party given by *Le Fou Parle* at the office on the rue de la Félicité, Alekos Fassianos strolled up to Petropoulos and taunted him: "You look like a lawyer."

Petropoulos retorted with an impish grin: "I am a lawyer!"

(Indeed, in 1949, he had studied law at the University of Thessaloniki, passing his exams and being classed among the top students. He had dropped out of law school after that year. Yet he continued to note, on the biographical résumés for his books, that he had "studied law.")

At other times, Petropoulos would claim to be a "grand professeur" at the Sorbonne.

"And your academic specialty?" someone would ask.

"Mounology," he would answer haughtily," "the art and science of the female pudenda."

In *Lousology*, he informs his reader on the title page that he is a Professor in the Parasitology Department of the Sorbonne.

Petropoulos was an aesthete, a hedonist, but also sometimes timid. He relished elegance for its own sake, but he also needed a mask.

CII

I'm disgusted by people who wear pajamas.
Pajamas make me think of petit-bourgeois interiors.
They make me think of senility and hospitals.

(from *After*)

CIII

One day we received a postcard from Turkey, featuring Nigarî's portrait of Suleiman the Magnificent. In Nigarî's interpretation, Suleiman combines refinement and savagery: a well-clipped white beard over which droops a Mongol mustache; fine dark eyes yet a rather thick neck; a vast white turban from whose elaborate folds sprouts an admonishing black feather; a luminous blue, yet otherwise primitive, unadorned gown. The card is dated 15 October 1986. Petropoulos had signed his name "Ilias Tourkos." Petropoulos was invited to Istanbul to speak about rebetic songs at a colloquium on Mediterranean folksongs. This was his only trip to the country whose culture he had described so often.

CIV

Some people told me to stay away from Elias Petropoulos.

One day in our living room, as the French poet E. and I were chatting over a cup of coffee, I mentioned Petropoulos and his album of rebetic songs. Well-versed in Modern Greek matters, E. dismissed both Petropoulos and his album immediately: "J'ai des grandes doutes sur le bien-fondé de son travail." This means: "I have great doubts about the seriousness with which his work has been conceived and is carried out."

D., a French linguist interested in homosexual slang, claimed that nearly all the words in *Kaliarda* had been invented. When I mentioned this to Petropoulos, he broke into laughter and exclaimed: "So I'm James Joyce!"

When I made a gaffe by giving the Greek novelist K. a signed bibliophilic copy of Petropoulos's *A Macabre Song* (this also occurred in our living room, over some warm morning coffee, and both Françoise and K.'s wife were present), the man put it on the floor, made a gesture with the back of his hand indicating that it could be thrown out, and declared: "I don't agree at all with what he writes." When the couple left, the novelist left the book on the floor.

Others said that Petropoulos's "ranting and raving" was incomprehensible. Some said that he was a liar and could not be trusted. Some shrugged their shoulders and avowed that they could not see how his books would ever interest non-Greek readers, the implication being that I was wasting my time translating and helping him.

CV

An English-language anarchist publisher, F., who was of Greek origin and with whom Petropoulos had exchanged letters, came to Paris for a few weeks. He went to see Petropoulos; the meeting went well; they were discussing the possibility of publishing *A Good Thief's Manual* in English. Petropoulos had high hopes that the manuscript—my translation—would be accepted. However, without asking permission, F. made the enormous mistake of giving out Petropoulos's address as a mailbox at which he could receive letters while he was in Paris. During their meeting, F. had not even mentioned this to Petropoulos, who was always extremely tense about his mail. A day or two later, a letter from F.'s wife arrived at 34, rue Mouffetard. Petropoulos went into a rage. He called me, shouting into the phone in both Greek and French. I tried to calm him down, suggesting that perhaps only F.'s wife had the address, and no one else. But it was impossible to appease him. Petropoulos forwarded the letter back to F.'s wife, without even letting F. see it. Absolutely furious, Petropoulos explained that this was an old Fascist and K. G. B. tactic for framing people. The French police could secretly inspect the mailbox and prove that Petropoulos (who constantly worried about the problem of possessing, and renewing, a foreign resident's permit) was corresponding with noted anarchists. Petropoulos evidently had a strong anarchist temperament, but he refused to belong to any official anarchist organization; and this was not the point, anyway.

Petropoulos was overly paranoid in this case, as he was in a few other situations that I eyewitnessed. But it is true that he had been in prison three times, had been sentenced in absentia to prison a fourth time for *The Good Thief's Manual* (and had not been later amnestied by the PA.SO.K Socialist government), and that obtaining or renewing one's *carte de séjour* in Paris could be a risky experience: if your request was rejected, you automatically became an illegal alien, but at the same time you had necessarily provided, on the forms, precise information about your whereabouts. Petropoulos increasingly feared that he would not be able to renew the permit, because of the conviction for *The Good Thief's Manual*, and thus that he could be extradited to Greece for a trial; he eventually decided to live in Paris without a *carte de séjour*. Moreover, F. had not respected the simplest rules of courtesy. A brutal falling-out between the two men occurred. As it turned out, I had an appointment that very afternoon to meet F. in a café on the place Contrescarpe. I had no way of contacting him ahead of time, so I went. The meeting lasted only a few minutes, time enough for me to explain Petropoulos's position and for F. to announce: "Actually, it doesn't really matter what happened, nor that he is an asshole. The other evening, I was reading a text of his that had been translated into French. From the purely literary point of view, it's very badly written. He has no idea of what a transition is. As an editor, I'm obliged to tell you this. Take my advice. Drop him."

CVI

On 17 August 1982, Petropoulos wrote to me. We were going to see each other soon.

> Yiani,
>
> Don't forget to ask me for photocopies of Yiorgos Ioannou's *Phylladio*, in which he insults me for over twenty pages. That way, you'll have an idea of what literary criticism in Greece is like.
> E.

Petropoulos's article "The Last Trip," published in *Yiati* (Nos. 121-122, July-August 1985), is dedicated to Ioannou's memory. During their dispute, which probably goes back to an article published in *Short Texts*, Petropoulos told me that I should "by all means" read and even translate Ioannou's short stories. In *After*, he recalls a conversation with the writer:

> One day (thirty years ago)
> Yiorgos and I,
> I mean the late Yiorgos Ioannou,
> were listening to the rebetic song that begins:
> "Don't despair, it won't be long."
> And he, bless him, turned to me and said:
> Elias, I would be proud
> to have written that!
> — You're right, Yiorgos, and me, too,

I'd be happy to write with such emotion...

CVII

I sometimes smoothed out, beforehand or afterwards, the abrasiveness of a first encounter with Petropoulos. I would take on the role of an intermediary, a diplomat. But reconciliation was not always possible. While I was living in Paris, there were friends of mine to whom I mentioned Petropoulos's name once, then never again. Getting along with Petropoulos implied accepting him on his own terms, almost completely. Yet the "almost" was actually a little broader than most people imagined. Humor always helped.

CVIII

After moving to Berlin for a year, Petropoulos sent me his new address on 25 October 1983. In a second letter mailed from Berlin and dated 7 November, he reports that Jacques Vallet, the editor-in-chief of *Le Fou Parle*, has sent him an "article by Robert (or Dimitris?) Kalogeropoulos." I laughed out loud when I read this. This was proof that Petropoulos had not discerned that I was the "Robert Kalogeropoulos" who had reviewed Mary Koukoules's *Loose-Tongued Greeks*, an anthology that I had translated, in the pages of *Le Fou Parle*.

I plead guilty to this conflict of interest. But as Vallet had avowed when he convinced me to take on the assignment, who else in Paris was in a position to review the book? I had concocted this particular pen name because Robert is my middle name and my hometown is Des Moines (the false French etymology of which is "Monks" or "Of the Monks")—whence the *kalogeros*, which means "monk" in Greek. I also wanted to use the suffix -*opoulos*, for obvious reasons. I had not realized that Koukoules and Petropoulos had a Greek friend whose name was Dimitris Kalogeropoulos. At any rate, I had sworn Vallet to secrecy and asked him to send the article to Petropoulos, so that I could appear surprised at seeing the review.

The final twist to this story is that the review appeared in *Le Fou Parle* with a computer printing error. In my typescript, I had begun a sentence in the first paragraph with the words "Pour ce registre linguistique...," which were garbled into "ÉÉ&É ce registre linguistique." When the Greek edition of Koukoules's anthology was going to appear in 1984, Petropoulos wanted to reproduce the entire French article on the inside flap of the front cover. I happened to be with him when he designed the book. For the inside flap, Petropoulos had made a photocopy of the article, reduced its size, then arranged it alongside excerpts of two Greek articles that were going to be placed just to the right of the French article. Proudly he showed me the paste-up book. It's true, Petropoulos had exquisite typographical taste, and I learned how to appreciate fine printing from him. I then perused the article, suddenly feigning that I had discovered a typo. It was of course not necessary to point out the typo. Petropoulos had been aware of it from the beginning.

"But what can we do?" he lamented disgruntledly. "If we tell the Greek typesetters to retype the French, they will make even more errors. It's a minor mistake. Sometimes it's better to let minor mistakes pass, at the proof stage, so that major ones will not be committed. Let the printers photograph the cover as I have designed it. The important thing is to show Greek readers that this book has been read abroad!"

(Forcing Greeks to acknowledge his internationalism and their provincialism was typical of Petropoulos.)

I nonetheless suggested that he correct the error by hand, since he was capable of such fine ink work. He judged that this would be even worse.

"It will look as though someone had changed the true words of the article."

I gave up.

Then I asked: "Who is this Robert Kalogeropoulos who wrote the article? I don't remember ever meeting anyone here with that name."

"I don't know," Petropoulos replied bluntly. "Mary and I thought that it was our friend Dimitris, but when we asked him he said no. Apparently Jacques received the article through the mail and decided to print it. There was not even an address on the manuscript."

Petropoulos, who could see through all sorts of tricks (having himself played so many practical jokes on others), seemed at a total loss this time.

"It doesn't really matter who the author is," he concluded abruptly, now irritated to an extent that convinced me—out of my long experience of working with him—that it was time to change the subject.

Just before changing the subject, though, I was tempted to reveal the secret. But I did not. This was the only practical joke that I successfully played on Elias Petropoulos.

CIX

Elias Papadimitrakopoulos came to Paris in April 1987, with his wife Niobe, to be treated for kidney stones. Françoise and I knew both of them well from our visit to Paros in August 1985. And I had corresponded with Papadimitrakopoulos ever since the autumn of 1983, when (thanks to "the other Elias," as I would speak of one to the other) I had read, then started translating, his short-story collections *Toothpaste with Chlorophyll* and *Maritime Hot Baths*. I have detailed in my book, *Into the Heart of European Poetry*, the essential role that Papadimitrakopoulos's prose played in the evolution of my own writing. He, too, was a mentor for me, through his style, literary sensibility, and encouragement. It is also important to know that Niobe's sister, Nausicaa Kataki, was Petropoulos's ex-wife and the mother of their one daughter, the architect Leda Petropoulos (who was born in 1961).

An evening or two before the ultrasound treatments were scheduled to begin, Mary and "the other Elias" invited Elias Papadimitrakopoulos, Niobe, Françoise, and me to have dinner together at the rue Mouffetard apartment.

As we entered, my immediate thought was: "Mais quelle mouche a piqué Elias (Petropoulos)?," as the French say. "But what fly has stung him?"

From the moment we arrived, he was in a furious mood. First, there was a problem with the dinner table: how the places had been set and its exact position in the living room. But whatever this problem was (and I remember helping both Eliases move the table slightly), it was solved. The other Elias (that is, Petropoulos) took his place at one head of the table. I sat down just to his left, then came Françoise (to my left) and, continuing around the table, there was Mary, Elias (Papadimitrakopoulos) and Niobe, who was thus sitting next to Elias (Petropoulos) and across from me.

Once again, Elias (Petropoulos) showed signs of being in a rage about something that was otherwise unclear. Although he never drank alcohol, he poured us all a glass of ouzo, including himself, rather quickly banged the bottom of his glass on the table, uttered a *yia chara*, took a sip. He hurriedly wanted us to eat. Not long afterwards, with increasing violence, he started criticizing the French.

The atmosphere darkened more when a piece of Italian cheese came onto the table. It was like a gorgonzola combined with a robiola, or perhaps it was a kind of dolcelatte. Different-flavored layers of blue and white cheeses alternated. Elias (Petropoulos) began arguing that the French were pretentious; that the Italians produced the best cheese in the world. "Look at this cheese!" he roared. "The French are incapable of producing cheese like this!" He served himself a generous portion.

I countered by citing examples of exquisite French cheeses: there are over four hundred varieties in France. This was to no avail.

After the meal, which was delicious, for Elias (Petropoulos) and Mary—like the other Elias and Niobe—knew how to cook up all sorts of rare Greek, Turkish and Middle-Eastern delicacies, we moved to the other part of the living room.

Elias (Petropoulos)'s fury against the French continued apace, putting Françoise, to say the least, in an uncomfortable position. She was the only French person present. I no longer remember the details of his diatribe as it evolved, but it had to do with François Mitterrand, then President of France, and with Colonel Kadhafi of Libya. Elias (Petropoulos) kept declaring: "Eh bien, il faut que la France baisse la culotte!," "Well, France is going to have to pull down her pants (and get a good spanking)!" No one else was speaking; it was impossible to interrupt him; Niobe was concerned about Françoise.

The other Elias and I teased him by suggesting that he should air his political views on French television. He was willing to do so! More seriously, I pointed out that a national foreign policy did not allow him to generalize about an entire people. But it was clear that his views, that evening, stemmed from deep wounds and resentment that could not be healed. This was not the only time that I had glimpsed the wounds. In other circumstances, they seemed related to the disappearance and probable murder of his father in 1944.

Finally, everyone except Elias (Petropoulos) was tired and wanted to sleep. It was one in the morning.

As we were leaving, Elias (Petropoulos) warmly embraced Françoise and specified that his remarks were not "personal." She shrugged the grim evening off and forgave him.

Down in the street, before showing the other Elias and Niobe how to return to their hotel on the rue des Écoles, we all talked for a while. "We call him "O Phonaklas," laughed Niobe, which I translated into French as "le braillard": a baby that "bawls" all the time.

After that, whenever referring to Elias (Petropoulos), Françoise and I often called him, affectionately, "O Phonaklas", "Le Braillard."

When I put down the telephone receiver, for example, I would say to Françoise in French: "I'm going to see Le Braillard later this afternoon. Would you like me to drop by the Greek grocery store on my way home?"

CX

Like many writers and artists, Elias Petropoulos could be excessively self-centered. There were times when I dreaded another phone call from him, having already received one or two or three daily during the past week. This occurred whenever he became impassioned about something: the *Dictionary of Family Names* that he was compiling (and that never appeared, though some of its inspiration is found in *Naming Streets and Squares* (1995); the letters to Melina Mercouri about the stamp that would commemorate the Shoah in Salonica; sodomy as the sexual preference of the Greeks; later, the art of Roland Topor, whom he admired intensely. He went on and on about these people or topics, not to mention about his many projects for future books. He became furiously obsessed with a given subject matter, though the obsession mostly ended once the article or book associated with it had been written and published. He moved on to a new topic. And all too soon, the passion and tension and fury built up once again.

This being said, at least as far as I was concerned, Petropoulos could be equally excessive in insisting that I look beyond him and his world. He understood perfectly well that our personalities and literary interests differed greatly. He sensed what I would like in Modern Greek literature, and sent me in that direction. Thanks to him, I read Elias Papadimitrakopoulos. Thanks to him, I read and translated work by Veroniki Dalakoura, Manolis Xexakis, and Thanassis Valtinos. He directed me to Alexandros Papadiamantis, then Georgios Vizyinos, then Emmanuel Roïdis; then back to Papadiamantis, whose stories he especially cherished and whom he calls "the paganist of Skiathos" in the first of his *Five Erotic Poems*, and elsewhere "the famous poor short-story writer." As for Nikos Gabriel Pentzikis, his own mentor, he wanted me to be aware of the man's accomplishments: he spoke often and in detail of Pentzikis's famous pharmacy in Thessaloniki, where he and other young Greek writers would meet, and even more often of the pharmacist's novels and poems; he talked of how Pentzikis had deeply influenced him by showing him "how to see." (In his essay on Pentzikis, Petropoulos writes this memorable homage: "Pentzikis showed me how to use my eyes. Slowly but surely I learned how to see things askew, diagonally, illogically, axonometrically, unorthodoxly.") But Petropoulos always added that Pentzikis's prose was too difficult for me. "There's no sense at this time in even opening those books," he declared after I had told him that I had purchased *Pragmatognosia* (Knowledge of Things) and *Palaiotera Poimata kai neotera peza* (Older Poems and More Recent Prose Texts). In an all too tangible and frustrating sense, the prose of not just Pentzikis but also other authors vanquished my Greek. Petropoulos encouraged me to persist. He would say that the Greek language was "a very old slut" and that his own "experiencing of her refinements would never be finished."

It may come as a surprise to specialists of Modern Greek literature that Petropoulos often praised the work, if not the personalities, of two writers with whom he had bitterly quarreled. I have mentioned Yiorgos Ioannou. There was also Dinos Christianopoulos, whom I evoked above in conjunction with one of Petropoulos's postcard pranks. The three had been friends early in their careers. In Thessaloniki, Petropoulos had been a member, from the second issue onwards, of the editorial committee of Christianopoulos's magazine *Diagonios*. In the special issue of *Mandragoras*, he explains that their dispute stemmed from a decision made alone by Christianopoulos to publish an attack on Vassilis Vassilikos, who later wrote the famous novel *Z* (1966), based on the assassination (on 22 May 1963) of the leftist deputy Grigoris

Lambrakis in Thessaloniki. Petropoulos was working as a journalist at the time of Lambrakis's assassination, covered the event, and was deeply shocked by it. (Yet one of Christianopoulos's most memorable poems is also devoted to the murder of Lambrakis.) Much later, Petropoulos published in *Knives and Pistols* a chapter entitled "Christianopoulos's Blunders." Theoretically, fundamental differences existed between Petropoulos and Christianopoulos, the most blatant examples of which were the former's proclaimed heterosexuality and atheism, and the latter's proclaimed homosexuality and attachment to Christianity. In other respects, perhaps their personalities were similar in uncomfortable ways. In any event, one afternoon Petropoulos, sitting behind his desk in the living room of the rue Mouffetard apartment, fingered through his address book, found Christianopoulos's name, and dictated the address to me. "Write to him," he ordered, "not mentioning my name. And tell him that you are interested in his poetry." Petropoulos had shown me sample poems from Christianopoulos's *Short Poems*, pointing out that the poet had an "extraordinary sensitivity."

I followed suit. I corresponded with Christianopoulos, eventually wrote two articles about his poetry and short prose.

CXI

"Sensitive" was a word that Petropoulos often used when describing, favorably, a certain kind of writer whose *intimiste* style could hardly be farther removed from his own. He could be harsh and abrasive in his prose and especially in his poetry: *Mirror for You*, *In Berlin*, *Never and Nothing*, and *After* offer overwhelming proof of this stylistic orientation. But if another writer possessed a subtly crafted style and evoked human feeling with sensitivity, it was likely that Petropoulos would view him favorably. He had a very high opinion of the short stories of Elias Papadimitrakopoulos, whose sensibility was likewise antipodal to his own. They remained close friends from their student years up to Petropoulos's death. In the afterword to *Never and Nothing*, Petropoulos reveals that Papadimitrakopoulos read all his manuscripts before they were published.

Tellingly, Petropoulos often expressed the idea that a personality included flagrant inherent contradictions. In his conversation, he sometimes cited the proverbial example of Stalin's kindness to children. In *The Good Thief's Manual*, he develops this very notion for the psychology of thieves. Here is another provocative example from the same book:

> Even as skinning, as a method of executing a martyr, has disappeared, so also has the role of the Executioner vanished. In the old days, the Executioner's trade was hereditary, and many Executioners left a good name behind them on account of their dexterity.
>
> The Torturers of Antiqua belong to no unions and enjoy no legal privileges. The Torturers of Antiqua are not allowed to bequeath their trade to their children. The Torturers of Antiqua work unofficially. *The work of the Torturer is both toilsome and tedious.* Usually the Torturer is an extremely nice fellow whose only worry is to do his duty as quickly as possible, then head for home. I am speaking very, very seriously.

Petropoulos was an iconoclast in the literal sense of the term. He sought to break images, to shatter them. Sometimes the shattering seemed gratuitous, and this attitude was unbearable to many people. But there were also grim truths in the *chaos* of shattered pieces lying on the ground. Petropoulos wanted us, often forced us, to look deeply into that chaos.

CXII

Petropoulos had a secret sensitive side, which comforted me on a few occasions. One of the most touching letters that I have ever received was his reply to a quick note that I had dashed off and dropped in a mailbox just before I took the métro, then the RER express train, for Charles de Gaulle Airport. My father had called the night before: my mother was dying. I cancelled my classes at the language school, packed, prepared to fly to Des Moines the next morning. Just before leaving the apartment, I remembered that I had an appointment scheduled with Petropoulos for a few days later and that we were going to work on a translation.

When I finally returned to Paris, after my mother's death, I found this note written in Greek and dated 10 October 1981. My mother had died on 19 October.

John,

When a human being is dying, one does not speak about books. I am very sorry about the terrible end of your mother's life. When you return, we'll talk about it.

Yia sou,
Elias

CXIII

"You ask me
— why are you so harsh?
I answer:
— out of tenderness."

(From *Never and Nothing*)

CXIV

I know.
I'm like a thistle for you.
Open me more deeply, and you'll find me.

(From *After*)

CXV

True stories and false rumors about Petropoulos's sex life, and the ways women were attracted to him, would fill an entire book. His oft-aphoristic and exclamatory erotic poems offer thought provoking evocations of sexual pleasure, giving an idea of the underlying motivations and consequences; to wit, some sample maxims:

Love cannot be forgotten by means of hate.

Hate ultimately arises as compensation for eros.
Anything that pleases me is moral.
(*Body*)

I know nothing more melancholy than the body of an entirely naked woman.
(*Body*)

Pleasure, the echo of Never.
(*Body*)

Death is the only worthy act of the body.
(*Body*)

Be lenient with the body's impulses.
I am not responsible for the evil that I do.
(*Body*)

Men are faithful only to their work.
Men consider eros to be an allegorical pause.
(*Body*)

Eros did not ask us whether we consented.
(*Body*)

From love derives melancholy,
Even as melancholy crushes love.
(*Body*)

But even the most beautiful woman is unable to chase away the dark thoughts of a melancholy man.
(*Suicide*)

...poor old me perceives the eroticism of a woman
even in the way she smokes
(*Five Erotic Poems*, II)

I never asked for advice and advice I am given
uninvited advisors petit-bourgeois babblers
they keep saying and prophesizing
that I'll be eaten by beautiful women
but it's my hope to be eaten by beautiful women
and pity on you, miserable men
(...)
your life is founded on silence and sadness
while I
love her in secret and she is beautiful
and elegant and I hug her in hiding
not a bird watches us
not a flower hears us
we kiss and the walls shake
flowing tears a salty taste at the gate
the Gate of Consolations
(*Five Erotic Poems*, V)

Sappho lisps: "The moon hath thet (etc.)
and I thleep alone." (Ya fuckin' deserve it, old tart.)
(*Mirror for you*)

In my land they all write serious poetry,
But I prefer charlatans and to-and-froetry.
(*Mirror for you*)

CXVI

I rarely asked him questions about his personal life. Many of our conversations were technical, about the translations on which we were working. Otherwise, Petropoulos would speak in detail about his always numerous projects for new books, handing me outlines, notes, illustrations, and page layouts. He would describe the work of other writers and artists with whom he wanted to acquaint me. He liked to show me drawings, engravings, and paintings made by his artist-friends, or catalogs for their upcoming exhibits. He would hand me photos or articles that he had cut out of newspapers or magazines. While preparing some

"European coffee," he would tell me to leaf through a book or album that he had just bought or been given.

Of course, many of those photos, articles, books, albums, drawings, engravings, and paintings dealt with or depicted sex. I remember several well-illustrated, though rather cheap, albums about the erotic art of various civilizations. We had just finished correcting proofs at the Mérat brothers' printing shop. I was walking with Petropoulos to a taxi stand on the rue de Rennes when he spotted the series in a remainder bin outside a small bookshop. He bought the entire series. Later, once the taxi had let us off on the place de la Contrescarpe, I helped him to carry the books up the stairs to his apartment. At all times, he had his eagle's eye open for anything that might help, highlight, or fuel his work. Not long after arriving in France, as he was strolling through the Paris flea market, he came across an album of old drawings. They gave a good indication of the modes of dress during the Ottoman Empire. He forthwith published the album, with commentary, as *Album turc* (1976).

Now and then, Petropoulos told me stories about his sexually turbulent Greek past; only a few times, about what was going on in the present. One afternoon, when he was fifty-seven or fifty-eight years old, we were sitting next to each other in the living room of the rue Mouffetard apartment. This spatial equality itself was rare, for Petropoulos almost always remained behind his desk when I was visiting, even when our work was finished and we were chatting. That day, he announced: "Who knows how many years I have left? I still have lots of fucking to do, lots of books to write!" He looked at me straight in the eyes and added: "The two are equally important!"

Important for what exactly? If one could answer this question with scrupulous honesty, one would understand Petropoulos's fury and drive and motivation much better.

From *Body*: "The grammar of kisses is as indispensable / as the grammar of words."

In a hand- and typewritten bio-bibliographical document that he prepared for the special issue of *Mandragoras*, he looked back on his life as having been graced with "passion and poetry."

On his desk, he had a penholder on which photographs of naked derrieres had been pasted.

CXVII

Such was his tension, sexual and literary energy, humor, ambition, not to mention despair (melancholy), by which I mean his constant awareness and defiance of death. I often had the impression that Petropoulos, via his oeuvre, intensely struggled with death—not as an abstract, romantic, category or metaphor but rather as a threatening tangible reality that had gruesomely devoured his father and some of his childhood friends (like his Jewish sidekick Samico). He regularly told me that his masterpiece was not the *Rebetic Songs* anthology, but instead an enormous photograph album "in progress" entitled *The Cemeteries of Greece*. The irony is that this book, on which he had labored for over thirty years, was not quite completed at his death: seven or eight pages of inside explanatory material needed to be written. Because Petropoulos always worked hard to finish projects and see them through to publication, this failure is telling. It is almost unbelievable. The album was published posthumously in 2005 as *Ellados koimitiria*, with illustrations by Costas Tsoclis and reproductions of Petropoulos's handwritten instructions about how it should be printed.

CXVIII

What about the drawings of graves that fill out what Petropoulos considered to be his "most beautiful book," *The Graves of Greece*? At first glance, it seems that he has one artistic shortcoming: the rendering of human figures. The three mourners over a grave in Preveza (on page 20) are hesitatingly rough and simplified, as is the grave over which they are mourning, when compared to the finely rendered curvilinear shapes of the wrought-iron crosses alongside them on the next page or elsewhere in the album. Perhaps these three mourners, who are the only human presences in the album excepting a few mustachioed busts atop some gravestones from Kalamata, are designed to ferry us more readily—on the Epirotean dirges that, or so we imagine, they are singing—into the realms of Death, otherwise objectified in Petropoulos's drawings by cemetery artifacts void of their customary human accompaniment. Most of the graves in Petropoulos's album are not freshly dug, shadowed by family bereavement, but rather chanced upon long after all the descendents have died or moved away. They are sketched in their neglect and disrepair.

Is this album of iron-wrought crosses and tombstones "macabre"? In his brief preface, Petropoulos claims that two things held up an earlier publication of the book, a small sampling of which had appeared in a chapbook issued in 1974 by Study in Greece, the school run by Katharine Butterworth: his constant problems with the Greek police and the Ministry of Justice, and "the indifference shown by Greek publishers toward such an expensive and macabre book." This is why Petropoulos privately printed *The Graves of Greece*, as he had previously done with *Rebetic Songs*, *Kaliarda*, and a few other volumes.

The adjective "macabre" surprised me when I first read this text that I was going to translate. I had already seen the drawings and the page layout of the entire album. The word "macabre" had not entered my mind. The secret lies in the 220-gram brown *papier canson* on which the drawings are reproduced, and in the layout, which has been carefully conceived for each page. Each page is bordered at the top and at the bottom by a long thick black line. The page numbers and the names of the localities where the drawings were made are printed just above the top black line; the drawings themselves are naturally found in the space between the two black bordering lines. However, the drawings have been arranged, in this space, in ways differing greatly from page to page. This gives the album as a whole a sort of merriness, even a certain jocularity; considering the subject matter, this is a tour de force. On some pages are three drawings, or six, or twelve, or sixteen, or twenty-three, or just one. The graves, gravestones, slabs, and crosses have been twisted and turned so that several perspectives are dizzyingly visible on the same page. On page 49, to take a subtly droll layout, Petropoulos has neatly arranged eleven upright wrought-iron crosses with a twelfth one that has been bent over by time, weather, or vandalistic hands. On page 109, a bottle of olive oil has fallen over. Here and there, on a few drawings, grass or weeds have sprouted around a gravestone or slab otherwise removed from its mortuary context. In order to get a good view of the ossuary of one Ioannis A. Dhimas, Petropoulos has stealthily opened the lid.

These graveyard irons and marbles, which would be icily morbid to our eyes were we fulfilling familial duties in a cemetery, are transformed by Petropoulos's ink pen, metamorphosed into images that, in this multifarious arrangement, transcend their gloomy, indeed macabre, state. Ironically, the graves are full of life. The artist has captured their being, namely as objects infused with vital folkloristic traditions of the Greek people. In comparison, the wastefully enormous hyper-realistic canvases of the French artist Jean-Olivier Hucleux, who depicts the slick marbles and cheap plasters of French cemeteries in all their catholicity, are very macabre. As opposed to Hucleux's paintings, Petropoulos's drawings are permeated with love and respect for the traditions and customs of the Greek people.

Therefore call him also, with respect to *The Graves of Greece*, a sort of *psychopompos*, guiding us to the gates of *our* unique afterworlds: these grave slabs and stones, these marble and iron crosses. And this inveterate atheist would insist that there is absolutely nothing else "beyond" them, except nothingness.

CXIX

The erotic collages and greeting cards that I received from him through the mail usually included illustrations cut out of men's magazines. Petropoulos would paste them on elegant thick "Arches" paper that he had saved from one of his bibliophilic projects at the Mérat brothers' printing shop. (He never wasted paper. At the printing shop, he would keep anything and everything that had been discarded when pages were measured and cut.) For his greeting cards, he then penned a message in a cartoon bubble alongside the (inevitably naked) woman's mouth. One of the collages that I received features a naked woman lying on her side, her lower regions fully visible in the forefront of the picture. In the bubble, she is sighing: "Happy Easter."

Just before his death, as I was leafing through *A History of the Condom*, I was struck by the notion that this particular book—teeming with pornographic images—was not pornographic at all. Think of the final scene of Guiseppe Tornatore's film *Cinema Paradiso* (1989), in which the old projectionist has bequeathed to the young main character a homemade film consisting of all the kissing scenes that the village priest had scissored out of each movie. Perhaps *A History of the Condom* is a hymn to eroticism in this sense, as well as an at once defiant and melancholy expression of Petropoulos's ever-tense, heightened, awareness of death.

CXX

Today eroticism
seems commonplace.
As banal as the Parthenon.

(from *After*)

CXXI

He was an unlikely teacher, I an unlikely pupil.
So much separated us, or should have—but did not.
He was born in 1928, I in 1952, but Petropoulos liked the company of younger writers and artists.

Although he detested American foreign policy, he appreciated American culture and American writers. He often asked me what Gregory Corso was writing and where he was living. I did not know. He slipped into the crowd at a poetry reading that Allen Ginsburg gave in Paris. He was curious about William Styron, who was considered to be a great novelist by many French critics. Styron's books fell from my hands. Petropoulos was also intrigued by Charles Bukowski, who had likewise suddenly become famous in France. I was rereading Nathanial Hawthorne. I was translating the short prose of Elias Papadimitrakopoulos, whose own style and narrative technique were liberating me from the traditional American short story. Soon I would turn to contemporary French short prose. By the 1990s: Jacques Réda, Philippe Jaccottet, Yves Bonnefoy, Pierre-Albert Jourdan, Louis Calaferte, and others.

He was an atheist, I an agnostic attached to and troubled by my Puritan, Protestant origins. Petropoulos sensed this, respected this, teased me about it while I was translating his erotic poems.

He could stare hard at brute facts, meticulously examine objects from all angles, immerse himself in the outside world. He could also be gentle, tender. This is little known. What he taught me most deeply was how to look objectively at the outside world.

He was never at ease in France, in French, among the French. We had both arrived in the country at more or less the same time. Thanks to Françoise, I quickly felt assimilated into France, French, Frenchness. As my knowledge of French literature grew, I kept telling Petropoulos that there were many more interesting French writers than he imagined. He would not believe me. Absolutely not believe me.

As far as I know, he never played a musical instrument, but his fingers were long, thin, supple, graceful—like a pianist's. But it was I who liked classical piano music. He launched me into the harsh, moving beauty of rebetic songs, which eventually formed a chapter of my life. By those years, he was not listening to recorded rebetic songs. He would listen to American jazz while he was writing in order to drone out background noise. I wrote in silence. Besides his Modern Greek translations from the *Palatine Anthology*, some of his poems were also put to music and recorded.

I ended up writing a book of prose and poetry entitled *The Apocalypse Tapestries*, based on the "Apocalypse Tapestries" in the Chateau of Angers as well as on the Book of Revelations. Petropoulos translated the Book of Revelations into Modern Greek while he was in prison, and published his version as *The Apocalypse of John* (1979).

To what extent is Montaigne's quip ("Because he was he, because I was I") appropriate to my relationship with Elias Petropoulos?

CXXII

Was he a friend? In the loose sense that this term has acquired, the answer is yes. After only two or three work sessions (I was struggling with *The Good Thief's Manual*) and despite our age difference, we spoke to each other with the familiar Greek *esy*, with the familiar French *tu*. This linguistic transformation occurred spontaneously, in the midst of one of Petropoulos's explanations. He started using the informal form, without asking my permission. I followed suit. There was no mutual agreement, as often happens. I would never have initiated the informal form, but I felt at ease when using it with him. By the way, Petropoulos once wrote, and recounted occasionally, that he never used the familiar form of address with Nikos Gabriel Pentzikis.

As regards the equality implied by the deeper, stricter sense of the word "friendship," Petropoulos was a mentor, not a friend. This is not to say that reciprocal affection was absent from our work sessions.

In these reminiscences, I have called the man "Petropoulos." In real life, I called him "Elias," pronouncing the name in the French way, even when I was speaking Greek.

We would shake hands firmly when I arrived, when I left. During the 1990s, when I saw Petropoulos only rarely, we would embrace each other whenever meeting, like the French, kissing each other on each cheek. And embrace each other when we parted company.

CXXIII

August 29, 2003

I sat down on the chair to the side of the bed, put my hand on the back of his left hand, told him (the white lie) that I was in Paris for the day, had heard that he was sick, had decided to drop by the clinic. "*Poly arrostos*," "very sick," he countered in a whisper. He had aged greatly since I had last seen him. His beard had become sparse, was now fully white. Then I added that, in all events, I was happy to see him again. I told him that Françoise was thinking about him, as were Veroniki Dalakoura and Katharine Butterworth, both of whom had confided messages to me by e-mail.

I reminded him of all the good work that we had done together; to this he murmured "*nai*," "yes." I reminded him of how much he had written, of the magnificent monument that he had left for future generations of Greeks. "I haven't read your most recent books," I confessed. "Mary is going to give me copies. That way, I'll be able to see what sort of mischief you've been up to!"

His eyes drifted over to the television screen, across which were flying silver fighter planes. Missiles were being shot from the planes. Then rows of pilots, with helmets tucked under their arms, were saluting an officer. The program seemed to be about the air force of some country that was not France.

He rolled his head back to me. I told him that I was grateful for all that he had taught me, that if I had managed to write a few books, it was in great part because of him. "You made me work hard on the translations, you in fact taught me how to work hard and precisely, then you encouraged me to find my own way," I stated. "Above all, you taught me how to keep my eyes open, wide open. I often think about what you wrote about Pentzikis, your own mentor. What you said about him, let me say it now about you."

He whispered "*efcharisto*," "thank you." He was too weak to continue. So I spoke again. "I have some good news. A collection of essays is coming out in January, followed by a volume of prose and poetry later in the year." "Bravo," murmured Elias; then he closed his eyes briefly.

Mary Koukoules, who had been standing down the hallway, came in and asked him if he wanted to drink some water. He declined. She nonetheless poured some mineral water into a paper cup and held it out to him. He declined again. Then she opened a small box of Greek loukoums and held it out to me. "These little *loukoumakia* are delicious," she remarked, taking one herself and making a sign to me with her eyes that it would be good if we could entice him into eating one. Turning to him, she inquired. He raised his eyebrows slightly, the Greek sign for saying no. He had barely eaten for weeks, and was now often refusing to drink water as well. He raised his right hand, grasped with difficulty the triangular ring hanging above the bed and, pulling himself up ever so slightly, readjusted himself in the bed. He didn't seem to want anyone to help him. Mary suggested that we have a cup of coffee. "There is a café on the rue Linné," she said.

Still touching the back of his hand, I stood up, leaned down over him, explained that we were going out for a very short while. "Take a rest," I added. "We'll be back soon."

When we returned, he was staring at the television. A quiz show was on. I once again sat down on the chair, put my hand on the back of his hand, though I knew that I should not stay long. He turned his head feebly; he now seemed to be in pain.

Struggling to find words that would be worthy but not too sad, I repeated part of what I had already said about my gratitude, adding that there were so many other younger writers, artists, and photographers who had benefited from his rigor, his knowledge, and especially his courage to write exactly what he thought should be written, whatever the consequences. He had ordered Mary to let no friends come upstairs to his bedside in the clinic; she had made an exception for me. I thus felt, during those last few minutes with Elias Petropoulos, that I was indeed the representative of many *confrères* and *consœurs*—some known to me, others not—who had implicitly entrusted me with similar messages of gratitude. It was my responsibility to communicate them to him. I spoke in French, not very eloquently, with the impression nevertheless that it pleased him to hear such words. I added that, after so much work, after so much writing, he needed a rest.

"Repose-toi," I repeated.

Then I stood up, bent over, kissed him on the forehead.

I said: "*yia sou, Maître*," "good-bye, Maître."

It had been our long-standing habit to call each other, not by our first names, but rather by this antiquated French appellation. We had found it, strangely enough, in a rebetic song. Before I could straighten up, he strained to move. With his right hand, he reached behind my head, pulling me back toward him, kissing me on both cheeks. Again I said "*yia sou, Maître*," then left the room.

CXXIV

Before our final long telephone chat, in September 2002, our most recent talk together had taken place at Le Contrescarpe café, located in the like-named square and near the rue Mouffetard apartment. We had sat outside, side by side, in the exceptionally warm air of an autumn noon. We had observed the square. Across it, at the beginning of the rue du Cardinal-Lémoine and to the left, is the apartment where Ernest Hemingway first lived when he came to Paris. Across the square, down the rue Descartes and on the right, is the building in which Paul Verlaine died (and in which Hemingway had a room and wrote his first stories). Petropoulos of course knew this, and perhaps more, but he was not especially interested in the fine details of American expatriate and French literary history. I ordered a *ballon* of red Côtes du Rhône wine,

Petropoulos a Coca Cola. He sent it back to the kitchen when the waiter served it without ice.

After I had visited him in the clinic and knew that I would never see him again, I thought of buying a bottle of Greek wine that I could take back to Angers and drink in his honor when he died. There was no hope left: he was going to die soon. And I knew that I had to prepare myself for the event. I thought of wine even though Petropoulos never drank alcoholic beverages. When Françoise and I lived in Paris, we used to buy Greek products at a shop on the rue de Bazelles, at the bottom of the rue Mouffetard, not far from the Saint-Médard Church.

So that day (29 August 2003), after leaving Petropoulos, I walked to the Greek grocery shop, carrying a heavy sack containing *The String*, *A History of the Condom*, and a German translation of rebetic songs—three books that Mary Koukoules had given me. I also had one of my own manuscripts with me. I had worked on it in the Angers-Paris train.

The Greek shop was closed. The steel shutter out front had been rolled down completely. There was no sign posted on the shutter, but the two brothers (if indeed the owners were still the same) were probably on vacation in their native Crete. I had wondered if they would remember me.

I walked back up the rue Mouffetard. The street was crowded on that Friday afternoon. Music was blaring from the Greek restaurants. They were not for me that day.

I took a seat outside Le Contrescarpe café, at more or less the same table at which Petropoulos and I had sat a few years before. There was only one other customer there, a plump elderly man reading *The International Herald Tribune*. Not far from where I was sitting, a policeman and a policewoman were listening to a delivery-truck driver explaining that in order to deliver his products to a Greek restaurant down the street, he had to park there "for only three minutes." The policewoman shook her head, took out her ticket book. The driver was fuming. In the meantime, the waiter of Le Contrescarpe had come outside. Standing next to me, he too watched the delivery-truck driver arguing with the impassible policewoman.

At last he turned to me. I ordered a large salad and, not a *ballon*, but rather a half-liter pitcher of red Côtes du Rhône wine.

CXXV

And I said to my wife:
—when I die like a dog, here in Paris,
burn my corpse in the crematorium
then toss the ashes into a sewer.
This is my testament.

— *Never and Nothing*

We were the first to leave the columbarium of the Père Lachaise Cemetery—Jacques Vallet, the French photographer Daniel Colagrossi, the Turkish journalist Sinan Fisek, the Greek artist Dimitris Souliotis, the Turkish political cartoonist Selçuk Demirel, Phaedon Koukoules and I. We turned right, headed down the rue des Rondeaux, searching for a sewer opening between the parked cars. Jacques and Phaedon looked the most actively; the rest of us tagged along. Mary Koukoules was about sixty feet behind us, cradling the bag (which enclosed the urn) with her right arm. Walking with her were a dozen or so other men and women, most of them Greeks. Nikolas Syros was gripping his bouzouki. It must have been Katia Koukoules who was carrying the bouquet of sunflowers. The sun on that Saturday afternoon, the 13th of September, was shining warmly, not too hot. There was no wind. The Greek word for "beautiful," *oraios*, came naturally to mind, and I declined it in my mind—*oraios, oraia, oraio*—listening to those magnificent open vowels which, in this context, gave the word an almost archaic, sacred resonance, as if the word were being uttered for the first time at some funeral rite, at the dawn of civilization.

Along the curb of the rue des Rondeaux, Jacques and Phaedon each found a water outlet. Street sweepers open these outlets at dawn, releasing streams of water that flow through the gutters. It is in fact essential to understanding Paris to be able to imagine the city, at dawn, with water flowing through gutters everywhere. Just in front of such outlets is an opening, covered by a grating, which leads down to the sewer conduits. Some twenty years before, Elias Petropoulos had spoken to me about a German artist who would steal the rags, or *serpillières*, which sweepers leave near the outlets; the artist had a way of using these filthy rags on his canvases. Yet in front of the outlets that Jacques and Phaedon had found, the sewer holes were too small for our purposes; in addition, there was hardly room for even one person to stand between the fenders of the parked cars. Phaedon quipped in Greek, then in French: "He's keeping us running till the very end."

We passed the rue Émile-Landrin, the rue Achille, the rue Eugénie-Legrand, all three of which are short side streets.

By this time the rue des Rondeaux had begun to descend, following the downward slope of the cemetery, whose high stonewall rose just to our right. It was shady in that narrow street; branches from the cemetery trees had grown up and over the wall. Jacques remarked that if we walked a little farther, we would surely find a larger sewer hole at the bottom, since the gutter water from the outlets would necessarily have to return to the sewers. We arrived at the corner formed by the rue Charles-Renouvier. There, a sign signaled a dead-end further down the rue des Rondeaux.

The last section of the rue des Rondeaux was indeed a quiet impasse. The cemetery wall continued on the right; on the left there were two rather small apartment buildings. And at the very end of the street, which was also blocked off by a high wall, there was another, larger, sewer opening. It, too, was covered with a grating. As the second group, with Mary and Katia, caught up with us, I moved away to the right, squeezed my way between the fenders of two parked cars, and stood on the sidewalk near the wall. I would have liked to lean against that wall, for I felt tired and a little dizzy and tears were welling in my eyes, but a sloping concrete extension at the base prevented me from doing so. It had been built so that men could not approach the wall and urinate. Some had done so nonetheless; I took a few steps back toward the group.

At this point, as the others were forming a half-circle about fifteen feet back from the grating, a fat woman and an even fatter bearded man came out on a first-floor balcony that overlooked the street. They seemed to be slightly drunk. The man mumbled something about his being the owner not only of his apartment but also of the sewers beneath it, in the street below, then the woman asked more distinctly what we were doing there. Someone answered that it was a ceremony. The woman countered: "A ceremony for rats?" The man was getting angrier about our presence in the street; his wife gave him a push on the shoulder, ordered him inside. She continued to watch us, disapprovingly. Scattering ashes in the way that Mary was going to scatter them was, of course, illegal.

By this time, Mary and Phaedon had squatted down and were removing the glass urn from the black bag. It was shaped like a big jar and enveloped in a purple towel, which Phaedon unwrapped. There was a lid scotch-taped on, and a black ribbon around the neck. The ashes were not really gray, but rather off-white. I thought of the dust of the Attic, but a more accurate analogy would be the way cinders, from certain volcanoes or even bonfires, are charred white, not black. I was not standing close enough to see precisely, but it seemed that there were bits of bone among the ashes as well. Mary and Phaedon removed the lid. In the meantime the sunflowers had been set on the curb, just above and behind the grating.

Carrying the urn, Mary went over to the grating, squatted, said something in Greek and, without further ado, she poured the ashes between the bars of the grating, into the sewer. Ash dust rose in the air, causing two or three of the onlookers to move back. Photos were taken. With their hands, Mary and Phaedon then carefully brushed the remaining ashes—those that had been stopped by the grating bars—into the hole. Finally Mary stood back up, raised the urn above her head, and smashed it hard against the grating, murmuring something else that I could not comprehend from afar. Phaedon again came over, helped his mother to push the broken pieces between the bars. One piece—the bottom of the urn—was still too big, so Mary broke it again against the grating, then pushed the pieces into the sewer. Phaedon found the black ribbon. It, too, disappeared into the hole.

The woman on the balcony called out: "Is what you are doing legal?"

No one paid attention to her. Eventually she, too, became absorbed in what followed.

Nikolas approached with his bouzouki, knelt on one knee alongside the grating, and began singing a rebetic song in the deep hoarse voice typical of this kind of music. His way of playing the bouzouki, his singing, and the very lyrics of the song were all extremely moving. I had in fact translated the song nearly a quarter-century before, with the help of Elias Petropoulos. It begins :

> When I die put me in a lonely place
> an' don't forget my bouzouki — wow man! — consolation for
> an ace...

The song laments the death of a *mangas*, an underworld hoodlum. Figuratively at least, Elias Petropoulos was now joining all the other *manges*, in Hades, which I could also now imagine as a crowded netherworld pantheon of *poètes maudits*. He would be in good company, and so would they.

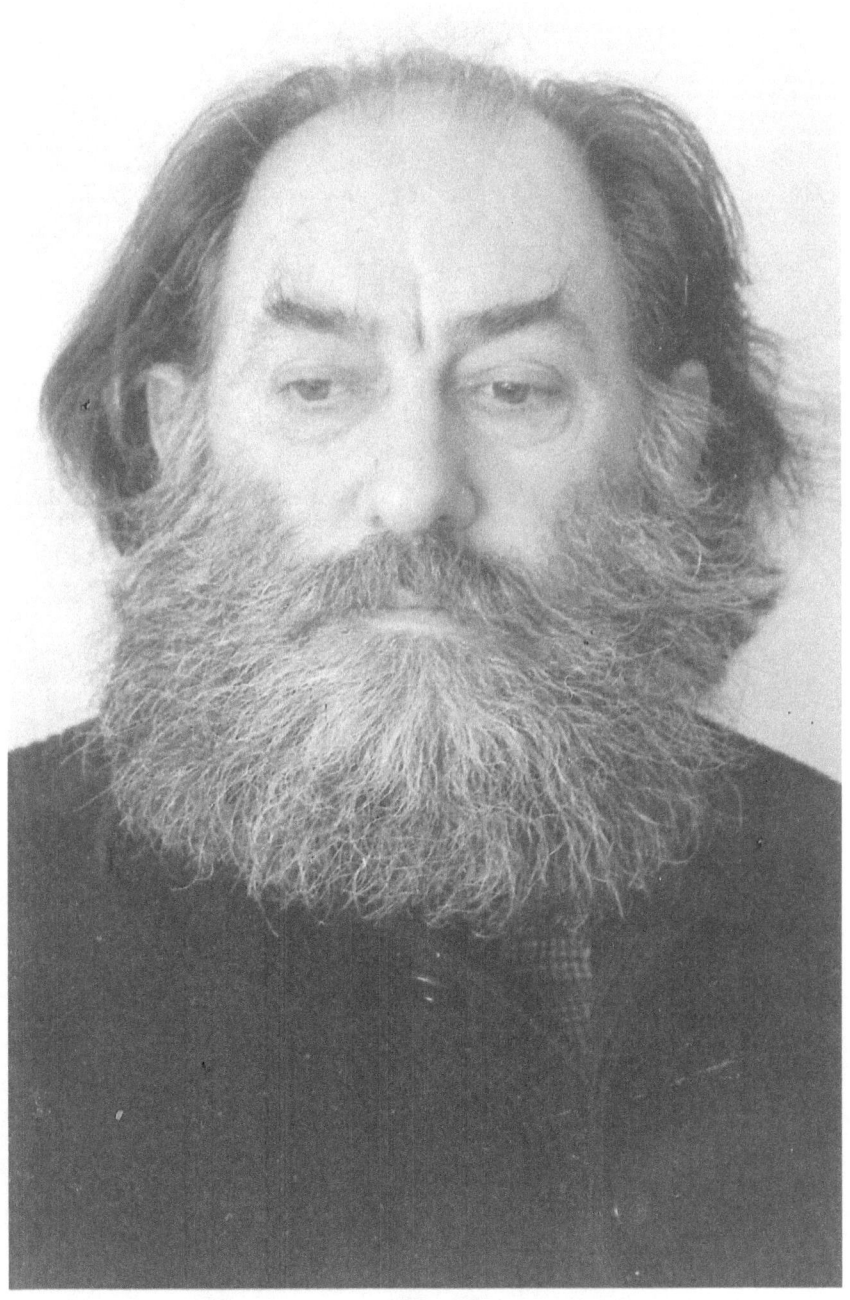
Elias Petropoulos by Vassilis Liapas, c. 1980, Paris.

Petropoulos's parents, Sophia (second from left) and Nikos (far right), with their children (Elias, Zoista and Soulis) in Salonica, Greece, c. 1936.

Jewish chest of Salonica, drawn from memory by Petropoulos in Paris, May 23, 1985. Image courtesy of John Taylor.

Petropoulos as a young child (age 6) in Salonica, 1934. Image courtesy of the Gennadius Library, Athens.

Petropoulos's student identification card from the University of Salonica, where he studied law, 1946. Courtesy of the Gennadius Library, Athens.

Petropoulos age 19, sitting with Vania (the Russian), a member of the Pan-Macedonian National Liberation Front, a resistance group associated with the communist party, 1947.

Petropoulos and the writer Nikos Gabriel Pentzikis standing outside the latter's pharmacy in Salonica, April 30, 1959.

Gathering of writers and artists in Kavala, Greece, 1965. (Left-Right) Nikos Gabriel Pentzikis, Elias Papadimitrakopoulos, Yiorgos Ioannou (face hidden), Takis Kanellopoulos, Nausica Kataki-Petropoulos, Niobe Papadimitrakopoulos, Elias Petropoulos and Pavlos Moskhidis.

Petropoulos with Yiorgos Ioannou at a gathering in Salonica, 1963.

Petropoulos seated next to the singer Alexandra. Also pictured (on the left) are rebetic musicians Vassilis Tsitsanis and Yiannis Papaioannou, 1971.

Drawing of Petropoulos by rebetic lyricist Nikos Mathesis made during the former's imprisonment at Korydallos prison, 1972-1973.

Drawing of Petropoulos made by a fellow inmate during his confinement in Trikala Prison, 1969.

Petropoulos standing against a plaque erected in memory of poet Kostas Karyotakis, who took his own life with a revolver at that same spot on July 21, 1928. Photo taken on January 3, 1975 in the town of Preveza, Greece. Image courtesy of Mary Koukoules.

Petropoulos and Mary Koukoules in Coye-la-Forêt, c. 1980s.

Petropoulos's apartment in Athens, at 47 Voukourestiou Street, where he was living when he met Mary Koukoules, January 1974. Images courtesy of Mary Koukoules.

John Taylor and Petropoulos in the woods near Coye-la-Forêt. Photo taken by the author's wife Françoise Daviet-Taylor during their visit to Petropoulos and Mary Koukoules's country home north of Paris, 1979.

Petropoulos's student identification card for his studies in Turkology, undertaken at the Sorbonne from 1975-1977. Image courtesy of the Gennadius Library, Athens.

John Taylor in Coye-le Forêt on August 31, 1980, photo taken by Petropoulos.

(Left-Right) Alekos Fassianos, Elias Petropoulos, Jacques Vallet and John Taylor at the book launch for "Mirror for You" (1983) in Paris. Photo taken on April 12, 1983 by Vassilis Liappas.

Petropoulos eating in a crêperie in Coye-la-Forêt, c. 1980s.

The writer Elias Papadimitrakopoulos and his wife, Niobe, who is a poet. Image courtesy of Dimitris Kanellopoulos.

Petropoulos and Alekos Fassianos sitting at a cafe in St Germain, Paris, dated March 16, 1977. The print features drawings by Fassianos and color tinting and toning. It was used on the back cover of the 1979 Kedros edition of "Rebetic Songs." Photo taken by Dimi Argiropoulou. Image courtesy of the Gennadius Library, Athens.

Front cover for the first edition of Petropoulos's "The Brothel" (1980), with artwork by Alekos Fassianos. Note the slogan printed along the edge, reading: "throw the Americans out of Greece."

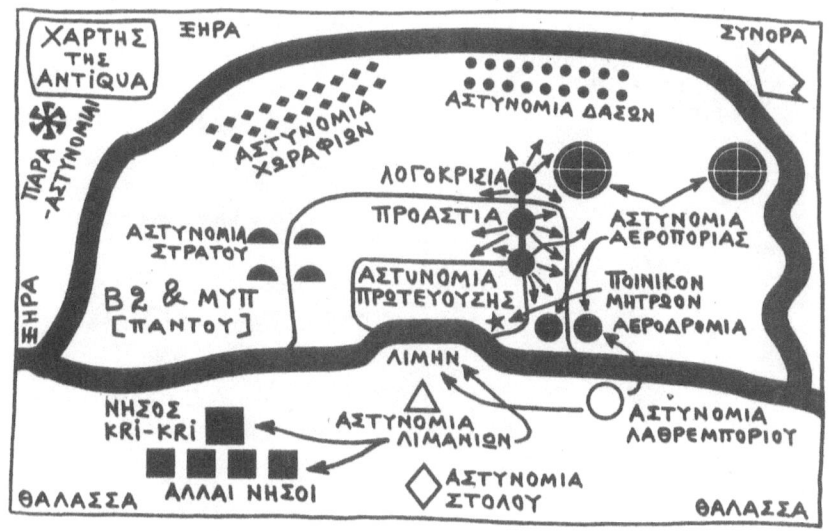

Petropoulos's drawing for the Map of Antiqua from his "Good Thief's Manual" (1979).

Two visual aids drawn by Petropoulos for Taylor's translations of "Balconies in Greece" (1981) *and lyrics in the Rebetic Songs anthology.*

Elias Petropoulos
c/o Byzantinisches Seminar
Unter den Eichen 78/79
1000 Berlin 45

21-12-1983

John, βλέπω πώς δουλεύεις
σάν άράπης! Καλή σου τύχη, λοιπόν.
Πάντως, πρόσεχε πολύ-πολύ τόν Παπαδια-
μάντη. Είναι όλο παγίδες. Καί, βασικά,
τό κείμενο = καθαρεύουσα, καί, οἱ διάλογοι =
= λαϊκή γλώσσα (ἰδίωμα τῆς Σκιάθου). Θά
σοῦ στείλω τίς διευθύνσεις πού ζητῆς.
Αὔριο θά ἔχω γραφομηχανή. Πῆρες ὅλες
τίς κριτικές πού ταχυδρόμησα?

διά σου
 ’H. le Juif

Card sent by Petropoulos to John Taylor from Berlin, dated December 12, 1983. Petropoulos signs off as "le Juif" (the Jew).

Petropoulos and an unknown companion at a party at the Künstlerhaus Bethanien on Mariannenplatz, Berlin. Photo taken by Wolfram Jacob and included in an album preserved at the Gennadius Library, Athens, dated January 18, 1984.

Writer Kostas Tachtsis, Petropoulos and John Taylor at the Greek embassy in Paris, November 11, 1986.

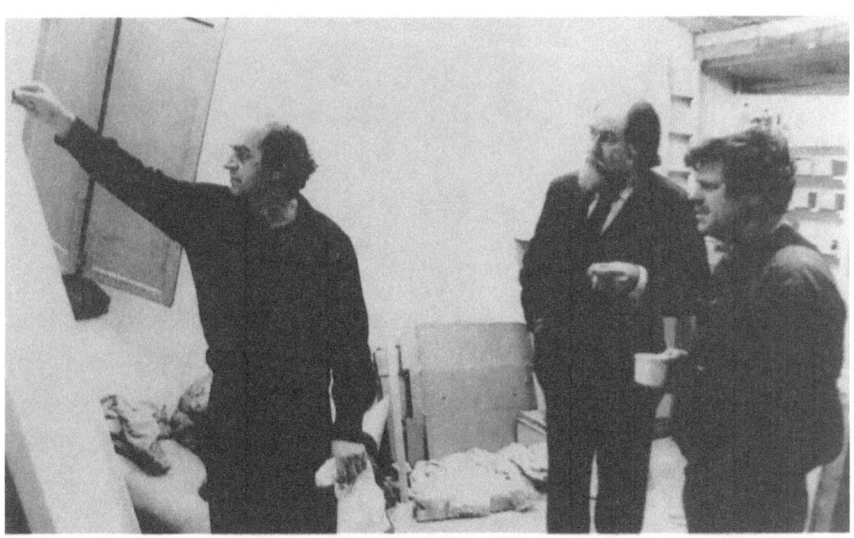

(Left-Right) Alekos Fassianos, Petropoulos and artist Costas Tsoclis. Photo taken at Tscolis's atelier in Paris on January 23, 1985. Fassianos is drawing a portrait of Tsoclis.

Petropoulos and Mary Koukoules (center), along with the writer Ersi Sotiropoulos who gives a typical insult gesture, Paris, 1990s. Image courtesy of Mary Koukoules.

Petropoulos, Mary Koukoules and Reinhold Aman, the editor of "Maledicta", in Paris, c. early 1980s. Image courtesy of Mary Koukoules.

Petropoulos reclining on a bed in Paris. Image courtesy of the Gennadius Library, Athens.

Petropoulos lighting a cigarillo inside his office and study on 34 rue Mouffetard, Paris, late 1990s.

Photo of Petropoulos taken by Gilles Berquet at a studio session on August 22, 1998. Reproduced with permission © Gilles Berquet.

Photo taken by Gilles Berquet on August 22, 1998. Reproduced with permission © Gilles Berquet.

Petropoulos in a Parisian cafe, c. 1990s.

Roland Topor's illustration for the front cover of Petropoulos's book "The Jews of Salonica" (1983).

Still from Kalliopi Legakis's documentary on Petropoulos, "A World Underground" (2005). *In accordance with his last will and testament, Mary Koukoules pours Petropoulos's ashes down a Parisian sewer, September 13, 2003.*

APPENDIX

FOR ELIAS PETROPOULOS

Four hours later I awoke
from a dream, saying *Yia sou,
Ilia*; then much louder: *Yia sou, Ilia!*
(as if we were waving good-bye, you
leaning out the window of the sleeper, I
standing on the chilly, near-deserted platform,
the train already pulling out of the Gare
d'Austerlitz—for Thessaloniki—
but in fact you were flying slowly up
and away from where I was pondering
your apparition,
into the Night of Nights,
and of course you were wearing
your knit tie, yet not your customary dark, but rather a
cream-colored, three-piece suit).

Très élégant, Maître,
I would have said back then
and you would have added slyly: *Toujours.*
Or perhaps more sternly: *Il le faut.*

How strange I thought (watching you soar
toward a blackness that was, surprisingly,
pinpricked with very dim stars),
I never called you *Ilia* when saying good-bye
as the taxi dropped me off on the place d'Italie,
or from a step on the spiral staircase leading down
from the rue Mouffetard apartment
where we had labored over songs, slang,
your *Ugly Poems*, grammatical refinements,
and surely not after that sunny afternoon—so unexpected—
when you wanted simply to stroll
in the Jardin du Luxembourg then sit on a bench,
but *Elias*, or much more often, *Maître*—as you also
almost always addressed me after, for example,
I had picked up the receiver, uttered a *Hello—*

                                                   Maître?—

and occasionally when,
an hour later,
from behind your desk and with a cigarillo
burning between your pianist-like fingers, you spoke
seriously (or sarcastically, angrily, admiringly)
of poetry, politics, pornography or the
etymology of, say, the French word *périple*.
Or *orthographe*.
Or Gorbatchev.
Or Pentzikis's pharmacy, where medication
was rarely sold but the loftiest literature
discussed. He was your *daskalos, didaskalos,*
you wrote in your homage. (You, my *teacher, elementary school teacher*.) Or—
three or four times—your father's
tragic death.

                                       One incurable wound.

And you

played child's pranks too
(in order to forget those wounds, perhaps):
phony phone calls concluding
in laughter, anonymous
erotic collages
left in friends' mailboxes.
The friends of course knew
who the mailman was.

...this flurry of remembrance
at once confusing and acute,
before I emerged from half-sleep, made an effort
to peer into the bedroom's utter darkness,
searching for the slightest sheen
of white ceiling

                (and nothing else)

yet there

you were again floating through the Night of Nights,
though much further away
from the Here and Now that you, through me, still also inhabited,
if barely. You were receding fast,
faster, toward those specks of light that you
would not have overlooked—periods, commas,
semi-colons
that should be in italics, or not. Every
detail counted, I knew, as you
had taught me every detail counted. So

I corrected my initial farewell—the one
uttered after the unremembered dream—
as I might have rectified an error in a first draft, and said,

mustering my courage: *Yia sou,*

Maître.

These words I managed to whisper twice

before you disappeared
into the Chaos or the Constellations.

                  (read at the Columbarium of Père Lachaise Cemetery
                                     on the 13th of September, 2003)

TWO TEXTS ON "KALIARDA": GREEK GAY SLANG

The following two articles originally appeared in *Gay Books Bulletin* (No. 9, Spring-Summer 1983) and *The Cabirion / Gay Books Bulletin* (No. 11, Fall-Winter 1984). I have added an excerpt from Kimon Friar's translation of the long title page of *Kaliarda* (as he published it in his *Books Abroad* article of October 1972), made minor stylistic corrections, and introduced the Greek alphabet for the Kaliarda terms. I have also suppressed certain remarks and footnotes, or parts thereof, when the information is included elsewhere in this book or in the bibliography. It was nonetheless necessary to maintain a few repetitions because context is important in certain places.

BENAVIS TA KALIARDA?

Well, probably not. But even if you do not speak Greek homosexual slang, and even if you do not *benavis* (μπενάβεις) Greek, the recently published fourth edition of Elias Petropoulos's *Kaliarda: An Etymological Dictionary of Greek Homosexual Slang* (1982) may very well snatch your fancy; that is, if you are a dabbler in languages and have a penchant for disreputable argots.

Disreputable argots indeed! For this lexicon of, as Petropoulos specifies, "about 3000 words used by the 'passive' (κίναιδος *kinaidhos*) but not by the 'active' (κολομπαράς *kolombaras*) Greek gay" has enjoyed no smooth publishing history. When the first edition was privately printed and distributed by Petropoulos in 1971, the Junta in power at the time banned the book as "pornography" and by 1972 had sent its compiler off to the clink for seven months. Back to the clink I should say, for in fact he had just been released after a five-month stretch for his long poem, *Body*. In 1969 Petropoulos had already been behind bars for five months because of his anthology of Greek underworld folk songs, *Rebetika Traghoudhia*, also printed and distributed at his own expense. But what the uniformed guardians of "Helleno-Christian Civilization" (as they put it) did not suspect is that the three prison terms only facilitated the encounters so necessary to the work of a folklorist specializing in Greek subcultures and the Greek underworld. Such as when in Korydhalo Prison during his *Kaliarda* stretch Petropoulos ran into the very person—a homosexual named Perla—who had helped him on the first edition. Perla subsequently furnished about 150 additional terms and expressions now included in this most recent edition. This story as well as that of the *Kaliarda* censorship trial are told in the long appendix, and a few etymological and orthographic corrections to the original edition are made. On the long title page, Petropoulos calls his project "an amateur linguistic investigation" and adds that it is "an explanatory and, in large part, etymological lexicon, scrivened for the use of philologists, policemen, folklorists, psychiatrists, king's guards, linguists, firemen, men of letters, philanthropists, sociologists, snobs, theologians, sailors, the unemployed, informers, academicians, the curious, and, in general, peculiar people."

Petropoulos thinks that the word *kaliarda* (καλιαρντά) may derive from the French word *gaillard* ("lively," "sprightly," "bold," "bawdy," "ribald," "hale and hearty," "jolly"), but among Greek gays the word connotes something "bad," "ugly," "curious," or "queer." There are several other ways of designating Greek homosexual slang, a few of which are translatable: Kaliardi, Kaliardo, Tsinavota, Liardo, Doura Liarda, Latinika ("Latin"), Vathia Latinika ("Deep Latin"), Etrouska ("Etruscan"), Loubinistika, and Frangoloubinistika. The language of the *kinaidhos*[1] may also be divided into a sort of "common" Kaliarda and a much more esoteric Kaliarda; that is, the aforementioned Doura Liarda, Deep Latin, or Etruscan. Doura Liarda words, denoted with an asterisk in the lexicon and making up about ten percent of the words collected, would be unknown and often incomprehensible to most Greek *kinaidhi*. Thus various synonyms of "sperm," such as λαχανιαζόζουμο *lakhaniazozoumo* "panting juice" (with a pun on the Greek λαχανόζουμο *lakhanozoumo* "vegetable juice"), τρεμόζουμο *tremozoumo* "trembling juice," and τεκνοκαλλιεργίστρα *teknokallieryistra* "that which cultivates boys," belong to Doura Liarda. Common Kaliarda terms for "sperm" are σαρμελόζουμο *sarmelozoumo* "penis juice," κουραβελτόζουμο *kouraveltozoumo* "fuck juice," μπουλκουμέ *boulkoume* (unknown etymology), and φλόκι *floki* (probably some association with words meaning "pubes").

The various terms for "pederast" are likewise divisible into Kaliarda and Doura Liarda. To Doura Liarda belong μοντερνόπουρος *modernopouros* "old modernizer," τεκνοροκανατζής *teknorokanatzis* "boy nibbler," τουρλολιγούρης *tourlolighouris* "he who craves plump swellings," and ψυχοτραγόπουρος *psykhotraghopouros* "soul priest" (whereas the Kaliarda term for "priest," τραγοπουρός *traghoupouros*, literally means "old he-goat"). The Kaliarda terms for "pederast" are κολόμπος *kolombos*, κολόμβος *kolomvos* (both derived from the Greek term for "pederast," κολομπαράς *kolombaras*), and χριστόφορος *khristoforos*. The astute would-be Kaliardophone will already have noticed that the latter is a play on the former; i.e., "Christopher Columbus." A middle-aged pederast who pays a *kinaidhos* for his pleasure is a μπαλαμό *balamo* (unknown etymology). The unknowing little boy who falls prey to an older homosexual is a "cake" (κέκ *kek*) or "cupcake" (κεκάκι *kekaki*).

It is often extraordinarily difficult to establish the etymologies of Kaliarda terms, let alone translate them. Besides those deriving directly from Modern Greek, many English, French, Italian, and Turkish words come into play and several terms are borrowed from the language of the Gypsies. Μπούκουρος *boukouros* "beautiful" is perhaps from Albanian. The word ότρος *otros* "other" is from Spanish. A Kaliarda term is often a garish alloy of two or three roots from two or three different languages. How to translate a word like Ανιματσούρνος *Animatsournos*? The word means Kharos (the modern folk version of the ancient Greek Charon) or, literally, the "soul thief" or "soul pickpocket," but it has been forged from the Italian word *anima* "soul" and from a word of Gypsy origin, *tsourno*. *Tsourno* (τσουρνό) refers to a type of pickpocketing: the pickpocket, a friend of the *kinaidhos*, hides under the bed and at a sufficiently orgiastic moment rifles the pederast's pockets. Remembering that such a term to the ears of a Greek unacquainted with Kaliarda sounds just as bizarre and exotic as it does to us, we can only leave the term as it stands, translating Ανιματσούρνος by "Animatsournos."

For other examples of Kaliarda words concocted from different languages, let's take a look at a few of the several compounds employing γκοντο- *godo-*, which naturally comes from our own English word "God":

γκοντοαφιόνα *godoafiona* "religion," derived from γκοντο- and from Greek αφιόνι *afioni*, which itself comes from the Turkish *afyon* "opium"; in other words, "God's opium."

γκοντοδούλα *gododhoula* "angel," derived from γκοντο- and from Greek δούλα *dhoula* "slave"; in other words, "God's slave." Add, in Kaliarda, the Turkish word bas "chief" to the above and we obtain μπάς-γκοντοδούλης *bas-gododhoulis* "archangel."

Γκοντοκόντρα *Godokontra* "Hell," derived from γκοντο- and from Greek κόντρα *kontra* / Italian *contra* "against"; in other words, "God-against."

γκοντορελιά *godorelia* "wind," derived from γκοντο- and probably from Gypsy *ril* / *rila* "fart." In Romanian slang, *ril* means "fart" and *rila* means "penis." In other words, γκοντορελιά probably means "God's fart."

Although I have interpreted each word (γκοντορελιά *godorelia* = *God's fart* = wind) in the above examples, it must always be kept in mind that the non-initiated Greek speaker is hardly better off than we are. If it's both Kaliarda and Greek to us, it's at least Kaliarda to him! Like all secretive argots, Kaliarda is consciously designed so as not to be understood outside a tightly closed group. And Kaliarda is spoken at the speed of lightning.

Where each component of a compound word, but not necessarily the word itself, would be comprehensible to a non-initiated Greek speaker, it is more justifiable to translate each component into English; such as in another Kaliarda synonym of Kharos / Charon, Μαυρονταβάς *Mavrodavas* "Black Pimp." But even here, where μαύρος *mavros* "black" is a Greek word, νταβάς *davas* (of Turkish origin) is from Greek underworld slang. This, however, is rare. According to Petropoulos, only about ten words from Tsaboukalidhiki, the lingo of the Greek underworld, are used in Kaliarda; and only about twelve Kaliarda words, in underworld slang. Likewise, words of Russian and German origin are virtually nonexistent in Kaliarda; of course, they are hardly common in Greek, either. One noticeable absence is that of the word πούστης *poustis*, the most common pejorative term in Modern Greek for "homosexual." Πούστης, which we might translate as "faggot," only appears in one compound, πουστόμαγκας *poustomangas* "rough and tough faggot"; the *mangas* (or *rebetis*) is the Greek underworld tough guy. On the other hand, Kaliarda has over forty synonyms for the Greek term *kinaidhos*, the most common of which is αδελφή *adhelfi* (as well as αδερφή *adherfi* or αδρεφή *adhrefi*) "sister." In passing, the term for "brother" is άφακος *afakos*, literally "he who is not to be fucked" (privative *a-* plus English *fuck*); a synonym is κουτζίνος *koutzinos* "cousin" (from Italian *cugino* "cousin"). I have placed the other synonyms of *kinaidhos* in an appendix at the end of this article.

Besides its ability to forge new compounds from the roots of several languages, Kaliarda has charming onomatopoeias. The word for "sewing machine" is τσικτσίνω *tsiktsino*, which Petropoulos derives from the sound of a machine sewing away: *tsik-tsik-tsik-tsik*. Since a train goes *fous-fous-fous-fous*, one of the many words for "train" is φούς-φούς *fous-fous*. "Masturbation" is ντάπ *dap*, derived both from direct onomatopoeia (*dap-dap-dap-dap*) and from another word of onomatopoeic origin, ντούπ *doup*, which means "beating" or "thrashing." Φσί-φσόλ *fsi-fsol* "intercourse" might be of onomatopoeic origin, if it is not from German soldier slang, *ficki-ficki* "fucky-fucky." To the Greek ear, a burning fire goes *khor-khor-khor-khor*; consequently, "fire" is χορχόρα *khorkhora*. The subtlest onomatopoeia of all is certainly φιοφιόρι *fiofiori* "a fold in a piece of cloth or clothing."

There are several other grammatical and lexical idiosyncrasies of Kaliarda that are worth noting. One is that almost all nouns and adjectives are used in the feminine case, even when this obliges the speaker to transform staid masculine and neuter words into freakish-sounding feminines. Sometimes, as Petropoulos notes, "pseudo-colloquial or pseudo-foreign endings" are playfully attached to the root word. The word ροσολιμαντέ *rosolimadé* "licking" derives from the pseudo-foreign μαντέ *madé* and from the Kaliarda ροσόλι *rosoli* "saliva." Ροσόλι itself comes from *rosolio*, the name of an Italian cordial typically flavored with orange blossom, cloves, cinnamon, or rose petals. When foreign words are brought into Kaliarda, they are sometimes, but not always, given Greek endings (e.g., κλοσόνι *klosoni* "bell," from French *cloche* "bell"). And, of course, often the pronunciation of a Greek word is simply altered (e.g., Kaliarda φούσι *fousi* "light," from Greek φως *fos* "light") in order to obscure its meaning. An argot constantly defends itself against comprehension from the outside, and Kaliarda is no exception. Whence the need felt by hardcore *kinaidhi* to alter the pronunciation of Kaliarda terms into Doura Liarda neologisms. The verb δικέλω *dhikelo*, of unknown etymology, is the Kaliarda term for "I see" or "I look at."[2] In Doura Liarda, it is transformed into κουέλω *kouelo*. The verb κουέλω is then employed in new Doura Liarda compounds that do not always correspond to those formed with the original Kaliarda term δικέλω; that is, even if the second component of the compound formed with κουέλω is not itself a Doura Liarda term. Employing ροσόλι *rosoli* once again, in Doura Liarda we obtain κουελορόσολο *kouelorosolo* "tear," literally "eye saliva." Another Doura Liarda term for "tear" is κουελοφλόκι *kouelofloki* "eye sperm." Add the Greek verb σφαλάω *sfalao* "I shut" to κουέλω *kouelo* and we obtain a Doura Liarda term for "I sleep," κουελοσφαλάω *kouelosfalao*, literally "I eye-shut." Analogous δικέλω-compounds (employing the same components) are not listed in the lexicon, although this is, of course, by no means a proof of their nonexistence. The reverse also seems true. In Kaliarda, "dizziness" and "giddiness" are expressed by the compound δικελόσβουρα *dhikelosvoura* "I watch a spinning-top." But the Greek word σβούρα *svoura* "top" is not listed as being combined with κουέλω.

More than Greek underworld slang, which is a sort of Modern Greek with slang terms inserted, Kaliarda is nearly a language in itself. A Greek *kinaidhos* can speak at ease almost without resorting to Modern Greek at all. In Kaliarda, only very few Greek words (e.g., και *kai* "and," όταν *otan* "when," γιατί *yiati* "since") are necessary, along with two particles (θα *tha*, να *na*) required in the construction of verbal tenses. Articles are generally not used in Kaliarda where they would be in Greek. Kaliarda even has its own prepositions, such as νάκα *naka* "without" (unknown etymology) and ντόπα *dopa* "after" (from Italian *dopo* "after"). "No" and "not" are expressed by a single word, νούκου *noukou*. "Together" in Kaliarda is καρμπονέ *karbone* "carbon" (i.e., "carbon copy"). The words τζάκα *tzaka* and its Doura Liarda equivalent τζάκατα *tzakata* (of unknown etymology if not from the Turkish *çak* "until") can be employed as conjunctions, adverbs, or prepositions with many different meanings: "as soon as," "like," "as," "where," "when," "near," "in front of," "here." This increases their unintelligibility. Similarly, there are two multi-purpose verbs in Kaliarda: αβέλω *avelo* and its Doura Liarda equivalent βουέλω *vouelo*. These verbs can mean "I give," "I take," "I can," "I put," "I take out," "I have," "I am," "I want"; indeed, nearly whatever the speaker wants them to mean. In Greek underworld slang there is an analogous verb, κουσουμάρω *kousoumaro*. Petropoulos has collected over eighty *avelo*-phrases and nearly forty with *vouelo*. Here are a few examples:

αβέλω αίτνα *avelo aitna* "I have a pimple," literally "I have a Mt. Aetna."

αβέλω βιολέτα *avelo violeta* "I pay," literally "I give violets."

αβέλω κράκρα *avelo krakra* "I am thirsty," literally "I have krakra" (onomatopoeia).

αβέλω νορμάλ *avelo normal* "I fall down (on my stomach)," literally "I assume a normal position."

αβέλω πακέτο *avelo paketo* "My genitals bulge under my pants," literally "I put out my package."

αβέλω φρομάζ Υμηττού *avelo fromaz Ymittou* "I have a dirty penis," literally "I have Hymettus cheese." In colloquial Greek, "cheese" (τυρί *tyri*) means "sperm." Φρομάζ comes from the French word *fromage* "cheese." Mt. Hymettus is the famous mountain overlooking Athens.

βουέλω μουνόπασχα *vouelo mounopaskha* "I have my period (menstruation)," literally "I have cunt-Easter."

βουέλω σεμελόπηγη *vouelo semelopiyi* "I urinate," literally "I turn on my penis fountain."

One additional grammatical observation made by Petropoulos in this new edition of *Kaliarda* is that when a *kinaidhos* wants to say "he fucked me" (active voice) he says instead "we were taken" (παρθήκαμε *parthikame*), employing the first-person plural of the verb "to take" (παίρνω *pairno*) and the passive voice. Sometimes παρθήκαμε is intentionally mispronounced as παρφούκαμε *parfoukame*.

The most important reason behind Kaliarda's autonomy from Modern Greek is that Greek *kinaidhi* have devised words for all sorts of objects and aspects of everyday life. It would be a great error, indeed, to have the impression that Kaliarda is constituted exclusively of sexual terms. For example, Greek foods have special Kaliarda names which, Petropoulos reports, one may hear being cried out from waiter to cook in the Athenian tavernas in which homosexuals hang out. Certainly most of you have tasted that delicious Greek (but in truth, Turkish) speciality, *dolmadhes*, little grapeleaf-wrapped balls of rice with herbs and spices. Well, in Kaliarda, *dolmadhes* go by the name of αμπελομπομπίτσες *ambelobombitses*, "little bombs from the vineyard." Similarly, macaroni noodles are called σωλήνες *solines* "pipes." Less colorfully, "veal meat" is simply κάρνο *karno*, a slight transformation of the Italian word *carne* "meat." Turkish coffee may be called, curiously, νυφοκουκούλα *nyfokoukoula* "bribe's bonnet"; synonyms are καημοζούμι *kaimozoumi* "yearning or sorrow juice," πφε *pfe* (an intentional phonetic perversion of the Greek καφές *kafes* "coffee"), and τουρκόσουπα *tourkosoupa* "Turkish soup." Greek *kinaidhi* have invented words for animals, plants, flowers, colors, professions (including several kinds of doctors), relatives, shades of beauty and ugliness, diseases and deformities, metals, various aspects and figures of religion, money, and even the four seasons. In Kaliarda, for example, "summer" is ξελογιάρα *kseloyiara* "seducer."

Not to forget nicknames, proverbs, curses, and place names! Paris, for instance, is Μουτζότοπος *Moutzotopos* "Cunt Place," in the sense of "Place where there are many cunts (i.e., women)." The term derives from two Greek words, τόπος *topos* "place" and μούτζα *moutza*. In Kaliarda, μούτζο *moutzo* (from Greek μούτζα *moutza* or *moudza*) means "the female pudenda." But in Greek, *moutza* is the name of an insulting gesture, equivalent in impact and aggression to our "finger," in which the palm of the hand with all five fingers spread out is flashed at another person. In Kaliarda, this typical Greek gesture is the "five-drachma curse," the ταλιροκατάρα *talirokatara*.

If Paris is known for its women, London is renowned (at least among Greek homosexuals) for its "sisters"; the British capital is, in any case, Αδερφοχώρι *Adherfokhori* "Sister City." Italy becomes Γκράνταμπότα *Grandabota* for obvious reasons and an Italian is transformed into a "Little Great Boot" (Γκράνταμποτάκι *Grandabotaki*), that is a "Little Italy." The Postal Savings Bank of Athens is "Shylock's Hut" (Σαιλοκότσαρδο *Sailokotsardho*). The Acropolis (in Greek, Ακρόπολι *Akropoli*) is irreverently mispronounced so as to mean "White Ass" (Ασπρόκωλη *Asprokoli*); sometimes it is simply "Tourist Trap" (Τουριστόφακα *Touristofaka*). And the language of Socrates and Alkibiades becomes καραπουρόλιγκα *karapourolinga*, which translates into something like "terrible mushy old lingo."

One of the dictionary entries that got Petropoulos in trouble in 1971, a year in which both Vice President Spiro Agnew (Anagnostopoulos) and Commerce Secretary Maurice Stans visited Athens, the latter conveying President Richard Nixon's "warm love" to the Junta, arose from the unfortunate fact that in Kaliarda the Greek word πρεσβεία *presvia* "embassy" means "public toilet."[3] The conscientious lexicographer was obliged to report—and it was cited in the accusation against him—that Greek gays were calling the public toilets at Omonia Square in Athens "The United States Embassy." Those located at City Hall had been christened "The Embassy of the United Arab Republic" and those at Syntagma Square "The Embassy of Great Britain." Syntagma Square itself goes by the name of Γερμανόγκρεκα *Germanogreka*, apparently because Greek gays can meet German tourists there. Because of its fountains Omonia Square is called Κανουλού *Kanoulou*, a deformation of the Greek κάνουλες *kanoules* "faucets." One nickname that Petropoulos did not include in the 1971 edition was Σπειροχαιτόπουρος *Spirokhaitopouros* "Old Spirochete" (i.e., "Old Syphilis Germ"), the Greek homosexual appellation for the Junta leader, Colonel George Papadopoulos. Since "Papadopoulos" is also the brand name of a well-known Greek biscuit, the term μπισκοτότεκνο *biskototekno* "biscuit boy," which in Kaliarda means "infantryman," soon came to signify a "lackey of Papadopoulos." The Kaliarda term for "fascist" is τζασροβεσπάκης *tzasrovespakis*, which derives from the Kaliarda affix τζασ *tzas* and from ροβεσπάκης *rovespakis* "democrat" (from "Robespierre"). Τζασ connotes "flight," "banishment," "expulsion," "outflow," "without," and sometimes "giving." The Kaliarda verbs τζασάρω *tsasaro* and τζασέρνω *tzaserno* mean "I flee," "I break," "I drive away," "I scatter," "I damage," "I hunt," "I liberate." Τζάσε! *tzase!* means "get out of here!" All these connotations go into our original word, *τζασροβεσπάκις*. Would the polyglot punning ingenuity of Greek *kinaidhi* have given James Joyce an inferiority complex?

When Greek *kinaidhi* sing, they sing in Kaliarda, inventing lyrics to the tunes of popular songs. When they are speaking Kaliarda and suddenly wish to express their thoughts with a proverb, the proverb is unflinchingly delivered in Kaliarda as well. "Τζάκατα δικέλεις ντούμα χορχόρα αβέλεις τ' άχατα" / *"Tzakata dhikelis douma khorkhora avelis t'akhata,"* a Greek gay might be inclined to muse: "Where there's smoke, there's fire." While speaking Modern Greek, however, *kinaidhi* invent their own particular proverbs on the spot in Greek: "Ο κώλος είναι το μουνί του μέλλοντος" / *"O kolos inai to mouni tou mellondos,"* "The ass is the cunt of the future." In Steve A. Demokopoulos's article "The Greek Gays have a Word for It" (*Maledicta*, vol. II, 1978, pp. 33-39), the thirty Greek homosexual curses listed in Petropooulos's lexicon are translated into English.[4] They are typically outlandish:

> I hope you become shriveled and lose your teeth and look like an old tortoise!
> (Που να σαφρακιάσεις και να σου τζάσουν τα ντίλια και να καταντήσεις σαν πουρή χελώνα!)
>
> I hope that when they bury you, dearie, your ass doesn't decay, for what you did to me!
> (Που να σε θάψουνε και να μη λιώνει ο κώλος σου, κουφάλα, απ' το κακό που μούκανες!)
>
> I hope that your piles hang like a bunch of grapes!
> (Που να σου κρεμαστούν τα καριόλια σαν τσαμπιά σταφύλια)

In Kaliarda, a more direct way of letting off your steam is the word-saving χάλε κουλά! *khale koula!* "eat shit!" (χάλε from Kaliarda χάλω *khalo* "I eat," which is of Gypsy origin [note Romanian slang *hali* "I eat"], and *κουλά* perhaps from Greek κουλές *koules* "tower" [from Turkish *kule* "tower"] or from Italian *culo* "ass," "bottom"). If you desire to express your admiration for something, say λατσά! *latsa!* "great!" "beautiful!" "brilliant!", an exclamation that is of Gypsy origin.

An esoteric slang, an argot, is never *only* a collection of words and phrases—a "slang dictionary"—but also comprises a variety of gestures, "argotic gestures," as important to the argot's comprehensibility for the insider as they are to its incomprehensibility to the outsider. In his introduction to the lexicon, Petropoulos describes spoken Kaliarda as being "accompanied by eloquent gestures and grimaces and antics and smirks and effeminate body movements." In the new edition, eleven photographs of such Greek homosexual gestures are included. Fortunately, within a year or so Petropoulos will be publishing his *Panorama of Gestures in Greece*, in which several drawings by the Turkish artist Selçuk Demirel, as well as Petropoulos's photographs, will depict "homosexual gestures"; appropriate Greek or Kaliarda phrases (with an English translation) will accompany each picture. [This book was in fact never published.]

Eleven years have passed since Petropoulos printed his first *Kaliarda*, but what the folklorist pointed out then has lost little of its truth today: "From the viewpoint of literary exploitation and literary investigation, Kaliarda is a completely unknown and virgin language." Indeed, research on Kaliarda has barely begun. [I wrote this article in 1982, but I have come across next to no research on the topic since then.] Comparative studies should be carried out, contrasting from several angles (psychological, sociological, linguistic, etc.) the Greek gay with his European and especially Middle Eastern counterpart. The homosexual tradition of Ancient Greece must likewise be taken into account. Petropoulos would not wish us to ignore the "topography" of the places at which Greek *kinaidhi* meet or hang out—in Athens, behind the Hilton Hotel on King Constantine Avenue after midnight, early in the morning on Favierou Street (No. 44), in the public toilets on Omonia and Syntagma Squares and behind City Hall, in Taverna Grika on Astrous Street (No. 92), in Taverna Stelaki on Kifissou Avenue, etc., etc., etc. In Petropoulos's book *The Brothel* (1980), we learn that most Greek whorehouses use *kinaidhi* as maids. This, too, is a subject that needs investigating. One of Petropoulos's most important contributions to the study of Greek folklore has been his insistence on the role of the city, "street," and Greek underworld (*hypokosmos*) in the propagation of folk customs and traditions. Do Greek *kinaidhi* belong to the underworld? In his introduction to *Kaliarda*, Petropoulos tells us that they do, although to its periphery. This question should also be explored in greater depth. The philological and linguistic research on Kaliarda that could be done is evident. And what about Greek lesbianism? A starting point could be the several Kaliarda terms for "lesbian": γκουνιότα *gouniota* (probably of French origin: e.g., *gouine* "lesbian"), μαντάμ-γκού *madam-gou* (from γκουνιότα), σεμναδερφή *semnadherfi* "modest or decent sister" (from Greek), τζιβιτζιλού *tzivitzilou* (from Kaliarda τζίβ-τζίβ *tziv-tziv* "lesbian intercourse" [probably onomatopoeia]), σιβιτζιλού *sivitzilou* (phonetic transformation of τζιβιτζιλού), and σιβίτζω *sivitzo* (from σιβιτζιλού).

But then there is the problem of the freedom of the press in sexual matters. Petropoulos originally intended to include a 45-rpm record of Kaliarda speech with the third edition of the lexicon in 1980. This idea, dating back to 1971, was naturally impossible to carry out during the Dictatorship of the Colonels. But every Greek record must pass through a governmental censorship office and the Kaliarda record was not approved by this office during the recent Karamanlis government. At about the same time (1980), coinciding with the entry of Greece into the European Economic Community, one of the requirements for which is a democratic form of government, the Greek government conducted and won three censorship trials dealing with "pornographic" publications: on October 24, against the publisher of *Betty*, the autobiography of a transvestite; on October 26, against the homosexual magazine *Amfi*; on November 3, against the publisher of a Greek translation of the Marquis de Sade's classic *La Philosophie dans le boudoir*. On October 23, the government had already won a much-publicized trial to ban *The Good Thief's Manual* (1979), our lexicographer's best-selling parody of the Greek police and judicial system. The charges: slanderous attacks against the Greek judiciary, the Greek police, and the Greek Orthodox Church. As a "habitual offender," Petropoulos was sentenced *in absentia* to eighteen months in prison and a large fine. The folklorist, fortunately living in Paris at the time, became a "wanted man" for the Greek authorities. But naturally all this changed with the coming to power of the PA.SO.K Socialist Party in October, 1981. . . .

But no, it didn't! Last spring (1982), trials were conducted against a cinema owner who had shown *Emmanuelle* (and the like), as well as against the satirical magazine *Scandal*. The PA.SO.K government of Papandreou decided to retain the "Press Law" passed in 1979 during Karamanlis's tenure but whose tenants go back to laws promulgated during the dictatorship of Metaxas in the late 1930s. Under this law, any prosecuting attorney can take legal action against any book or magazine that he finds "immoral" or "contrary to the interests of national security." This law suppresses the journalistic right to unnamed sources and makes certain topics, such as the armed forces and foreign agents, "taboo." Under this law, publishers, editors, writers, and journalists also run the risk of far severer sanctions than in the past. And as I was typing these pages—and I am now retyping them— Petropoulos informed me that just yesterday (9 September 1982) the Greek police raided Athenian bookstores and seized recently published translations of, once again, the works of le divin Marquis.[5] Couple these events with the rampant censorship carried out by several groups in the United States and, alas!, it has been a tough year for μπούκια *boukia* "books," as Greek *kinaidhi* would say.

One can get mad at politicians and Greek gays are no exceptions. Kaliarda possesses several depreciatory "titles" for the loftier positions of the governing class. A "minister" is a μινιστέρος *ministeros* (from Greek μινίστρος *ministros*, from Italian *ministro*) or, more injuriously, a μινιστροπουρός *ministropouros* "mushy old minister." The head of the lot, the prime minister, is called, naturally, the πρίμος-μινιστροπουρός *primos-ministropouros* or, simply, the πριμάτσος *primatsos* (superlative degree of πρίμος *primos* "first," from Italian *primo*). There is another synonym of "prime minister," πρωτονταβάς *protodavas*, of particular interest to both the citizen and political scientist. My most attentive Kaliarda students will already have ascertained its literal meaning.

THE KALIARDA SYNONYMS OF "KINAIDHOS"

Note: For the sake of clarity and precision, I have employed the Greek word κίναιδος *kinaidhos* "passive homosexual" in my translations below.

This is because of the socio-cultural differences that (I suspect) exist between homosexuality in Greece and homosexuality in America and most other parts of Europe. In a proper translation, one would need to substitute derogatory American or English synonyms for *kinaidhos* (e.g., queer, faggot, fag, fairy, pansy), since most of the terms below carry demeaning or degrading connotations. But even this would not be doing justice to the esotericism of Kaliarda. The logical idiom for the translation of such terms is, of course, "The Queens' Vernacular" (as in Bruce Rogers's famous lexicon, 1972).

αγλαρογκόμενα *aghlarogomena* "night-owl *kinaidhos*," literally "non-slumbering dame" (from privative *a-* + Greek γλαρώνω "I slumber" + Greek underworld γκόμενα "dame").

αγλαροπουρός *aghlaropouros* "old night-owl *kinaidhos*" (from Kaliarda πουρί "old," in turn from Greek *pouriv* "porous stone," with negative connotations of "mushy," "sloppy," "rotten," even "tartar" on the teeth).

αγλαρότεκνο *aghlarotekno* "night-owl boy" (see τεκνο *tekno* below).

αδελφή *adhelfi*, literally "sister."

αδερφάρα *adherfara* "eminent *kinaidhos*," literally "big or large sister" (in Greek, -αρα is an augmentative suffix).

αδερφή *adherfi*, literally "sister" (another pronunciation of αδελφή).

αδρεφή *adhrefi* "sis" (colloquial variant of αδελφή / αδερφή).

ανέμη *anemi*, literally "spool"; in particular, a *kinaidhos* who makes extremely effeminate gestures and movements; from the image of a spool, spinning wheel, and yarn.

ανεμόμυλος *anemomylos*, literally "windmill"; in particular, a *kinaidhos* who makes extremely effeminate gestures and movements; from the image of a windmill turning.

αρτίστα του βωβού *artista tou vovou* "old and expert *kinaidhos*," literally "artiste of the silent films" (from Italian *artista* + Greek βωβός *vovos* "silent").

βλαχοντάνα *vlakhodana* "provincial *kinaidhos*," literally "hick whore" (from Greek βλαχο- *vlakho-* [connotes "hick"] + Greek πουτάνα *poutana* "prostitute" [phonetic word play: πουτάνα το ντάνα]).

γιδοτεκνοσυντήρητη *yidhoteknosyntiriti* "provincial *kinaidhos*," literally "kept by young she-goats" (from Greek γίδα *yidha* "she-goat" + *τεκνό* [see above] + Greek verb συντηρώ *syntiro* "I provide for").

διαπομπού *dhiapompou* "*kinaidhos* accompanied by young boys," literally "pilloried one" (from Greek verb διαπομπεύω *dhiapompevo* "I put in the pillory" and Greek πομπεμένη *pompemeni* "escorted").

διπλό-μπατιμάν(ι) *dhiplo-batiman(i)* "escorted *kinaidhos*," literally "double battement" (from the French dancing term *battement*, "an extension of the free foot in any direction followed by a beat against the supporting foot").

δίσκος *dhiskos* "active and passive homosexual," literally "disk" in the sense of "musical record"; i.e., it can be played on both sides.

επιτάφιος *epitafios* "*kinaidhos* accompanied by a group of beautiful, well-dressed boys," literally "funeral procession"; also the "Good Friday procession" and in particular the religious carving representing Christ's tomb that is carried in this procession.

ετρούσκος *etrouskos*, literally "Etruscan."

ζουγκλολουμπίνα *zoungloloubina* "wholehearted hardcore *kinaidhos*," literally "jungle fag" (from Greek ζούγκλα *zoungla* [from English *jungle*] + λουμπίνα [see below]).

κάππα *kappa*, literally "kappa," the first letter of the Greek word κόρη *kori* "girl," "maiden" (see κόρη below).

καραμπινές *karabines* "hardcore *kinaidhos*" (from Karliarda καρα- *kara*-, an intensifying and augmentative affix [from Turkish *kara* "black"] + Greek μπινές *bines* "pansy").

καραλουμπού *karaloubou* "bad *kinaidhos*" (from Kaliarda χαρα-, an intensifying and augmentative affix [from Turkish *kara* "black"] + λούμπα [see below]).

καραλούμπω *karaloubo* "bad *kinaidhos*" (from Kaliarda χαρα-, an intensifying and augmentative affix [from Turkish *kara* "black"] + λούμπω [see below]).

κεραυνός *keravnos* "completely toothless *kinaidhos*," literally "thunderbolt."

κεραυνού *keravnou* "toothless *kinaidhos*"; variant of κεραυνός.

κλούβα *klouva* "destitute street *kinaidhos*, prostitute, breeched-out *kinaidhos*," literally "paddy wagon" (from Greek underworld slang, apparently because the police pick up such *kinaidhi* with one).

κορακοβλαστήμω *korakovlastimo* "extraordinarily fat *kinaidhos* (or woman)," literally "cursing crow"; according to one interpretation, because the pallbearers (in colloquial Greek, the "crows") will curse when they have to carry the casket.

κόρη *kori*, literally "girl" or "maiden."

κοτούλα *kotoula* "young stud who will nevertheless accept the passive role," literally "little hen" (from Greek underworld slang κότα *kota* "hen," a prisoner who accepts the passive homosexual role while in prison but who is not otherwise a passive homosexual).

κόφ-μεσίκ *kof-mesik* "*kinaidhos*-prostitute," literally "slut with chic" (from Greek underworld slang κόφα *kofa* [from κουφάλα *koufala*] "slut" + Greek με *me* "with" + French *chic*).

κροτάλω *krotalo* "destitute street *kinaidhos*" whose passing creates a "sensation"; from Greek κρότος *krotos* "noise," "fuss," "sensation."

κρυφή *kryfi* "crypto-*kinaidhos*," literally "crypto"; closet queen.

κρυφή *kryfo* "crypto-*kinaidhos*, literally "crypto"; closet queen.

λαίδη *laidhi*, literally "lady" (from English).

λατέρνα *laterna* "*kinaidhos* with make-up on," literally "barrel organ" (from the decorations on a barrel organ; the Greek word λατέρνα comes from Italian).

λέδη *ledhi*, literally "lady" (from English).

λούμπα *louba* (from λουμπίνα).

λουμπέσκο *loubesko* (from λουμπίνα, with a suffix of Rumanian origin).

λουμπίνα *loubina* (it is not improbable that this word derives from "Columbine," associated with a festival that up until the Second World War used to take place in Athens on Shrove Monday and Lenten Sundays. Homosexuals dressed up in Spanish costumes and as cabaret singers used to perform dances around a sort of May pole, the γαιτανάκι *yaïtanaki*. At the time, this was their only public appearance and the festival was often prohibited by the police. Some translators transliterate λουμπίνα and its derivatives as *loumbina*, etc.)

λουμπουνιά *loubounia* (from λουμπίνα).

λούμπω *loubo* (from λούμπα, from λουμπίνα).

λουτροκαμπίνες *loutrokabines* "homosexual apartment owner"; in newspaper want ads in Greece, the word means a bathroom including a toilet.

μισογουνού *misoghounou* "*kinaidhos* who has his privates depilated," literally "fur hater."

μοντερνότεκνο *modernotekno* "young *kinaidhos*," literally "modern boy" (from the widespread belief among *kinaidhi* that homosexuals are "with it"; see τεκνο *tekno*).

μούμια *moumia* "old but well-preserved *kinaidhos*," literally "mummy."

μπάιρον *bairon* "polite, noble, elegant, well-bred *kinaidhos*" (from Lord Byron).

μπιτζανού *bitzanou* "*kinaidhos* who is starving" (unknown etymology).

νεροχύτης *nerokhytis* "*kinaidhos* who works in a brothel," literally "kitchen sink" (according to Petropoulos, many Greek brothels use *kinaidhi* as maids).

ντάμντελαρί *damdelari* "*kinaidhos* who sells himself in the street," literally "dame de la rue."

ντόβας *dovas* "odious, repugnant *kinaidhos*" (unknown etymology).

ζεφωνισμένι *ksefonismeni* "*kinaidhos* of lower-class origin," "destitute *kinaidhos*," literally "he who is yelled at" (from Greek verb ξεφωνίζω *ksefonizo* "I yell"; such *kinaidhi* are often hailed with the shout σύκα! *syka!* "figs!" as they pass; see also συκιά *sykia* and σύκο *syko* below).

ξεκωλήθρα *ksekolithra* "provocative, ostentatious, hardcore *kinaidhos*" (from Greek underworld slang ξεκωλιάρα *ksekoliara*, a pejorative term for passive homosexual).

ξεσκισμένι *kseskismeni* "street *kinaidhos*" (from Greek underworld slang ξεσκίζω *kseskizo* "I humiliate," "I dishonor").

ξεσκίστρα *kseskistra* "*kinaidhos*-prostitute" (see ξεσκισμένι).

πλέν-λουμπινιά *plen-loubinia* "hardcore *kinaidhos*," literally "full or stuffed fag" (from Spanish *pleno* "full" + λουμπίνα [see above]).

πουστόμαγκας *poustomangas* "tough guy *kinaidhos*," literally "faggot-hoodlum" (the *mangas* is the Greek underworld tough guy).

συκιά *sykia*, literally "fig tree" (see *σύκο*).

σύκο *syko* "underage *kinaidhos*," literally "fig" (see ξεσκισμένι).

ταραφόλουμπα *tarafolouba* "*kinaidhos* obviously belonging to the world of homosexuals" (from Greek underworld slang ταράφι *tarafi* "person belonging to the same group as we do"; "one of us" + λουμπίνα [see above]).

ταραφολουμπέσκο *tarafoloubesko* "obvious *kinaidhos*" (from ταραφόλουμπα).

τεκνό *teknó* "boy," "catamite" (from Greek τέκνο *tékno* [note change in accent]: in Greek Orthodox monasteries, every elderly monk has his τέκνο).

τζαζκαραμπαζού *tzazkarabazou* "hip-swaying, mincing, smirking *kinaidhos*," literally "effusion of screwing and unscrewing" (from Kaliarda affix τζαζ *tzaz-* "flight," "banishment," "effusion," "giving" + Kaliarda verb καραμπάζω *karabazo* "I screw").

τζιναβοτός *tzinavotos* "tricky *kinaidhos*," "*kinaidhos* who knows his way around the world of homosexuals" (probably of Gypsy origin; note Kaliarda verb τζινάβω *tzinavo* "I understand," "I feel," "I employ trickery"); employed as adjective.

τζιναβοχειροκρότης *tzinavokhirokrotis* "partisan of or sympathizer with *kinaidhi*," literally "fag applauder" (from τζιναβοτός *tzinavotos* + Greek χειροκροτώ *khirokroto* "I applaud"); not a synonym of *kinaidhos*, of course.

υψομετρού *ypsometrou* "provincial *kinaidhos*" (from Greek υψόμετρον *[h]ypsometron* "hypsometer."

φιλέλληνας *filellinas* "polite and noble *kinaidhos*," literally "philhellene."

φιόγκος *fiongos* "*kinaidhos* who passes himself off as a stud"; literally "bow" (from Greek φιόγκος *fiongos* "bow," "knot," from

Italian *fiocco* "tassel"; also colloquial Greek τζιτζιφιόγκος *tzitzifiongos* "coquettish person," "decent, well-bred person").

φρανσή *fransi*, literally "Frenchman," by extension "Frenchy" (from French *français*).

ψωραδερφή *psoradherfi* "lower-class *kinaidhos*," literally "scab sister" (from Greek ψώρα *psora* "psoriasis," "scabies").

---

1. Kaliarda is spoken by the "passive" homosexual, the *kinaidhos* (plural: *kinaidhi*). The Greek distinction between "passive" and "active" homosexuals goes back to Antiquity: see the thorough discussion of *erastes* "lover" and *eromenos* "beloved" in K. J. Dover's *Greek Homosexuality* (New York: Vintage Books, 1978). The word *kinaidhos*, in ancient Greek, is of uncertain etymology. A critical examination of the several hypotheses is found under *kinaidos* in the *Real-Encyclopädie der Classischen Altertumswissenschaft*. The reader should also consult Pierre Chantraine's *Dictionnaire étymologique de la langue grecque* (Paris: Klincksieck, 1968) and note the explanation of the Italian cognate (*cinèdo*) in Carlo Battisti and Giovanni Alessio's *Dizionario etimologico italiano* (Florence: G. Barbera, 1968) and especially in Salvatore Battaglia's *Grande Dizionario della lingua italiana* (Turin: Unione Tipografico, 1964). We find the term used in the sense of "passive homosexual" at least as far back as Plato. In *Gorgias* (494e; translation by B. Jowett), Socrates asks Callicles: "But what if the itching is not confined to the head? Shall I pursue the question? And here, Callicles, I would have you consider how you would reply if consequences are pressed upon you, especially if in the last resort you were asked, whether the life of a catamite (*kinaidos*) is not terrible, foul, miserable? Or would you venture to say that they too are happy, if they only get enough of what they want?" *Kinaidos* lives on in Latin literature as *cinaedus*.
2. Modern Greek has no infinitive, so I have translated all verbs into the first-person singular.
3. According to Petropoulos (in his interview with Schofield Coryell in *Afrique-Asie*, No. 248, 14-17 September 1981, pp. 55-59), a main reason behind his recent troubles with the Greek government is his association with protests against United States military bases in Greece. The information about Agnew, Stans, and Nixon is taken from Richard Clogg's *Short History of Modern Greece* (London: Cambridge University Press, 1979, p. 193).
4. The newly born Kaliarda enthusiast should also consult the following articles: Hélène Ioannidi, "Caliarda: la langue secrète des homosexuals grecs," *Topiques*, No. 20, October 1977; Jean-Luc Hennig, "Kaliarda," *Libération*, 16 December 1977; Theodor Kallifatides, "Den Farlige Lexicografen," *Svenska Dagbladet*, 16 July 1978; Steve Demakopoulos, "A Greek Gay is a Greek Gay is a Greek Gay. . .", *Maledicta*, Vol. VI, 1982, pp. 45-51. The first person to review *Kaliarda* was the noted translator Kimon Friar (*Books Abroad*, October 1972). In these articles, the

reader will find Kaliarda terms translated and analyzed that I have not dealt with here.

5. See *Libération* (10 September 1982, p. 19) and *Le Monde* (17 September 1982, p. 14). The Greek police arrested Themis Banoussis, the owner of Exantas Press, for having published *120 Journées de Sodome*, *La nouvelle Justine*, and *L'Histoire de Juliette sa soeur*. Exantas Press, a well-known publishing company specializing in the avant-garde and in translation (especially from French), was also the publisher of *La Philosophie dans le boudoir*, seized and banned by the Karamanlis government and banned definitively by the Papandreou government after Exantas Press made an appeal. In protest against these measures, forty-seven Greek publishers announced that they would collectively publish one of Sade's works and distribute it free of charge. The Socialist government has ordered the arrest of all of them (see the *International Herald Tribune*, 16 September 1982, p. 2). The Greek Minister of Culture, the former actress Melina Mercouri, has refused to comment on these violations of the freedom of the press. As for Greek homosexuals, the PA.SO.K party is on record (see *Libération*, 10 September 1982) as having referred to them as "repugnant earthworms" and "sub-humans."

KALIARDA REVISITED

By publishing a long article on Greek homosexual argot in *Gay Books Bulletin* (No. 9), I hoped to incite philologists, linguists, sociologists, psychologists, and Neo-Hellenists to investigate a field opened up by Elias Petropoulos's *Kaliarda: An Etymological Dictionary of Greek Homosexual Slang*. To date, several articles and reviews have served as useful presentations of a few terms of the argot to a public unfamiliar with Greek. Indeed, it is noteworthy that the dictionary has received more serious attention abroad than in Greece, where Petropoulos's writings are systematically either ignored by academics or smeared by journalists and literati with the most hysterical scandal and controversy; when the folklorist's writings are praised in Greece, the encomiums can be equally hysterical. One impatiently awaits a critical confirmation or refutation of the positions advanced by Petropoulos, not just in *Kaliarda*, but also in his many other books and photograph albums concerning urban folklore, popular architecture, the Greek underworld, Greek prison life, folk music, slang, and the multicultural history of Thessaloniki.

Nearly all the non-Greek articles and reviews have highlighted the bizarre compounds found in Kaliarda, which can be oft-garish concoctions of two or three roots from two or three different languages. The Kaliarda term σούκρα *soukra* "sugar" (from French *sucre*), for example, is employed in or creates the following Kaliarda compounds and derivatives:

σούκρα-βεριτά *soukra-verita* "naked truth," literally "sugar truth." From Italian *verità* "truth."

σούκρα-μαντόσκονη *soukra-mantoskoni* "pastry dough," literally "sugar flour." From Kaliarda μαντόσκονη *mantoskoni* "flour" (from Kaliarda μαντό *manto* "bread" [see Messing's Romany etymology below] and Greek σκόνη *skoni* "dust," "powder").

σούκρα-μπούζ *soukra-bouz* "custard," "jelly," "gelatin," literally "sugar ice." From Kaliarda μπουζ *bouz* "cold," "icy," "frozen" (from Greek μπούζι *bouzi* "ice," "icy" [from Turkish *buz* "ice"]).

σουράρω *soukraro* "I sweeten," "I sugar."

σουκρατζέ *soukratzé*, the ζαχαροπλαστείο *zakharoplastio* or "sweet shop" similar to an ice cream parlor in which one can eat Greek pastries; the suffix *tzé* gives a French flavor to the word, but not to the pastries!

σούκρικο-μαντό *soukriko-manto* "pastry," "sweet," literally "sweet bread." From Kaliarda μαντό *manto* "bread" (see Messing's Romany etymology below).

σούκρικος *soukrikos* "sweet" (adjective).

σουκροβαίζω *soukrovaizo* "chocolate," literally "sugar blackness." From Kaliarda βαίζω *vaizo* "black" (from Albanian *bajze* "girl"; Petropoulos notes that most harem girls were Arabs; in Greek, Arabs are often [e.g., in folksong lyrics] described as being "black").

σουκροζουζούνι *soukrozouzouni* "bee," literally "sugar bug." From Greek ζουζούνι *zouzouni* "bug," "insect."

σουκροκαρύδα *soukrokarydha* "baklava" (a Greek pastry), literally "sugar nut." From Greek καρύδα *karydha* "nut."

σουκροπουρός *soukropouros* "confectioner," literally "mushy old sugar man." From Kaliarda *pouros* "old," "mushy."

What needs to be kept in mind, however, is that like all languages and argots Kaliarda is also full of less colorful words and phrases. Σαρκοδομή *sarkodhomi* "bone" literally means something like "what gives flesh structure"; but its two duller synonyms are σπάλα *spala* (from Greek σπάλα *spala* "shoulder," "shoulder blade" [from Italian *spalla* "shoulder"] and μπόνι *boni* (from English *bone*). Στακοζά *stakoza*, of unknown etymology, simply means "thus." Γότσι *ghotsi* "wristwatch" and γούντι *ghoudi* "wood" come unpretentiously into Kaliarda from English. Φέγι *feyi* "leaf" simply derives from the French *feuille*.

The time has come, in other words, to begin to examine Kaliarda not as a compilation of philological monstrosities (as most of the articles and reviews have done), but rather as, simply, Greek homosexual slang. Two of the most obvious places to start are with words for which Petropoulos found no etymology and with those for which an uncertain etymology could be challenged or confirmed. Let the research on Kaliarda begin!

I am happy to report that Dr. Gordon M. Messing, a specialist of both Greek and Romany at Cornell University, in a personal letter sent to me on 6 June 1983, was able to confirm or to propose Romany derivations for several Kaliarda terms whose etymologies were hitherto uncertain or unknown. As a stimulus to further research, I have listed below the terms that Dr. Messing examined, interjecting into his explanations Petropoulos's own definitions and etymologies.

μπαλαμό *balamo* "middle-aged pederast who pays a passive homosexual" is a Romany word used in various dialects to mean "non-Gypsy merchant" or the like; oddly enough, in

Greek Romany it is the standard word for "Greek." [For Petropoulos the etymology of *balamo* is unknown.]

μπούτ *bout* "much," "many" = Romany *but* "much," "many."[For Petropoulos the etymology is unknown; he notes in passing the English *butt* and the Turkish *buut* "distance," "range."]

κουλό *koulo* "shit"; *koul-koul* "shit" = Romany *kul* "shit." [Petropoulos notes that *koulo* is perhaps from the Greek κουλές *koules* "tower" (from Turkish *kule* "tower") or from the Italian *culo* "ass," "bottom."]

λατσός *latsos* "good" = Romany *latsó* "good." The adverb *latsá* is on the Greek pattern of καλά *kala* "well," "beautiful," "great," etc. [Petropoulos posited a Romany origin for the term.]

καλιάρντω *kaliardo*, καλιαρντή *kaliardi*, καλιαρντά *kaliarda*, etc. Heavens, not from *gaillard*! This is a common Romany term for "Gypsy." It is originally a participial form meaning "blackened," but eventually *kaliardó* came to mean "black" and both it and the normal term for "black," *kaló*, were used in the sense of "dark-complexioned person," and so "Gypsy." That a slang or covert language should be named "Gypsy language" is not unusual (especially when it contains many Gypsy words): a similar low-life speech in Spanish is known as *Caló*.

τα *ta* is probably not the Greek neuter plural article but rather Romany *ta* (also *tay*, *thay*) "and."

μαντό *manto* "bread" looks like Romany *manró* "bread." Could Petropoulos's informant have gotten this form a little skewed? In Romany, the word appears as *manró*, *marnó*, *mandró*, etc. [For Petropoulos the etymology of μαντό is unknown.]

μπενάβω *benavo* "I speak" is clearly formed on the first person singular of Romany *phenav* "I say." The verb is very Gypsy-like in appearance but the Gypsies don't use it to mean "speak." [Petropoulos posited a Romany origin for this term.]

τζάω *tzao* "I flee," "I slip away," "I drive out" and *tzase!* "go away!" are from Romany *dzav* "I go," *dza!* "go!" Tzinavo "I understand," "I feel," like benavo (see above), is from the first person singular of Romany *dzenav* "I know."[Petropoulos posited a Romany origin for this term.]

μπούκουρος *boukouros* "beautiful" is of course from Albanian *bukur* "beautiful," a Balkan word usually brought into relationship with Rumanian *bucurie* "joy" despite the semantic jump. [Petropoulos posited a probable Albanian origin for the term.]

In the third (1980) and fourth (1982) editions of *Kaliarda*, Petropoulos had included similar etymological corrections, many of which had to do with Romany.

Petropoulos had corresponded with and met Messing. When I showed him the latter's annotations, and especially the proposed etymology of *kaliarda*, he reminded me that a philologist should be cautious and that there were sociological factors that had led him to derive the word from "gaillard."

BIBLIOGRAPHY

This bibliography can be complemented by the one provided by Maria Dousi in the special issue of *Mandragoras* (October 1997-October 1998), especially for articles about Petropoulos from the years 1958-1980.

Collected Works:
Άπαντα, Athens: Nefeli, 1990-

Individual Books, chapbooks, special offprints, bibliophilic editions, and albums:

Νίκος Γαβριήλ Πεντζίκης (Nikos Gabriel Pentzikis), Thessaloniki, privately printed, 1958 / Athens: Grammata, 1980, with reproductions of paintings by Pentzikis / Expanded edition: Athens: Patakis, 1998. (Text also published in *Μικρά κείμενα*.)

Παύλος Μοσχίδης (Pavlos Moskhidis), Thessaloniki: *Diagonios* (special offprint of the magazine), 1959. (Republished in *Μικρά κείμενα*.)

Γιώργος Παραλής (Yiorgos Paralis), Thessaloniki: *Diagonios* (special offprint of the magazine), 1959. (Republished in *Μικρά κείμενα*.)

Κάρολος Τσίζεκ (Karolos Tsizek), Thessaloniki: *Diagonios* (special offprint of the magazine), 1959. (Republished in *Μικρά κείμενα*.)

Μποστ (Mentis Bostantzoglou or "Bost"), Thessaloniki: Bost's first artist's album, 1959. (Republished in *Μικρά κείμενα*.)

Θεσσαλονίκη, 1865 (Thessaloniki, 1865), Thessaloniki: *Ζυγός* (special offprint of the magazine), 1959. (Republished in *Μικρά κείμενα*.)

Χαρακτική / Π. Τέτσης (Engravings by Panayiotis Tetsis), Thessaloniki: *Ζυγός* (special offprint of the magazine), 1960. (Republished in *Μικρά κείμενα*.)

Γιώργος Δέρπαπας (Yiorgos Derpapas), Thessaloniki: *Εικόνες* (special offprint of the magazine), 1966. (Republished in Μικρά κείμενα.)

Ελύτης Μόραλης Τσαρούχης, (Elytis Moralis Tsaroukhis), Athens, privately printed, 1966 / Athens: Pleias, 1975 / Athens: Grammata, 1980 / Athens: Patakis, 1996.

Ρεμπέτικα τραγούδια (Rebetic Songs), Athens: privately printed, 1968, illustrated by Takis Sideris / Athens: Kedros, 1979, illustrated by Alekos Fassianos / New edition in 1992, with subsequent editions in 2000, 2003, 2006.

Γλωσσάριο των Ρεμπέτηδων (Rebetic Glossary), privately printed, 1968 (first included in original edition of Ρεμπέτικα τραγούδια, then available as separate offprint). (Republished in *Μικρά κείμενα*.)

Σώμα (Body), Athens: album by the artist Pavlos Moskhidis, 1969, bilingual, with a translation into English by Nikos Germanacos. (Another edition of this album exists, with a German translation of *Σώμα* by Alexander Schmidt.) The long-poem *Body* later appeared in the magazine *Τραμ*, Nos. 3-4, February 1972; and two times in *Κούρο*: No. 9, 1972, and No. 27, 1974. The poem was announced for publication in the June 1976 issue of *Τραμ*, but the corresponding pages were left blank as a protest against censorship. Republished in the 1980 edition of *Ποιήματα*, then in the 1993 edition, as well as in the French edition *Poèmes*.)

Καλιαρντά (Kaliarda: An Etymological Dictionary of Greek Homosexual Slang), Athens: privately printed, 1971 / Athens: Pleias, 1974 / Athens: Nefeli, 1980, 1982 (Collected Works, 1993).

Μνήμη Νίκου Καχτίτση (Nikos Kachtitsis in memoriam), privately printed, 1972 (with Elias Papadimitrakopoulos).

Αυτοκτονία (Suicide), Athens: secretly printed at the Tolidhis Brothers' printer's shop, 1973. (Republished in the 1980 edition of *Ποιήματα*, then in the 1993 edition, as well as in the French edition *Poèmes*.)

Η περιπέτεια ενος συγγραφέως (The Adventures of a Writer), Athens: privately printed, 6 August 1974. (See *Καπανταήδες και μαχαιροβγάλτες*, pp. 277-278.)

Α. Καναβάκης (Anakreon Kanavakis), Thessaloniki: Ζυγός (special offprint of the magazine), 1974.

The Graves of Greece, drawings by Elias Petropoulos, Athens: Study in Greece, 1974. (A chapbook exhibiting some of the sketches later included in the 1979 edition.)

Πέντε ερωτικά ποιήματα (Five Erotic Poems), Athens: privately printed, 1975. (Republished in the 1980 edition of *Ποιήματα*, then in the 1993 edition, as well as in the French edition *Poèmes*.)

Της φυλακής (From the Jails), Athens: Pleias, 1975, with an English summary ("From the Jails") by Katharine Butterworth / Athens: Nefeli, 1980.

Ιωάννου Αποκάλυψις (The Book of Revelations), illustrated by Alexis Akrithakis, translated into Modern Greek by Elias Petropoulos, Athens: Pleias, 1975 / Athens: Nefeli, 1980 (Collected Works, 1991).

La Voiture grecque, cover by Anakreon Kanavakis, with drawings and photographs by Elias Petropoulos, translated by Françoise Huart, Paris: Moments, 1976. (Greek text in *Μικρά κείμενα*.)

Cages à oiseaux en Grèce, cover by Anakreon Kanavakis, with drawings and photographs by Elias Petropoulos, translated by Françoise Huart, Paris: Moments, 1976. (Greek text in *Μικρά κείμενα*.)

Le Kiosque grec, cover by Anakreon Kanavakis, with drawings and photographs by Elias Petropoulos, translated by Jean-François Trocmé, Paris: Moments, 1976. (Greek text in *Μικρά κείμενα*.)

Album turc, Paris: Moments, 1976.

Υπόκοσμος και καραγκιόζης (The Underworld and Shadow Theater), Athens: Grammata, 1978, 1979, 1980, 1985, 1986, 1990 / Expanded edition in Nefeli Collected Works, 1996.

Ψειρολογία (Lousology: The Book of Lice), illustrated by Elias Petropoulos, Athens: Grammata, 1979 / Nefeli Collected Works, 1991.

Ο τουρκικός καφές εν Ελλάδι (Turkish Coffee in Greece), cover and illustrations by Elias Petropoulos, Athens: Grammata, 1979 / Nefeli Collected Works, 1990.

Εγχειρίδιον του καλού κλέφτη (The Good Thief's Manual), illustratred by Jean Kerleroux, Athens: Nefeli, 1979 / Expanded edition, with 100 new illustrations, in Nefeli Collected Works, 1990.

The Graves of Greece, bibliophilic edition, drawings by Elias Petropoulos, translated by John Taylor, Paris: Atelier Mérat, 1979.

La présence ottomane à Salonique, cover by Abidin Dino, preface by Clément Lépidis, translated by Véronique Perl, Athens: Grammata, 1980.

Salonique: l'incendie de 1917, cover by Abidin Dino, preface by Jacques

Lacarrière, Thessaloniki: Barbounakis, 1980. (Greek text in *Μικρά κείμενα*.)

Μικρά κείμενα 1949-1979 (Short Texts 1949-1979), Athens: Grammata, 1980.

Δώδεκα τραγουδάκια από την Παλατινή Ανθολογία (Twelve Little Songs from the Palatine Anthology), illustrated by Alekos Fassianos, translated into Modern Greek by Elias Petropoulos, Athens: Nefeli, 1980.

Επιστολαί προς μνηστήν (Letters to a Fiancée), illustrated by Alekos Fassianos, Athens: Grammata, 1980. (With Elias Papadimitrakopoulos.)

Το μάτι του βοδιού (The Oeil-de-Boeuf Window), Thessaloniki: Epimitheas, 1980.

Παλιά Σαλονίκη / Old Salonica, bilingual, Greek text translated by John Taylor, Athens: Kedros, 1980.

Ελληνικές σιδεριές / Ironwork in Greece, cover by Costas Tsoclis, photographs by Elias Petropoulos, bilingual, Greek text translated by John Taylor, Athens: Nefeli, 1980.

Το μπουρδέλο (The Brothel), cover by Alekos Fassianos, illustrations by Elias Petropoulos, Athens: Grammata, 1980 / Nefeli Collected Works, 1991.

Ποιήματα (Poems), illustrated by Alekos Fassianos, Athens: Nefeli, 1980. (Replaced by the expanded 1993 edition of Ποιήματα.)

Το μπαλκόνι στην Ελλάδα / Balconies in Greece, bilingual, cover and seven collage illustrations by Alexis Akrithakis, photographs by Elias Petropoulos, Greek text translated by John Taylor, Athens: Hatzinikoli, 1981.

Tsoclis's Tree, bibliophilic edition illustrated by Costas Tsoclis, bilingual, translated by John Taylor, New York: Iolas-Jackson Gallery, 1982. (Greek text in 1993 edition of *Ποιήματα*.)

Ξυλόπορτες Σιδερόπορτες στην Ελλάδα / Wooden Doors Iron Doors in Greece, illustrated by Costas Tsoclis, bilingual, Greek text translated by John Taylor, Athens: Kedros, 1982.

Τα μικρά ρεμπέτικα (The Short Rebetic Songs Reader), illustrated by Alekos Fassianos, Athens: Kedros, 1982, 1984 / Nefeli Collected Works, 1990.

Η αυλή στην Ελλάδα / Courtyards in Greece, illustrated by Alekos Fassianos, bilingual, Greek texts translated by John Taylor, Athens: Phorkys, 1983. (Includes two prose texts, respectively by Alekos Fassianos and Elias Papadimitrakopoulos.)

Mirror for You, bibliophilic edition illustrated by Alekos Fassianos, bilingual, translated by John Taylor, Paris: Atelier Mérat, 1983. (Greek text republished in 1993 edition of *Ποιήματα*.)

Les Juifs de Salonique / In Memoriam / The Jews of Salonica, bibliophilic edition, cover and one drawing by Roland Topor, translated into French and English by Françoise Daviet and John Taylor, Paris: Atelier Mérat, 1983.

A Macabre Song, bibliophilic edition illustrated with a collage by Elias Petropoulos, postscriptum by Pierre Vidal-Naquet, translated by John Taylor, Paris: Atelier Mérat, 1985. (Greek original later published in *Ιχνευτής*, No. 19, March 1987.)

In Berlin: Notebook 1983-1984, bibliophilic edition illustrated by Michael Bastow, translated by John Taylor, Paris: Atelier Mérat, 1987. (Greek text in 1993 edition of *Ποιήματα*.)

Πτώματα, πτώματα, πτώματα... (Corpses, Corpses, Corpses...), Athens: Nefeli (Collected Works), 1990.

Ρεμπετολογία (Rebetology), illustrated by Anakreon Kanavakis, Athens: Kedros, 1990.

Ο μύσταξ (The Mustache), Athens: Nefeli (Collected Works), 1990.

Το άγιο χασισάκι (Saint Hashish), Athens: Nefeli (Collected Works), 1991.

Η μυθολογία του Βερολίνου (The Mythology of Berlin), illustrated by the author and others, Athens: Nefeli (Collected Works), 1991.

Topor: Τέσσερεις εποχές (Topor: Four Seasons), illustrated by Roland Topor, bilingual, translated into French by Mary Koukoules, Athens: Nefeli (Collected Works), 1991.

Ποιήματα (Collected Poems), preface by Jacques Lacarrière, illustrated by Michael Bastow, Corneille, Anakreon Kanavakis, Sarandis Karavouzis, Yiorgos Sikeliotis, Roland Topor, Costas Tsoclis, Alekos Fassianos, Elias Petropoulos, Athens: Nefeli (Collected Works), 1993. (Includes *Λόγος Επικήδειος, Σώμα, Αυτοκτονία, Πέντε Ερωτικά Ποιήματα, Το Δέντρο του Τσόκλη, Καθρέφτης γιά Σένα, In Berlin / Σημειωματάριο 1983-1984, Επιστολή στον Α. Καναβάκη, Ο απρόσιτος, Τσιτσολίνας Εγκώμιον.*)

Τα Ακόλαστα Σονέτα του Αρετίνου (Pietro Aretino, *Sonetti Lussuriosi*), translated into Modern Greek by Mary Koukoules and Elias Petropoulos, Athens: Nefeli (Collected Works), 1992.

Η εθνική φασουλάδα (The National Bean Soup), Athens: Nefeli (Collected Works), 1993.

Η φουστανέλα (The Fustanella), Athens: Nefeli (Collected Works), 1993.

Ποτέ και τίποτα (Never and Nothing) and *Μετά* (After), illustrated with collages by Elias Petropoulos, preface by John Taylor, Athens: Nefeli (Collected Works), 1993. (Republished in 2004 as *Ποτέ και τίποτα / Jamais et rien.*)

Τα σίδερα. Η λάσπη. Τα μπαστούνια. (Irons. Mud [Shoe Scrapers]. Canes.), Athens: Nefeli (Collected Works), 1994.

Κυρίως αυτό (Mainly That: Selected Collages), Athens: Nefeli (Collected Works), 1994 (plus several subsequent printings through 2003). (The collages have been exhibited three times in Greece and, notably, in October 1994 at the Agkathi Art Gallery in Athens.)

Το ταντούρι και το μαγκάλι (The Tendour and the Brazier), Athens: Nefeli (Collected Works), 1994.

Η ονοματοθέσια οδών και πλατειών (Naming Streets and Squares), illustrated by Alexis Veroukas, Athens: Patakis, 1995.

Καρέκλες και σκαμνιά (Chairs and Stools), Athens: Nefeli (Collected Works), 1995.

Το παράθυρο στην Ελλάδα (Windows in Greece: A Study in Architecture), cover and two collages by Alexis Akrithakis, bilingual, Greek text translated by John Taylor, Athens: Nefeli (Collected Works), 1996.

Άρθρα στην Ελευθεροτυπία (Articles Published in the Newspaper *Eleftherotypia*), illustrated by Alexis Veroukas, Athens: Patakis, 1996.

Η τραγιάσκα (Hats and Caps), illustrated by Alexis Veroukas, Athens: Patakis, 2000, 2003.

Ιστορία της καπότας (A History of the Condom), cover by Marina Kanavakis, with several illustrations by Anakreon Kanavakis, Athens: Nefeli (Collected Works), 1996, 1999, 2003.

Τέσσερεις ζωγράφοι: Αντώνης [Anton] / Βιτάσταλη / Δουραλη / Σουλιώτης (Four Artists: Anton, Vitastali, Dourali, Souliotis), Athens: Nefeli (Collected Works), 1999.

Καπανταήδες και μαχαιροβγάλτες (Knives and Pistols), illustrated by Dimitris Souliotis, Athens: Nefeli (Collected Works), 2001.

Ο κουραδοκόφτης (literally "The Shit-Cutter" / The String: A Foreword and Twenty-Eight Articles), cover by Alexis Veroukas, Athens: Nefeli (Collected Works), 2002.

Παροιμίες του υποκόσμου (Underworld Proverbs), Athens: Nefeli (Collected Works), 2002.

Ποτέ και τίποτα / Jamais et rien, illustrated by the photos of Phaedon Koukoules, bilingual, translated into French by Mary Koukoulès and Jacques Vallet, Athens: Nefeli, 2004.

Μετά / Après, illustrated by the photos of Phaedon Koukoules, bilingual, translated into French by Mary Koukoules and Jacques Vallet, Athens: Nefeli, 2004.

Ελλάδος Κοιμητήρια (The Cemeteries of Greece), illustrated by Costas Tsoclis, Athens: Nefeli, 2005.

Translations of Books:

Corps, illustrated by Corneille, translated into French by Mary Koukoules, Paris: Moments, 1976.

Suicide, illustrated by Alekos Fassianos, translated into French by Jean-François Trocmé, Paris: Moments, 1976.

Rebetika: Songs from the Old Greek Underworld, translated by Katharine Butterworth and Sara Schneider, illustrated by Khronis Botsoglou, New York / Athens: Komboloi, 1975. (Greek original of Petropoulos's introduction in *Μικρά κείμενα*. This edition also includes essays by Markos Dragoumis, Ted Petrides, and Sakis Papadimitriou. See John Taylor's translation below.)

Poèmes (includes *Corps, Suicide, Cinq poèmes érotiques, L'Arbre de Tsoclis, Miroir pour toi*, and *In Berlin*), illustrated by Michael Bastow, Corneille, Alekos Fassianos, Yiorgos Sikeliotis, Roland Topor, and Costas Tsoclis, translated into French by Frédéric Faure and the author, Paris: Éditions du

Griot, 1991.

Rebetika: Songs from the Old Greek Underworld, illustrated by Alekos Fassianos, translated by John Taylor, London: Alcyon, 1992. (Greek original of Petropoulos's introduction in Μικρά κείμενα. This edition offers new translations of the fifty songs translated by Butterworth and Schneider, and provides versions of 150 more songs.)

Зошто не се враќам во Грција? (Why I Don't Go Back to Greece: Selected Poems), translated into Macedonian by Mary Koukoules and Liljana Kotevcka-Plevnes, Skopje: Detska Radost, 1993.

Türk Kahvesi Yananistn'da (Turkish Coffee in Greece), translated into Turkish by Herkül Millas, Istanbul: Iletiş im Yaymları, 1995.

La Grèce de l'ombre: chants rébetika, translated into French by Jacques Lacarrière and Michel Volkovitch, Saint-Cyr-sur-Loire: Christian Pirot, 1999.

Songs of the Greek Underworld: The Rebetika Tradition, translated by Ed Emery, London: Saqi Books, 2000.

Rebetiko: Die Musik der städtischen Subkultur Griechenlands, translated into German by Maximilien Vogel, Heidelberg: Palmyra, 2002. (See the bibliography of Rebetic Song translations and studies in this book.)

La Grèce de l'ombre: chansons rebètika, vol. 1, translated into French by Michel Volkovitch, Sèvres: Éditions Le miel des anges, 2014.

La Grèce de l'ombre: chansons rebètika, vol. 1, translated into French by Michel Volkovitch and with selected songs translated into English by John Taylor, Sèvres: Éditions Le miel des anges, 2017.

Translations published in magazines:

Πυγμή-φαλλός/ "Fist-Phallus," translated by Gerson Legman and Mary Koukoules, *Maledicta*, Vol. III, 1979, pp. 103-107.

"Och Gudskapade tortyren" (On Torture: Twenty-First Lesson of *The Good Thief's Manual*), translated into Swedish by Britt Arenander, *Amnesty International Bulletin* (Swedish section), October 1980, pp. 10-11.

"La Justice d'Antiqua" (Lessons Twenty-Nine and Thirty of *The Good Thief's Manual*), translated into French by Pascal Lhéry, *Le Fou Parle*, No. 15, December 1980, pp. 23-28.

"The Rebetic Songs," selection translated by John Taylor, *Maledicta*, Vol. 5, Nos. 1-2, 1981, pp. 25-30. (Includes an introduction by J. T.)

"The Rebetika," selection translated by John Taylor, *Journal of the Hellenic Diaspora*, Vol. 8, No. 4, Winter 1981, pp. 28-39. (Includes an introduction by J. T. and a translation of Petropoulos's text "Ο Χάρος" [Kharos] from Ρεμπέτικα τραγούδια)

"Turkish Coffee in Greece," translated by John Taylor, *Journal of the Hellenic Diaspora*, Vol. 9, No. 4, Winter 1982, pp. 53-61. (Excerpts from Petropoulos's book.)

"Les tombes bogomiles en Grèce?" (Bogomil Gravestones in Greece?), translated in French by Françoise Daviet and John Taylor, *Le Fou Parle*, Nos. 21-22, November-December 1982, pp. 53-54. (See Petropoulos's appeal to Melina Mercouri: "Σώστε τους τάφους της Βεύης", *Θεσσαλονίκη*, 15 January 1982.)

"The Ubiquitous Kiosk," translated by John Taylor, *Greek Accent*, Vol. 5, No. 5, March-April 1985, pp. 22-27. (Excerpts from Petropoulos's *Le Kiosque grec*.)

"The Jewish Wooden Chests of Salonica," translated by John Taylor, *Newsletter of the Jewish Museum of Greece*, No. 16, December 1985, pp. 5-6. A Judeo-Spanish translation appeared in *Aki Yerushalayim*, Nos. 28-29, January-July 1986, p. 37 (Jerusalem) and in *Salom*, 5 November 1986 (Istanbul). (See "Τα εβρέικα μπαούλα της Θεσσαλονίκης," *Ιχνευτής*, No. 8, January 1986.)

"Het tuitlampje (Lychnari)" (On Simple Lamps), translated into Dutch by Flip Lindo, *Lychnari* (Amsterdam), No. 1, March 1987.

Text about coffeehouses translated into German in *Griechenland*, edited by Armin Kerker, Hamburg: Argument, 1988.

In Berlin, translated into German by Armin Kerker, *Die Horen*, No. 153, 1989, pp. 159-175.

"Rebetologia: Monotone Schwätzerei in 24 Paragraphen" (translation of *Ρεμπετολογία*), translated into German, *Lettre International* (German edition), No. 8, Spring 1990. (A somewhat different version of this text was republished in *Rebetiko: Die Musik der städtischen Subkultur Griechenlands*, 2002—see above.)

"Selbstmord" (Suicide), translated into German by Helena Pekalis, *Lettre International* (German edition), No. 10, September 1990, pp. 86-88.

"De Griekse snor" (The Greek Mustache), translated into Dutch by Josien Anker, *Lychnari*, No. 3, 1989, pp. 8-11.

"Ah, Allegra," translated into French by Patricia Portier and Socrate C. Zervos, *Salonique 1850-1918*, Paris: Autrement, 1992, pp. 16-19. (This book was translated into Greek in 1994.)

Untitled text ["Ο απρόσιτος Τσόκλης," "Inaccessible Tsoclis"], translated by Eve Jackson, *Costas Tsoclis*, Athens: Adam Editions, 1992, pp. 10-25. (Greek text also in Ποιήματα.)

"I've always loved Piraeus," poem by Elias Petropoulos, translated by Ino Panagiotou, *Ο Πειραίας του Καραβούζη / Karavouzis's Piraeus*, Athens: Dexameni, 1995.

"Ein Spiegel für Dich" (translation of *Mirror for You*), *Lettre International* (German edition), No. 32, 1996.

"L'amour du trou du cul" (last chapter of *The Good Thief's Manual*), translated into French by Pascal Lhéry, *Anartiste*, No. 11, December 2007, pp. 21-24.

Selected Articles and Texts by Petropoulos:

"Η έκθεσις ζωγραφικής του Παύλου Μοσχίδη" (On the Painting Exhibit by Pavlos Moskhidis), *Μακεδονία*, 1949. (Republished in *Μικρά κείμενα*.)

"Οι θεσσαλονικείς ζωγράφοι" (Thessalonican Artists), *Μακεδονία*, 5 March 1956. (Republished in *Μικρά κείμενα*.)

"Η έκθεσις έργων Γαλάνη και Ρέγκου" (An Exhibit of Works by Galanis and Rengkos), *Μακεδονία*, 27 June 1956. (Republished in *Μικρά κείμενα*.)

"Τρείς εκθέσεις ζωγραφικής" (Three Painting Exhibits), *Μακεδονία*, 7 October 1956. (Republished in *Μικρά κείμενα*.)

"Δώδεκα θεσσαλονικείς ζωγράφοι" (Twelve Thessalonican Artists), *Νέα Πορεία*, October 1956. (Republished in *Μικρά κείμενα*.)

"Νίκος Φωτάκης και Σύρο Ντελ Νέρο" (Nikos Photakis and Syro del Nero), *Νέα Πορεία*, March 1957. (Republished in *Μικρά κείμενα*.)

"Πεντζίκης / Σαχίνης / Σβορώνος / Φωτάκης / Λεφάκης / Μοσχίδης / Νάτση" (On an Art Exhibit Comprising Work by Pentzikis, Sakhinis, Svoronos, Photakis, Lephakis, Moskhidis, and Natsi), *Νέα Πορεία*, May 1957. (Republished in *Μικρά κείμενα*.)

"Έκθεση Παύλου Μοσχίδη" (On an Exhibit by Pavlos Moskhidis), *Νέα Πορεία*, June 1957. (Republished in *Μικρά κείμενα*.)

"Οι λιθογραφίες του Γ. Σβορώνου" (Yiannis Svoronos's Lithographs), *Νέα Πορεία*, July 1957. (Republished in *Μικρά κείμενα*.)

"Η έκθεση γραφικής του Γ. Σβορώνου" (An Exhibit of Graphic Art by

Yiannis Svoronos), *Νέα Πορεία*, November 1957. (Republished in *Μικρά κείμενα*.)

"Η έκθεση του Λεωνίδα Χρηστάκη" (An Exhibit by Leonidas Christakis), *Νέα Πορεία*, November 1957. (Republished in *Μικρά κείμενα*.)

"Ο ζωγράφος Παύλος Μοσχίδης" (The Artist Pavlos Moskhidis), *Ζυγός*, 1959. (Republished in *Μικρά κείμενα*.)

"Η ιστορία της Θεσσαλονίκης και ο κ. Α. Λέτσας" (The History of Thessaloniki and Mr. A. Letsas), *Ελεύθερος Λαός* (Thessaloniki), 8 October 1961. (Republished in *Μικρά κείμενα*.)

"Κριτική κινηματογράφου" (Twenty-One Film Reviews), *Ελεύθερος Λαός* (Thessaloniki), 1962. (Republished in *Μικρά κείμενα*.)

"Φευγαλέες εντυπώσεις από την ταινία "Ουρανός" του Τάκη Κανελόπουλου και, εν μέρει, από τα τελευταία ποιήματα του Μανόλη Αναγωστάκη και του Γιώργου Ιωάννου" (Fleeting Impressions of the film "Ouranos" [Heaven] by Takis Kanelopoulos and, partly, of recent poems by Manolis Anagnostakis and Yiorgos Ioannou), *Διάλογος*, 1963. (Republished in *Μικρά κείμενα*.)

"Το διάγραμμα του ζωγράφου Γ. Παραλή" (The Diagram of the Artist Yiorgos Paralis), *Εικόνες*, 21 June 1963. (Republished in *Μικρά κείμενα*.)

"Η Θεσσαλονίκη καίγεται" (Thessaloniki is Burning), *Εικόνες*, 5 August 1966. (Greek original of text translated in *Salonique: l'incendie de 1917*; then republished in *Μικρά κείμενα*.)

"Η έλευση ενός δημιουργού" (The Arrival of a Creator: On Yiorgos Derpapas), *Εικόνες*, 26 August 1966. (Republished in *Μικρά κείμενα*.)

"Ένα άγνωστο έργο του Πικιώνη" (A Forgotten Architectural Work by Dimitris Pikionis), *Εικόνες*, 26 August 1966. (Republished in *Μικρά κείμενα*.)

"Το μνημείο των χιλίων εκτελεσθέτων" (On the Monument to the Thousand who were Executed by the German Army in Kalavryta), *Εικόνες*, Autumn 1966. (Republished in *Μικρά κείμενα*.)

"Σταμ. Σταμ. (είκοσι χρόνια από τον θάνατό του)" (Stamatis Stamatiou or "Stam. Stam.": Twenty Years after his Death), *Ζυγός*, 1966. (See the annotation to this text, when it was republished in *Μικρά κείμενα*.)

"Διάλεξη στον Πειραιά" (Lecture in Piraeus), published in a program distributed at Petropoulos's lecture (on rebetic songs) in the Municipal Theater of Piraeus, 2 February 1967; later republished every Tuesday, beginning on 14 November 1972, at the rebetic concerts that took place in Kytaro Hall during the Junta. (Republished in *Μικρά κείμενα*.)

"Το πουλοπάζαρο του Πειραιώς" (The Bird Market of Piraeus), *Άλφα*, 22 July 1967. (Translated and inserted into the introduction of *Cages à oiseaux en Grèce*; the Greek text is republished in *Μικρά κείμενα*.)

"Το ιμαρέτ της Καβάλας" (The Imaret of Kavala), *Άλφα*, 12 January 1968. (Republished in *Μικρά κείμενα*.)

"Η γλυπτική του Θύμιου Πανουργιά" (The Sculpture of Thymios Panouryias), Athens: Brithsh Council Catalogue, May 1969 (Republished in *Μικρά κείμενα*.)

"Ανακρέων Καναβάκης (λίγες νύξεις για την εκατόχρονη νεοελληνική γελιογραφία)" (Anakreon Kanavakis: A Few Remarks about a Hundred Years of Modern Greek Cartoon Drawing), *Ζύγος*, 1974. (Republished in *Μικρά κείμενα*.)

"Οι γυμνές κόρες του Σικελιώτη" (The Naked Girls of Yiorgos Sikeliotis), *Ζύγος*, February 1974. (Reprinted in the book *Κριτικές γιά το έργο του Γιώργου Σικελιώτη*, Athens: Hermes, 1975; then included in *Μικρά κείμενα*.)

"Υπόκοσμος και καραγκιόζης" (The Underworld and Shadow

Theater), *Αντί*, 7 August 1976. (Reworked, expanded, and then published as the book *Υπόκοσμος και καραγκιόζης*.)

"Odysseus Elytis, peintre" (On Elytis's Collages and Paintings), *Libération*, 25 October 1979, p. 12. (Text originally written in French.)

"Σώστε τους τάφους της Βεύης" (An Appeal to Melina Mercouri to Save the Ancient Bogomil Gravestones of Vevi), *Θεσσαλονίκη*, 15 January 1982.

"Salonique. 1943-1983. L'holocauste des Juifs de Salonique" (French version of Petropoulos's appeal to Melina Mercouri), translated by Françoise Daviet, *Libération*, 26 January 1982.

"Un appel d'Elias Petropoulos à Melina Mercouri, Ministre de la Culture du Gouvernement Grec," *Les Nouveaux Cahiers*, No. 68, Spring 1982, p. 79. (French version of Petropoulos's appeal to Melina Mercouri.)

"Το δέντρο του Τσόκλη" (Tsoclis's Tree), *Γιατί*, No. 85, July 1982. (Republished in the bibliophilic edition of *Tsoclis's Tree* and in the 1993 edition of *Ποιήματα*.)

"1912: τα πρώτα πολεμικά αεροπλάνα" (1912: The First Warplanes), *Μουσική*, No. 59, October 1982, pp. 64-67.

"Das Thema der Fremde im *Rebetiko*-Lied" (The Theme of the Foreigner in Rebetic Songs), translated into German by Gerhard Emrich, *Kultur im Migrationsprozess: Tendenzen einer neuen europäischen Kultur*, edited by Michael Fehr, Wuppertal: Museum Bochum / Sekretariat für gemeinsame Kulturarbeit, 1982, pp. 63-65. (Text written for this book.)

"Φαλλοκρατική Ετυμολογία" (Phallocratic Etymology), *Μουσική*, No. 66, April 1983, pp. 36-38. (Republished in *Ιστορία της καπότας*.)

"Ο Γκρέκο ήταν εβραίος;" (Was El Greco Jewish?), *Τομές*, July-September 1983, pp. 14-17.

"Τα μπαστούνια των παραθεριστών" (The Canes of Summer Vacationers), *Η Καθημερινή*, 22 January 1984. (Republished in *Τα σίδερα. Η λάσπη. Τα μπαστούνια.*)

"Τα χαρτονόμουτρα του Σκαρίμπα" (On the writer Yiannis Skaribas and Shadow Theater), *Η Καθημερινή*, 13 June 1985. (Republished in 1996 edition of *Υπόκοσμος και καραγκιόζης*.)

"Το τελευταίο ταξίδι" (The Last Trip: On the Exhibit "Le dernier voyage" in Monaco), *Γιατί*, Nos. 121-122, July-August 1985, pp. 55-59.

"Τα σίδερα (του σιδερώματος)" (Irons and Ironing), *Ιχνευτής*, Nos. 6-7, November-December 1985, p. 35-37. (Republished in *Τα σίδερα. Η λάσπη. Τα μπαστούνια.*)

"Τα εβρέικα μπαούλα της Θεσσαλονίκης" (The Jewish Wooden Chests of Thessaloniki), *Ιχνευτής*, No. 8, January 1986, pp. 18-19.

"Κάθε περιπετεία έχει τα μυστικά της" (Every Stroll has its Secrets), *Χάρτης*, No. 19, February 1986, p. 43.

"Χαριτωνίδου Εγκώμιον (1935-1985)" (A Tribute to Khariton Kharitonidis), *Χάρτης*, No. 19, February 1986. (Republished in *Ιστορία της καπότας*.)

"Κυνηγοί Κρανίων" (Skull Hunters), *Σχολιαστής*, No. 38, May 1986, pp. 33-35.

"Η λάσπη" (Mud and Shoe Scrapers), *Ιχνευτής*, No. 11, May-June 1986, pp. 20-24. (Republished in *Τα σίδερα. Η λάσπη. Τα μπαστούνια.*)

"Τα αναπαφώλια" (On Copulation Facilitation Devices), *Γιατί*, July-August 1986, pp. 30-31. (Republished in *Ιστορία της καπότας*.)

"Περί κλανιόλας" (On Fart-Gas Evacuators), *Σχολιαστής*, No. 42, September 1986, pp. 28-29.

"Posada: Viva la muerte" (On the Mexican Artist Posada), *Σχολιαστής*, November 1986, pp. 53-54.

"Ο Βενιζέλος και η γαλλική κατοχή του 1916" (Venizelos and the French Occupation of 1916), *Σχολιαστής*, No. 45, December 1986, pp. 52-55.

"Τσολιάς στ' ανάκτορα" (Evzone at the King's Palace: A Study of the Fustanella), *Ιχνευτής*, No. 17, January 1987, pp. 18-27. (Expanded into the book *Η φουστανέλα*.)

"Ο σοβιετικός κινηματογράφος" (Soviet Cinema), *Σχολιαστής*, No. 48, March 1987, pp. 53-54.

"Κυριαζής Χαρατσάρης" (On the Stage Director Kyriazis Kharatsaris), *Ιχνευτής*, No. 19, March 1987, p. 7. (Republished in 1996 edition of *Υπόκοσμος και καραγκιόζης*.)

"Ένα μακάβριο τραγούδι" (A Macabre Song), *Ιχνευτής*, No. 19, March 1987, pp. 14-15. (Greek original of the translation published in the bibliophilic edition of *A Macabre Song*.)

"Η ακατανοησία" (Incomprehensibility, that is on the Difficulties of Understanding Slang Terms Related to Hashish and Rebetic Songs), *Ιχνευτής*, No. 20, April 1987. (Republished in *Το άγιο χασισάκι*.)

"Το σερετιλίκι" (On the Type of Underworld Tough Guy Called a "Seretis"), *Γιατί*, No. 142, April 1987.

"30 χρόνια απ' το θάνατο της Μαρίκα Νίνου" (The Thirtieth Anniversary of the Death of the Rebetic Singer Marika Ninou), *Σχολιαστής*, No. 49, April 1987, p. 51. (Republished in *Το άγιο χασισάκι*.)

"Τα σκυλάδικα" (On the Kind of Taverna that was called a "Skyladiko," a sort of "Dive" or "Joint"), *Σχολιαστής*, No. 50, May 1987, pp. 46-47. (Republished in *Το άγιο χασισάκι*.)

"Ένας κακός Εβραίος" (An Unworthy Jew; a negative review of Alberto Nar's book "Οι συναγωγές Θεσσαλονίκης: τα τραγούδια μας," published in 1985, on the synagogues of Thessaloniki), *Ιχνευτής*, No. 21, May 1987.

"Τα ξημερώματα της 21ης Απριλίου" (On the Prime Minister Panayiotis Kanellopoulos and the Coup d'état of the Junta on 21 April 1967), *Σχολιαστής*, No. 54, September 1987, p. 36.

"Οι πόντιοι" (On the people from the Pontus), *Σχολιαστής*, No. 54, September 1987, pp. 46-47.

"Φάρσες της φυλακής" (Practical Jokes in Prison), *Εντευκτήριο*, No. 1, October 1987, pp. 15-20. (Republished in *Το άγιο χασισάκι*.)

"Αχ, αυτοί οι μπολσεβίκοι" (Oh, those Bolsheviks), *Ιχνευτής*, No. 25, October 1987.

"Λαική χαρτοκοπτική" (Folk Paper-Cuttings), *Ιχνευτής*, Nos. 26-27, November-December 1987, pp. 69-73.

"Περικαυλίδος λακωνική ιστορία" (A Short History of the Preservative), *Σχολιαστής*, December 1987, pp. 65-67. (Republished in *Ιστορία της καπότας*.)

"Τα γελοία ονόματα" (Ridiculous Names), *Αφιέρωμα στον Γιάνκο Α. Θωμόπουλο* (A Collection of Tributes to Yianko A. Thomopoulos), Athens: Ellinikis Onomatologikis Etaireias, 1988. (Also published in *Σχολιαστής*, December, 1988, and later in *Καπανταήδες και Μαχαιροβγάλτες*.)

"Η μυθολογία του Βερολίνου" (The Mythology of Berlin), *Ιχνευτής*, No. 28, January 1988, pp. 12-28. (Expanded into the book *Η μυθολογία του Βερολίνου*.)

"Κουρτ Τουχόλσκι" (Kurt Tucholsky: short introduction to Tucholsky, plus a text by Tucholsky), *Ιχνευτής*, No. 28, January 1988, p. 29-30. (Republished in *Η μυθολογία του Βερολίνου*.)

"Βρε, α σικητίρ!!!" (Fuck Off! Go to the Devil!: Against an exhibit, "German Resistance Movement 1933-1945," held in Athens at the Goethe Institut), *Ιχνευτής*, No. 28, January 1988, p.30. (Republished in *Η μυθολογία του Βερολίνου*.)

"Οι τάταροι στη Θεσσαλονίκη" (On a Red Army Squadron of Tatars in Thessaloniki) *Σχολιαστής*, April 1988.

"Βασανιστήρια και εξουσία" (On *Torture and Power* by Kyriakos Simopoulos), *Σχολιαστής*, April 1988, p. 61. (Republished in *Το άγιο χασισάκι*.)

"Η αηδιαστική ζωοφιλία" (On Disgusting Zoophilia and Animal Lovers), *Τέταρτο*, No. 36, April 1988, pp. 76-80.

"Μπαίνω στο 151" (On the Jewish Quarter "151" in Thessaloniki), *Σχολιαστής*, May 1988, pp. 65-67.

"Πτώματα, πτώματα, πτώματα" (Corpses, Corpses, Corpses), *Σχολιαστής*, June 1988, pp. 65-71. (Expanded into the book *Πτώματα, πτώματα, πτώματα...*)

"Καρέκλες και σκαμνιά" (Chairs and Stools), *Εντευκτήριο*, No. 3, June 1988. (Expanded into the book *Καρέκλες και σκαμνιά*.)

"Ένας εβρέικος γάμος στην Θεσσαλονίκη το 1890" (A Jewish Wedding in Thessaloniki in 1890: Presentation of a Forgotten Text by D. K. Vardouniotis), *Γιατί*, Nos. 156-157, June-July 1988, pp. 63-68.

"Στο σπίτι του ζωγράφου Aat Veldhoen" (At the Artist Aat Veldhoen's House), *Ιχνευτής*, Nos. 34-35, July-August 1988, pp. 4-11. (Republished in *Ιστορία της καπότας*.)

"Το ημερολόγιο τις Άννας Φράνκ" (Anne Frank's Diary), *Ιχνευτής*, September 1988, pp. 40-41.

"Ταπεινά εργόχειρα" (Humble Handiwork), Ιχνευτής, No. 36, September 1988, pp. 23-29.

"Ο Γκράφικερ Γιάννης Σβορώνος" (The Graphic Artist Yiannis Svoronos), Εντευκτήριο, September 1988, p. 34-35. (Republished in the catalog for an exhibit at the Thessaloniki Museum of Design in October 1997 and in the volume Δημήτρια '97, Thessaloniki: Thessaloniki Town Hall, 1997.)

"Βερολίνο 1918-1919" (Berlin 1918-1919: On the Spartacus Movement Uprising), Ιχνευτής, No. 37, October 1988.

"Τα γελοία ονόματα" (Ridiculous Names), Σχολιαστής, December, 1988. (See above Αφιέρωμα στον Γιάνκο Α. Θωμόπουλο, 1988; included in Καπαντσήδες και Μαχαιροβγάλτες.)

"Δόν Ζουάν η Ντόμ Χουάν" (On Translation, and on the Pronunciation of "Don Juan"), Εντευκτήριο, December 1988.

"Mémoire: Le tonneau à pointes - Elias Petropoulos," translated by Lucette Vidal, La Lettre sépharade, No. 9, August 1989. (http://www.lalettresepharade.fr/home/la-revue-par-numero/numero-09/memoire-le-tonneau-a-pointes---elias-petropoulos)

"Ο Τζογές της 'Βραδυνής'" (On the Columns Written in the Newspaper Vradyni by Sotos Petras, of interest for rebetology), Ιχνευτής, Nos. 47-48, September-October 1989, pp. 24-29. (Republished in Το άγιο χασισάκι.)

"Το βαρέλι με τα βελόνια" (The Barrel with Nails), Σχολιαστής, December 1989, pp. 52-55.

"Ο μύσταξ" (The Mustache), Ιχνευτής, No. 40, January 1989, pp. 14-23. (Expanded into the book Ο μύσταξ.)

"Η τρίπολη" (About the Word "Tripoli," which Appears in a Rebetic

Song), *Ο Παρατηρητής*, November 1989-January 1990, pp. 132-134. (Republished in *Το άγιο χασισάκι*.)

"Η εθνική φασουλάδα" (The National Bean Soup), *Σχολιαστής*, January 1990, pp. 50-53. (Expanded into the book *Η εθνική φασουλάδα*.)

"Ρεμπετολογία" (Rebetology), *Ιχνευτής*, No. 51, January 1990. (Expanded into the book *Ρεμπετολογία*.)

"Μποστ 1959" / "Μποστ 1989" (about the artist Mentis Bostantzoglou, "Bost"), *Σχολιαστής*, February 1990, pp. 53-55.

"Οι γιανιώτικες αργκό" (On the Origin of Twenty-Three Jargon Terms used by the Inhabitants of Yiannina), *Ιχνευτής*, Nos. 54-55, May-June 1990. (Republished in *Το άγιο χασισάκι*.)

"Η ομελέτα" (The Omelette), *Ιχνευτής*, Nos. 54-55, May-June 1990. (Republished in *Η εθνική φασουλάδα*.)

"Η διδασκαλία της αργκό" (On the Criminal Slang Taught in Police Schools), *Ιχνευτής*, Nos. 60-61, November-December 1990. (Republished in *Το άγιο χασισάκι*.)

"Τα τσόκαρα" (Wooden Shoes), *Επτάμισι*, Christmas 1991. (Republished in a new version in *Μανδραγόρας*, October 1997-April 1988; then included in *Καπανταήδες και Μαχαιροβγάλτες*.)

"Τα Βασιλικά Αλφαβητάρια" (The Royal Spellers), *Επτάμισι*, 6 December 1991.

"Ένα παλούκωμα στην Ανατολία" (An Impalement in Anatolia), *Επτάμισι*, 13 December 1991. (Republished in *Καπανταήδες και Μαχαιροβγάλτες*.)

"Τσιτσολίνας Εγκώμιον" (In Praise of La Cicciolina), translated into French by Socrate Zervos, *La Vulgarité*, edited by Pierre Kutzner, Brussels: Éditions de l'Université de Bruxelles, 1991 (Greek original in 1993 edition of *Ποιήματα.*)

"Οι επιπολαιότητες του Γιώργου Χειμωνά" (The Superficialities of the Writer Yiorgos Cheimonas), *Ελευθεροτυπία*, 25 January 1992. (Republished in *Άρθρα στην Ελευθεροτυπία.*)

"Το ταντούρι και το μαγκάλι" (The Tendour and the Brazier), *Επτάμισι*, 31 January 1992. (Expanded into the book *Το ταντούρι και το μαγκάλι.*)

"Γρυπάρης εις την καλιαρντήν" (On Kaliarda Parodies of poems by Gryparis and others, including Seferis), *Ιχνευτής*, No. 1 (second series), June-August 1992.

"Λακωνικό μνημόσυνο γιά τον Πεντζίκη" (A Laconic Requiem for Pentzikis), *Ελευθεροτυπία*, 15 January 1993. (Republished in 1998 edition of *Νίκος Γαβριήλ Πεντζίκης.*)

"Ο Μιμίκος και η Μαίρη" (Mimikos and Mary), *Ελευθεροτυπία*, 7 February 1993. (Republished in *Άρθρα στην Ελευθεροτυπία.*)

"Ένα πορτρέτο του Ρήγα" (A Portrait of Rigas Feraios), *Κυριακάτικη Ελευθεροτυπία*, 21 March 1993. (Republished in *Άρθρα στην Ελευθεροτυπία.*)

"Χίος: ο σεισμός του 1881" (Chios: The Earthquake of 1881), *Κυριακάτικη Ελευθεροτυπία*, 4 April 1993. (Republished in *Άρθρα στην Ελευθεροτυπία.*)

"Τι ήτανε το μαλακόφι;" (What was Crinoline?), *Κυριακάτικη Ελευθεροτυπία*, 17-18 April 1993 p. 29/V.

"Ο αδικημένος Γιώργος Μητσάκης" (The Unjustly Judged Rebetic Musician Yiorgos Mitsakis), *Κυριακάτικη Ελευθεροτυπία*, 23 May 1993. (Republished in *Άρθρα στην Ελευθεροτυπία.*)

"Ο Εθνικός Ήρωας Λάκης Σάντας" (The National Hero Lakis Santas), *Ελευθεροτυπία*, 31 May 1993. (Republished in *Άρθρα στην Ελευθεροτυπία.*)

"Το δάπεδο, το ποίημα του Γ. Θ. Βαφόπουλου και η μασονική συμβολική" (Masonic Symbolism in the Poem "The Ground" by George Vaphopoulos), *Ιχνευτής*, vol. 6 (second series), July-September 1993.

"Ερωτολογικά" (On Erotology), *Ελευθεροτυπία*, 31 July 1993. (Republished in *Άρθρα στην Ελευθεροτυπία*.)

"Το ντουλάπι που γυρίζει" (Revolving Cupboards), *Ελευθεροτυπία*, 16 September 1993. (Republished in *Άρθρα στην Ελευθεροτυπία*.)

"Η άλλη όψη της σελήνης" (The Other Side of the Moon), *Ελευθεροτυπία*, 27 October 1994. (Republished in *Άρθρα στην Ελευθεροτυπία*.)

"Τα ψιλά και τα λιανά" (Small Change and Petty Cash, with a pun on "Explain this to me clearly"), *Ελευθεροτυπία*, 4 June 1994. (Republished in *Άρθρα στην Ελευθεροτυπία*.)

"Το Ολοκαύτωμα του Χορτιάτη" (The Holocaust of Hortialis), *Ελευθεροτυπία*, 1 September 1994. (Republished in *Άρθρα στην Ελευθεροτυπία*.)

"Τα λάθη του Παπαδιαμάντι" (Papadiamantis's Mistakes), *Ιχνευτής*, No. 11 (second series), November-December 1994.

"Ο Δωδεκάλογος του Καρούζου" (On a Twelve-Line Poem by Nikos Karouzos [that was dedicated to Elias Petropoulos]), *Ελευθεροτυπία*, 17 December 1994. (Republished in *Άρθρα στην Ελευθεροτυπία*.)

"Λογοκρισία, Αυτολογοκρισία και Αγραμματοσύνη" (Censorship, Self-Censorship, and Illiteracy), *Ιχνευτής*, No. 14 (second series), July-September 1995. (Republished in *Ιστορία της καπότας*.)

"Ένα ομοσεξουαλικό ποίημα του Τερτσέτη" (A Homosexual Poem by Yiorgos Tertsetis), *Ιχνευτής*, No. 14 (second series), July-September 1995. (Republished in *Ιστορία της καπότας*.)

"Γραμμόφωνο, η, γραμόφωνο; / Φωνόγραφος, η, φωνογράφος" (On the Spelling and Pronunciation of "Grammophone" and "Phonograph"), *Φωνόγραφος*, Winter 1995. (Republished in *Καπανταήδες και μαχαιροβγάλτες*.)

"Ολίγα περί ρατσισμού" (A Few Things about Racism), *Ιχνευτής*, No. 13 (second series), April-June 1995.

"Η χουντική λογοκρισία" (Censorship under the Junta), *Ελευθεροτυπία*, 23 April 1996. (Republished in *Καπανταήδες και μαχαιροβγάλτες*.)

"Οι αμαρτωλές μηχανές" (The Sinful Machines: on Anakreon Kanavakis's Art), *Paraphernalia*, 1996 (artist's album by Kanavakis).

"Τα αναποδογύρισμα του καζανιού" (Overturning the Cooking Pot), *Ελευθεροτυπία*, 11 June 1996. (Republished in *Καπανταήδες και μαχαιροβγάλτες*.)

"Ο Μπιλίμπιν και οι Αιγυπτιώτες" (Billy Bean and Greek Egyptians), *Ελευθεροτυπία*, 12 August 1996.

"Καρούζος No. 2" (Annotations to an Unpublished Poem by Nikos Karouzos), *Ιχνευτής*, No. 17 (second series), Autumn 1996.

"Το τσουκάνι και το τζιρίτι" (An Etymological Study of the Words "tsoukani" and "tziriti"), *Ιχνευτής*, No. 17 (second series), Autumn 1996. (Republished in *Καπανταήδες και μαχαιροβγάλτες*.)

"Η κακογουστία των πολιτικάντηδων" (The Bad Taste of Political Schemers) *Η Εποχή*, 3 November 1996.

"Τα αντάρτικα τραγούδια" (Second World War Resistance Songs), *Ελευθεροτυπία*, 14 December 1996.

"Το χασίσι και οι ντρόγκες" (Hashish and Drugs), *Ιχνευτής*, No. 18 (second series), Winter 1996. (Republished in *Ιστορία της καπότας*.)

"Μόνον ο Τοπόρ με συγκρατεί" ("Only Roland Topor Retains Me"), *Ιχνευτής*, No. 18 (second series), Winter 1996. (See reference to same poem below, in *Η Εποχή*, 26 April 1997 and 18 May 1997.)

"Ο όλισβος" (A Study of the Word "olisbos", the dildo), *Μανδραγόρας*, Nos. 14-15, October 1996-February 1997. (Republished in *Ιστορία της καπότας*.)

"Η Ελλάς..., " (Greece...), *Η Εποχή*, 12 January 1997.

"Ερωτικά ήθη και έθιμα" (Erotic Morals and Customs), *Η Epochv*, 19 January 1997.

"Το πορνοβίντεο" (Porn Videos), *Η Εποχή*, 2 February 1997.

"Σιωπή και σιωπές" (Silence and Silences), *Η Εποχή*, 9 February 1997.

"Προς Θεού!" (For God's Sake!), *Η Εποχή*, 2 March 1997. (Republished in *Ο κουραδοκόφτης*.)

"Αποσπάσματα από την *Ιστορία της καπότας*" (Excerpts from *A History of the Condom*), *Μετρό*, 18 April 1997.

"Μόνον ο Τοπόρ με συγκρατεί" (Only Roland Topor Retains Me), *Η Εποχή*, 26 April 1997. (Excerpt of poem first published in *Ιχνευτής*, Winter 1996; excerpt of same poem, with a collage by Petropoulos, in *Η Εποχή*, 18 May 1997.)

"Τραγουδούσε μέσα από τα εντερά της" (She Sang with her Guts: Remembering the Rebetic Singer Sotiria Bellou), *Ελευθεροτυπία*, 18 August 1997.

"Ah, Roland . . .," the magazine *Έψιλον* of *Κυριακάτικη Ελευθεροτυπία*, 23 August 1997.

"Οι λαδάδες" (Oil Merchants, with pun on a family name and other meanings of the word), *Η Εποχή*, 20 July 1997.

"Ποίηση" (Twelve Short Poems), *Μανδραγόρας*, Nos. 18-19, October 1997-April 1998, pp. 46-47.

"Τα τσόκαρα" (Wooden Shoes), *Μανδραγόρας*, Nos. 18-19, October 1997-April 1988, pp. 48-50.

"Δανεικός επίλογος" (A Borrowed Epilogue), *Μανδραγόρας*, Nos. 18-19, October 1997-April 1998, p. 79. (Republished in *Ιστορία της καπότας*.)

"Τους χασικλήδες μη φοβού!" (Thou Shalt Not Fear Hash Heads!), *Kannabisstreet*, June 1998. (Republished in *Καπανταήδες και μαχαιροβγάλτες*.)

"Ο φίλος μου ο Σελτσούκ" (My Friend the Turkish Artist Selçuk Demirel), *Bestseller*, August 1998. (Republished in *Ο κουραδοκόφτης*.)

"Το κλαμπ και το κλομπ" (Underground Clubs and Billy Clubs), *Κυριακάτικη Ελευθεροτυπία*, 9 August 1998. (Republished in *Καπανταήδες και μαχαιροβγάλτες*.)

"Συνηθισμένα συγχωρετέα λάθη" (Customary Forgivable Mistakes), *Κυριακάτικη Ελευθεροτυπία*, 18 October 1998. (Republished in *Ο κουραδοκόφτης*.)

"Γιάννης Κ. Ανδρουτσόπουλος" (Yiannis K. Androutsopoulos), *Κυριακάτικη Ελευθεροτυπία*, 18 October 1998. (Republished in *Καπανταήδες και μαχαιροβγάλτες*.)

"Μικρό γλωσσάριο της φούμας" (A Short Glossary of Hashish Smoking), *Kannabisstreet*, December 1998. (Republished in *Καπανταήδες και μαχαιροβγάλτες*.)

"Οι κλούβες" (Cages), *Θεσσαλονίκη*, 8 December 1998. (Republished in *Καπανταήδες και μαχαιροβγάλτες*.)

"Η σφεντόνα και ο πετροπόλεμος" (Slingshots and Rock Fights), *Κυριακάτικη Ελευθεροτυπία*, 20 December 1998. (Republished in *Καπανταήδες και μαχαιροβγάλτες*.)

"Ο γαβριάς και το χαμίνι" (Brats and Street Urchins), *Κυριακάτικη Ελευθεροτυπία*, 24 January 1999. (Republished in *Καπανταήδες και μαχαιροβγάλτες*.)

"Ο καρικατουρίστας Τουρχάν" (The Turkish Caricaturist Turkan), *Ελευθεροτυπία*, 21 February 1999. (Republished in *Ο κουραδοκόφτης*.)

"Τα πατούμενα" (Shoes), *Θεσσαλονίκη*, 6 March 1999. (Republished in *Καπανταήδες και μαχαιροβγάλτες*.)

"Οι στραγγαλισμοί και η γκαρότ" (Stranglations and Garrotes), *Κυριακάτικη Ελευθεροτυπία*, 28 March 1999. (Republished in *Καπανταήδες και μαχαιροβγάλτες*.)

"Η σακαράκα και τα σπιρούνια" (Jalopies and Spurs), *Ελευθεροτυπία*, 4 April 1999. (Republished in *Καπανταήδες και μαχαιροβγάλτες*.)

"Οι σοφέρ" (Chauffeurs), *Κυριακάτικη Ελευθεροτυπία*, 2 May 1999. (Republished in *Καπανταήδες και μαχαιροβγάλτες*.)

"Η χαμαλίκα και η ζαλίκα" (On Camels Carrying Burdens on their Back and Shoulders), *Ελευθεροτυπία*, 23 May 1999. (Republished in *Καπανταήδες και μαχαιροβγάλτες*.)

"Τα γυφτολεξικά" (Gypsy Lexicons), *Ελευθεροτυπία*, Christmas 1999. (Republished in *Ο κουραδοκόφτης*.)

"Οι προπαπούδες των καπανταήδων" (The Great Grandfathers of Pistols), *Είκοσι Χρόνια*, Athens: Nefeli, 2000. (Republished in *Καπανταήδες και μαχαιροβγάλτες*.)

"Οι μπούρδες του Χριστιανόπουλου" (Dinos Christianopoulos's Blunders), *Κυριακάτικη Ελευθεροτυπία*, 16 January 2000. (Republished in *Καπανταήδες και μαχαιροβγάλτες*.)

"Η Σφαγή των Προξένων" (The Massacre of the Counsels),

Κυριακάτικη Ελευθεροτυπία, 23 January 2000. (Republished in *Καπανταήδες και μαχαιροβγάλτες*.)

"Πιάστα με το κουλό" (On Underhanded Kinds of Stealing), *Κυριακάτικη Ελευθεροτυπία*, 30 January 2000. (Republished in *Καπανταήδες και μαχαιροβγάλτες*.)

"Τσαμπουκαλίκια" (On Bullying and Swaggering), *Κυριακάτικη Ελευθεροτυπία*, 20 February 2000. (Republished in *Καπανταήδες και μαχαιροβγάλτες*.)

"Οι μποέμηδες" (The Bohemians), *Κυριακάτικη Ελευθεροτυπία*, 5 March 2000. (Republished in *Καπανταήδες και μαχαιροβγάλτες*.)

"Τα σκίτσα του Μάθεση" (Mathesis's Sketches), *Κυριακάτικη Ελευθεροτυπία*, 10 April 2000. (Republished in *Καπανταήδες και μαχαιροβγάλτες*.)

"Η αντιχουντική ΕΣΤΙΑ" (The Anti-Junta Newspaper *Estia* [which had written about Petropoulos while he was imprisoned]), *Κυριακάτικη Ελευθεροτυπία*, 16 April 2000. (Republished in *Καπανταήδες και μαχαιροβγάλτες*.)

"Ο ταμπουράς του Μακρυγιάννη" (Makryiannis's Tambouras), *Κυριακάτικη Ελευθεροτυπία*, 29 April 2000. (Republished in *Καπανταήδες και μαχαιροβγάλτες*.)

"Ο μυστήριος Σακαφλιάς" (The Strange Criminal Sakaphlias), *Κυριακάτικη Ελευθεροτυπία*, 7 May 2000. (Republished in *Καπανταήδες και μαχαιροβγάλτες*.)

"Κομπολόγια και μπεγλέρια" (On Worry Beads), *Κυριακάτικη Ελευθεροτυπία*, 28 May 2000. (Republished in *Καπανταήδες και μαχαιροβγάλτες*.)

"Οι χαρακίρηδες" (Those who Commit Suicide by Hara-Kiri),

Κυριακάτικη Ελευθεροτυπία, 4 June 2000. (Republished in *Καπανταήδες και μαχαιροβγάλτες*.)

"Τα μουρμούρικα" (On the Early Rebetic Songs that are called "Mourmourika"), *Κυριακάτικη Ελευθεροτυπία*, 18 June 2000. (Republished in *Καπανταήδες και μαχαιροβγάλτες*.)

"Ο Λάκκος στο Ηράκλειο" (The Area Lakkos, near Heraklion), *Κυριακάτικη Ελευθεροτυπία*, 9 July 2000. (Republished in *Καπανταήδες και μαχαιροβγάλτες*.)

"Τα κατόρθωμα του Βότση" (The Achievment of Nikolaos Votsis), *Κυριακάτικη Ελευθεροτυπία*, 13 August 2000. (Republished in *Ο κουραδοκόφτης*.)

"Το τσικρικόνι" (The Guinea Fowl), *Κυριακάτικη Ελευθεροτυπία*, 20 August 2000. (Republished in *Καπανταήδες και μαχαιροβγάλτες*.)

"Οι νέοι ρεμπετολόγοι" (The Young Rebetologists), *Κυριακάτικη Ελευθεροτυπία*, 3 September 2000. (Republished in *Καπανταήδες και μαχαιροβγάλτες*.)

"Ο Σαλομόν" (Salomon: On Dionysios Solomos), *Κυριακάτικη Ελευθεροτυπία*, 24 September 2000. (Republished in *Φιλολογική Σελίδα* on 30 September 2000, then included in *Ο κουραδοκόφτης*.)

"Δύο μυστήριες νεκρολογίες" (Two Strange Obituaries: On Nikos Karvounis and Nikos Zakhariadis), *Κυριακάτικη Ελευθεροτυπία*, 8 October 2000. (Republished in *Ο κουραδοκόφτης*.)

"Ώστε, οικουμενικός;" (On the Orthodox Term "Oecumenical Patriarch"), *Κυριακάτικη Ελευθεροτυπία*, 12 November 2000. (Republished in *Ο κουραδοκόφτης*.)

"Ο δέσμιος Ποιητής" (The Bound [Imprisoned] Poet: Kostas Samaras), 19 November 2000. (Republished in *Ο κουραδοκόφτης*.)

"Η Μαρία Κάλας" (Maria Callas), *Κυριακάτικη Ελευθεροτυπία*, 4 February 2001. (Republished in *Ο κουραδοκόφτης*.)

"Ο Άγγελος Προκοπίου" (Angelos Prokopiou), *Κυριακάτικη Ελευθεροτυπία*, 15 February 2001. (Republished in *Ο κουραδοκόφτης*.)

"Ο κουραδοκόφτης" (The String, literally "The Shit-Cutter"), *Κυριακάτικη Ελευθεροτυπία*, 4 March 2001. (Republished as the title article of *Ο κουραδοκόφτης*.)

"Οι κιζίλ-μπάσηδες" (On the word "kizil-basis"), *Κυριακάτικη Ελευθεροτυπία*, 22 April 2001. (Republished in *Ο κουραδοκόφτης*.)

"Το Ερωτικό Μουσείο της Βαρκελόνης" (The Erotic Museum of Barcelona), *Μανδραγόρας*, October 2001. (Republished in *Ο κουραδοκόφτης*.)

"Τιούργια" (On the Exclamation "Yiourgia"), *Πανδώρα*, November 2001. (Republished in *Ο κουραδοκόφτης*.)

"Δημήτρης Σουλιώτης: έρωτες και αλληγορίες και εφιάλτες" (Dimitris Souliotis: Loves and Allegories and Nightmares—Ten poems), *Dimitris Souliotis*, Athens: Yiayiannos Gallery, 2002, pp. 4-14. (See *Τέσσερεις Ζωγράφοι*.)

"Επιστολή της 2/11/1982 προς τον υπουργό Γ. Α. Μαγκάκη" (Petropoulos's Letter of 2 November 1982 to the erstwhile Minister of Justice, Yiorgos Alexandros Mangakis, asking not for a special amnesty in his own case, but rather that the Greek Press Law be repealed and that a new law establish freedom of the press for all writers and journalists), *Μανδραγόρας*, No. 37, October 2007.

Selected articles about and interviews with Petropoulos:

Article by Y. P. Savvidis, *Ταχυδρόμος*, 22 March 1958.

Article by Andreas Karantonis, *Η Καθημερινή*, 3 May 1966.

Article by Asteris Kovantzis, *Ημέρα*, 20 May 1966.

Article by Freddy Germanos, *Άλφα*, 17 October 1968.

Article in *Το Έθνος*, 21 December 1968.

Article by Dominique Grandmont in *Les Nouvelles Littéraires*, 1968.

"Rebetika Traghoudhia," review by Kimon Friar, *Books Abroad*, Spring 1969, p. 301.

Article by Freddy Germanos, *Ταχυδρόμος*, 13 February 1970.

Article by Vassos Varikas, *Το Βήμα*, 29 March 1970.

Article by G. N. Milarakis, *Θεσσαλονίκη*, 13 July 1970.

Article by Markos Dragoumis, *Γυναίκα*, 11 August 1971.

Article by Roland Jaccard, *Le Monde*, 3 December 1971.

Article by G. Kontoyiannis, *Το Βήμα*, 13 August 1972.

"Kaliarda," review by Kimon Friar, *Books Abroad*, October 1972.

"Jagd auf Jakob" (About Petropoulos's *Kaliarda*, Homosexuality, and Censorship), unsigned, *Der Spiegel*, 5 February 1973, p. 92.

Article by X. Philippidis, *Ακρόπολις*, 11 February 1973.

"Civil Wedding Ban Stays," by David Tonge, *The Guardian*, 7 May 1973.

Article by G. Kontoyiannis, *Το Βήμα*, 6 June 1973.

"Culture populaire et groupes marginaux: à propos des Rébétika grecs" (Folk Culture and Social Outcasts: On Greek Rebetic Songs), by Stathis

Damianakos, *Les Temps Modernes*, No. 330, January 1974, pp. 1447-1460.

"L'art contre la société: une culture dominée: le rébétiko" (Art against Society: Rebetic Music as a Dominated Culture), by Olivier Revault d'Allones, *La création artistique et les promesses de la liberté*, Paris: Klincksieck, 1973, pp. 143-178.

"Τι είναι το ρεμπέτικο τραγούδι;" (What are Rebetic Songs?), interview in *Γυναίκα*, 15 May 1974. (Republished in *Μικρά κείμενα*.)

Article by Giorgos Lianis, *Τα Νέα*, 7 June 1974.

Article by Kimon Friar, *The Athenian*, May 1975.

Article by Roderick Beaton, *The Athenian*, July 1975.

Article by Tasos Vournas, *Η Αυγή*, 1 November 1975.

Article in *Μακεδονία*, by N., 21 November 1975.

Article in *Θεσσαλονίκη*, by S. P., 25 November 1975.

Article by Fanis N. Kleanthis, *Τα Νέα*, 27 December 1975.

Article by Kaiti Romanou, *Η Καθημερινή*, 4 January 1976.

Article by G. Kontoyiannis, *Το Βήμα*, 18 January 1976.

Article by Anteia Frantzi, *Αντί*, 12 June 1976.

"Της φυλακής / From the Jails," review by Kimon Friar, *The Athenian*, November 1976, pp. 40-41.

Article by Tassos Vournas, *Η Αυγή*, 27 February 1977.

Article by Kimon Friar, *The Athenian*, June 1977.

Article by Maria Karavia, *Γυναίκα*, 20 July 1977.

"Caliarda: la langue secrète des homosexuels grecs" (Kaliarda: the Secret Language of Greek Homosexuals), by Hélène Ioannidi, *Topique: Revue Freudienne*, No. 20, October 1977, pp. 115-150.

"Kaliarda," review by Jean-Luc Hennig, *Libération*, 16 December 1977.

Article in *Αντί*, 31 December 1977.

Article by Ira Feloukatzi, *Τα Νέα*, 11 January 1978.

"The Greek Gays have a Word for It," by Steve A. Demakopoulos, *Maledicta*, Vol. II, 1978, pp. 33-39.

"Den farlige lexicografen" (article in Swedish about Petropoulos's life and work), by Theodor Kallifatides, *Svenska Dagbladet*, 16 July 1978.

Article by Nikos Papayiannis, *Ο Πολίτις*, 26 October 1978.

Article by D. Loukatos, *Το Βήμα*, 21 December 1978.

Article by M. G. Meraklis, *Διαβάζω*, July 1979.

"Ηλίας Πετρόπουλος: Εγχειρίδιον του καλού κλέφτη" (review of *The Good Thief's Manual*), unsigned, *Προϊνί*, 23 November 1979.

"Ακούω...βλέπω" (I Listen... I Look: review of *The Good Thief's Manual*), by Otovlepsies, *Τα Νέα*, 26 November 1979.

"Κατάσχεση βιβλίου" (The Confiscation of a Book), unsigned, *Ριζοσπάστης*, 30 November 1979.

"Κατασχέθηκε το βιβλίο 'Εγχειρίδιο του καλού κλέφτη'" (*The Good Thief's Manual* Confiscated), unsigned, *Η Αυγή*, 30 November 1979.

"Κατασχέθηκε το 'Εγχειρίδιο του καλού κλέφτη'" (*The Good Thief's Manual* Confiscated), unsigned, *Απογευματινή*, 30 November 1979.

"Κατεσχέθη το νέο βιβλίο του Πετρόπουλου" (Petropoulos's New Book Confiscated), unsigned, *Προϊνί*, 30 November 1979.

"Κατασχέθηκε το 'Εγχειρίδιο του καλού κλέφτη'" (*The Good Thief's Manual* Confiscated), unsigned, *Η Καθημερινή*, 30 November 1979.

"Κατασχέθηκε το 'Εγχειρίδιο του καλού κλέφτη'" (*The Good Thief's Manual* Confiscated), unsigned, *Τα Νέα*, 30 November 1979.

"Κυρώσεις γιά άσεμνα έντυπα και άλλα αντικείμενα" (Sanctions for Indecent Publications and other Topics), by Dimitris Vradynos, *Η Βραδυνή*, 30 November 1979.

"Δίωξι γιά το 'Εγχειρίδιο του καλού κλέφτη'" (A Ban for *The Good Thief's Manual*), unsigned, *Η Βραδυνή*, 30 November 1979.

"Κατασχέθηκε το 'Εγχειρίδιο του καλού κλέφτη'" (*The Good Thief's Manual* Confiscated), unsigned, *Το Βήμα* 30 November 1979.

"Κατασχέθηκε το 'Εγχειρίδιο του καλού κλέφτη'" (*The Good Thief's Manual* Confiscated), *Ελευθεροτυπία*, 30 November 1979.

"41 μαθήματα...κλοπής" (Forty-One Lessons . . . on How to Steal), unsigned, *Ελευθεροτυπία*, 1 December 1979.

"Απαράδεκτη ενέργεια" (Unacceptable Efficiency: On the Confiscation of *The Good Thief's Manual*), unsigned, *Η Αυγή*, 1 December 1979.

"Αναχρονιστική η νομοθεσία γιά την κατάσχεση" (Anachronistic Legislation about Confiscating Books), unsigned, *Ελευθεροτυπία*, 2 December 1979.

"Βους επί γλωσση..." (review of *The Good Thief's Manual*), by Yiorgos Ioannou, *Προϊνί*, 8 December 1979.

"Η επίσυμη Ελλάδα τον αφήνει εκτός τειχών" (Official Greece Leaves Him on the Other Side of the Walls), Letter by Costas Tsoclis, *Ta Néa*, 12 December 1979.

"Retour de la censure en Grèce" (The Return of Censorship to Greece: about *The Good Thief's Manual*), by Jacques Lacarrière, *Le Monde*, 14 December 1979.

Article by Themis Iatrou, *Ο Αθηναίος*, January 1980.

Article by Alekos Fassianos, *Ta Néa*, 5 January 1980.

"Ένα μνημείο γιά τα Ρεμπέτικα" (A Monument for Rebetic Songs: On the New Edition of Petropoulos's Anthology), by Kostas Stamatiou, *Ta Néa*, 16 February 1980.

Article in *Μεσημβρινή*, 29 February 1980.

Article by Nikos Zalaoras, *Διαβάζω*, March 1980.

Article by Tatiana Gritsi-Milliex, *Ελευθεροτυπία*, 2 February 1980.

Article by Aglaia Kremezi, *Ταχυδρόμος*, 6 February 1980.

Article by Thanasis Xiliotis (pseudonym of Elias Papadimitraklopoulos), *Αντί*, 14 February 1980.

Article by Veatriki Spiliadi, *Η Καθημερινή*, 30 February 1980.

Article by Elias Papadimitrakopoulos, *Η Καθημερινή*, 24 April 1980.

Article by Kostas Mavroudis, *Το Δέντρο*, May-June 1980.

Brief unsigned notice of new edition of *Ρεμπέτικα τραγούδια* in *Maledicta*, Vol. IV, No. 1, Summer 1980.

Article by Evgenios Aranitsis, *Ελευθεροτυπία*, 10 August 1980.

"Greek Coffee Shops Fall Victim to Pace of City Life," unsigned, *New York Times*, 10 August 1980.

Article by Valerios Ramphos, *Αμφί*, Autumn 1980.

Article in *Οικονομικός Ταχυδρόμος*, 2 October 1980.

"Les malheurs d'Elias Petropoulos" (The Trials and Tribulations of Elias Petropoulos, with an excerpt from *The Good Thief's Manual*), by J. F. D., *Libération*, 25 October 1980.

Article in *Διαβάζω*, November 1980.

Article by Ira Feloukatzi, *Τα Νέα*, 11 November 1980.

Article in *Οικονομικός Ταχυδρόμος*, by Kritovoulos, 13 November 1980.

Article by Tolis Yiannakis, *Ελευθεροτυπία*, 18 November 1980.

"Über den Kreislauf der Diebe: Zur Verurteilung des griechischen Schriftstellers Elias Petropoulous", (The Thievery Circuit: On the Indictment of the Greek Writer Elias Petropoulos), by Oswald Wiener, *Die Zeit*, 28 November 1980.

Unsigned notice about *The Good Thief's Manual*, actually written by Jacques Vallet, *Le Fou Parle*, No. 15, December 1980, p. 23.

"Ανορθόδοξι αντιμετώπιση του ύποπτου" (An Unusual Confrontation with Doubt: On *The Good Thief's Manual*), by Kostas Beis, *Ελευθεροτυπία*, 4 December 1980.

"Μας ρεζιλεύει διεθνώς η λογοκρισία μας" (About Oswald Wiener's Article on Censorship and Petropoulos in *Die Zeit* on 28 November 1980), unsigned, *Ελευθεροτυπία*, 9 December 1980.

Article by Yiorgos Ioannou, *Ελευθεροτυπία*, 18 December 1980.

"Elias Petropoulos condamné en Grèce" (Elias Petropoulos Sentenced in Greece), by Jacques Lacarrière, *Le Monde*, 19 December 1980.

Article by G. Ioakeimidis, *Αντί*, 19 December 1980.

Article in *Επίκαιρα*, 21 December 1980.

"Les incertitudes de l'alignement" (About Greek Foreign Policy, with a passage on *The Good Thief's Manual*), by Schofield Coryell, *Afrique-Asie*, No. 229, 22 December 1980, pp. 20-21.

Article by Nikos Bakounakis, *Πάνθεον*, 23 December 1980.

Τομές, No. 69, February 1981. Special issue with articles by Yiorgos Markopoulos, Zoe Nasioutzik, Dimitris Doukaris, Alekos Fassianos, and Elias Papadimitrakopoulos. (Papadimitrakopoulos's article was reprinted in special issue of *Μανδραγόρας*, Nos. 18-19, October 1997-April 1998, p. 33, as well as in his own collection of essays, *Παρακείμενα*, Athens: Kedros, 1983, pp. 44-53.)

"Bonnes moeurs" (Good Morals; article mentions *The Good Thief's Manual* controversy), unsigned, *Libération*, 21 February 1981.

"Έργο τέχνης η πορνογράφημα ο Μαρκήσιος ντε Σαντ;" (Are the Marquis de Sade's Books Works of Art or Pornography?), by Paulos Palaiologos, *Ελευθεροτυπία*, 1 March 1981.

"Des juges grecs condamnent le 'divin marquis'" (Greek Judges Indict the Divine Marquis), unsigned, *Le Monde*, 6 March 1981.

"Μια συζήτσηση με τον Ηλία Πετρόπουλο" (An Interview with Elias Petropoulos), by Nikos Bakounakis, *Πάνθεον*, 1 April 1981, pp. 26-29.

Article by Ilias Koutsoukos, *Θεσσαλονίκη*, 4 April 1981.

"Τέχνη κι ελευθερία" (Art and Liberty), by Evgenios Aranitsis, *Ελευθεροτυπία*, 5 April 1981.

"Λογοκρισία: το τέρας που πεθαίνει και ξαναγεννιέται" (Censorship: The Monster that Dies and is Born Again), by S. Alexandropoulou, *Κυριακάτκιη*, 5 April 1981.

"Το Εγχειρίδιον του καλού κλέφτη" (review of *The Good Thief's Manual*), by Evghenios Aranitsis, *Κυριακάτκιη*, 5 April 1981.

Article by Nikos Bakounakis, *Πάνθεον*, 14 April 1981.

Article by Olga Bati, *Γυναίκα*, 6 May 1981.

Article by Chr. Konstantopoulou, *Η Φωνή του Πειραιώς*, 9 May 1981.

Article by K. I. Tsaousis, *Ελευθεροτυπία*, 28 May 1981.

Article by Yiorgos Ioannou, *Η Καθημερινή*, 10 June 1981.

"Καταγγελια" (Accusation: on Petropoulos's Books about Thessaloniki), by Yiorgos Ioannou, *Η Λέξη*, July-August 1981, pp. 484-486.

"Un écrivain qui dérange" (A Troublesome Writer), by Schofield Coryell, *Afrique-Asie*, No. 248, 14 September 1981, pp. 58-59.

"Το εγχειρίδιον του καλού κλέφτη" (review of *The Good Thief's Manual*) by Ilias Koutsoukos, *Γιατί*, October 1981, pp. 41-44.

"Elias Petropoulos," by Clément Lepidis, *Révolution*, 30 October 1981, pp. 30-31.

"Elias Petropoulos: The *Mounópsira*," by John Taylor, *Maledicta*, Vol. 5, Nos. 1-2 (Elias Petropoulos Festshrift), 1981, pp. 11-24. (Greek translation by Vangelis Katsanis in *Ιχνευτής*, No. 5, October 1985, pp. 20-28.)

"Elias Petropoulos: A Presentation," by John Taylor, *Journal of the Hellenic Diaspora*, Vol. 8, No. 4, Winter 1981, pp. 7-28.

"A Greek Gay is a Greek Gay is a Greek Gay. . .," by Steve Damakopoulos, *Maledicta*, Vol. VI, 1982, pp. 45-51.

Article by Tatiana Gritsi-Milliex, *Ελευθεροτυπία*, 24 January 1982.

"Ο Σιωνισμός" (Zionism: on Petropoulos and his Appeal to Commemorate the Shoah of the Jews of Thessaloniki), by N. Laimoglou, *Ορθόδοξος Τύπος*, 5 February 1982.

"Απάντηση στον Ηλία Πετρόπουλο" (Group letter in reply to Petropoulos's Appeal to Commemorate the Shoah of the Jews of Thessaloniki), in Otoblepsies's column, *Τα Νέα*, 10 February 1982.

Article by Yiannis Kamilaris, *Ελευθεροτυπία*, 14 February 1982.

"Ο λόγος της Πιάτσας, το λεξικό της Πιάτσας και η μόδα Ηλίας Πετρόπουλος" (Words of the Underworld, the Lexicon of the Underworld, and the Fashionable Popularity of Elias Petropoulos), by Angelis Diplas, *Αντί*, No. 200, March 1982, pp. 53-55.

"Les Juifs de Salonique: un génocide oublié" (The Jews of Salonica: A Forgotten Genocide), by Schofield Coryell, *Différences*, No. 10, April 1982, pp. 36-37.

"Νά γιορτασθούν τα 40 χρόνια του ολοκαυτώματος των Εβραίων της Θεσσαλονίκης" (On Petropoulos's second appeal to Melina Mercouri about the Jews of Thessaloniki), *Θεσσαλονίκη*, 2 April 1982.

"Πετρόπουλος ψάλλων" (Petropoulos Psalmodying Again: On the Appeal to Melina Mercouri about the Jews of Thessaloniki), *Ελευθεροτυπία*, 2 April 1982.

"Qui est G. Legman?" (Who is Gershon Legman?), by John Taylor, *Le Fou Parle*, No. 20, April-May 1982, pp. 55-56. (This article, which mentions Petropoulos, was translated into Greek and published in *Ιχνευτής*, Nos. 34-35, July-August 1988, pp. 46-47.)

Article by Veatriki Spiliadi, *Ελευθεροτυπία*, 7 July 1982.

Article in *Libération*, 10 September 1982, p. 19.

Article in *International Herald Tribune*, 16 September 1982, p. 2.

Article in *Le Monde*, 17 September 1982, p. 14.

"Autour du *rébétiko*, la chanson des mauvais garçons" (About *Rebetika*, the Songs of Bad Boys), by Michel Grodent, *Le Soir* (Brussels), 21 September 1982.

"Η σκληρότητα είναι η ευγένεια του αιώνα μας" (Harshness is the Politeness of our Century), by Leonidas Christakis, *Διαβάσε γιά να Διαβάσεις*, No. 1, October 1982.

"*Maledicta*" (On the Journal *Maledicta*), by John Taylor, *Le Fou Parle*, Nos. 21-22, November-December 1982, pp. 71-72. (This article, which mentions Petropoulos, was translated into Greek and published in *Ιχνευτής*, Nos. 34-35, July-August 1988, pp. 48-49.)

"Dans les marges d'*Europalia*: l'autre Grèce de Petropoulos" (In the Margins of the Europalia Festival: the Other Greece of Elias Petropoulos), by Michel Grodent, *Le Soir* (Brussels), 22 November 1982. (Greek translation: "Στο περιθώριο των Ερωπαλίον: Η Ελλάδα του Ηλία Πετρόπουλου," *Μεσημβρινή*, 7 December 1982.)

Article by Kostas Stamatiou, *Ta Νέα*, 24 December 1982.

"Petropoulos, Paris'te Türk-Yunan kültür ortaklıgını arastırıyor" (Article in Turkish about Petropoulos's life and work), by Okay Gönensin, *Cumhuriyet*, 25 December 1982, p. 8.

"Δέκα Πέζα Κείμενα" (Ten Prose Texts, with several passages about Petropoulos), by Yiorgos Ioannou, *Φυλλάδιο*, Nos. 5-6, 1982, pp. 33-37, 45, 61-62, 65, 71.

"*Rebetiko Tragoudi* as a Generic Term," by Stathis Gauntlett, *Byzantine and Modern Greek Studies*, Vol. 8, 1982-1983, pp. 77-102.

"Unbequem der Rechten wie der Linken: Der Fall des exilierten Griechen Elias Petropoulous" (As Uneasy for the Right Wing as for the Left Wing: The Case of the Exiled Greek Writer Elias Petropoulos), by Eberhard Rondholz, *Frankfurter Rundschau*, 15 January 1983.

Article by N. Emonidis, *Η Καθημερινή*, 20 January 1983.

"Les démagogues d'Athènes" (On Commemorating the Shoah of the Jews of Thessaloniki), by Victor Malka, *L'Arche*, April 1983, pp. 86-87.

"Elias Petropoulos: Folklorist-in-Exile," by John Taylor, *Greek Accent*, Vol. 3, No. 9, May-June 1983, pp. 25-27, 46-47.

"L'architecture: mémoire populaire" (about Petropoulos's Photo Albums and Concept of Popular Architecture), by John Taylor, *Le Fou Parle*, No. 24, May-June 1983, pp. 58-59.

"Vidal-Naquet: autour des 'héros' du ghetto de Varsovie" (this article about Pierre Vidal-Naquet and the Warsaw Ghetto includes a passage about the album *Les Juifs de Salonique / In Memoriam / The Jews of Salonica*), by Michel Grodent, *Le Soir* (Brussels), 7-8 May 1983.

Article by Manolis Xexakis, *Διαβάζω*, no. 69, 18 May 1983.

"Benávis ta kaliardá?", by John Taylor, *Gay Books Bulletin*, No. 9, Spring-Summer 1983, pp. 14-19.

"Elias Petropoulos sur Radio libertaire en 1983: 'J'ai obtenu la première carte d'identité de l'histoire de la Grèce avec la mention 'athée,'" *La voie du jaguar, informations et correspondance pour l'autonomie individuelle et collective*, interview with Jacques Vallet, Jean-Luc Hennig and Christian Zeimert on 17 June 1983 on the French radio station *Radio libertaire*. » (https://lavoiedujaguar.net/_Elias-Petropoulos_)

"Καταγγελία" (Accusation: article mentions *Kaliarda*), *Πατρίς* (Πύργου-Ηλείας), unsigned, 1 July 1983.

"Για τον Πετρόπουλο" (about John Taylor's article on Petropoulos in *Greek Accent*) *Ελευθεροτυπία*, unsigned, 4 August 1983.

"Η αυλή στην Ελλάδα" (review of *Courtyards in Greece*) by Ilias Kephalas, *Τομές*, No. 88, October-December 1983, p. 60.

"Un album de souvenir [*Les Juifs de Salonique: In Memoriam*, par Elias Petropoulos]," review by John Taylor, *Les Nouveaux Cahiers*, No. 74, Autumn 1983, p. 80.

"Οι κυρίες της αυλής—κατά Ηλία Πετρόπουλο" (The Women of the Courtyards—According to Elias Petropoulos), by Freddy Germanos, *Ελευθεροτυπία*, 20 November 1983.

"Η αυλή στην Ελλάδα" (review of *Courtyards in Greece*), by Dimitris Stamelos, *Ελευθεροτυπία*, 8 December 1983.

"Η ιστορία τις λέξης αυλή" (The Story of the Word "Courtyard": review of *Courtyards in Greece*), by Angeliki Vassilakou, *Εξόρμιση*, 10 December 1983.

"Άλμπουμ...Άλμπουμ" (review of *Courtyards in Greece*), *Τα Νέα*, 31 December 1983.

"Η νοσταλγία τις απλής ζωής" (Nostalgia for the Simple Life: on *Courtyards in Greece*), unsigned review, *Ναυτική Ελλας*, No. 603, January 1984, p. 33.

"Η αυλή στην Ελλάδα" (Courtyards in Greece), *Συλλογές*, No. 4, January 1984, p. 13.

Article by Leonidas Christakis, *Ιδεοδρόμιο*, March 1984.

"Aufenthaltserlaubnis 'erschlichen'" (On the exhibit for Messaoud

Chebbi at the Kunstlerhaus Bethanien in Berlin), by Thomas Wulffen, *Zitty*, 13 April 1984, p. 7.

"Death in Greece," by Melanie Wallace, *Journal of the Hellenic Diaspora*, Vol. XI, No. 1, Spring 1984, pp. 39-46.

"Elias Petropoulos," unsigned, *Newsletter of the Jewish Museum of Greece*, No. 12, May 1984.

"Kaliarda Revisited," by John Taylor, *The Cabirion*, No. 11, Fall-Winter 1984, pp. 10-11.

"*The Jews of Salonica: In Memoriam*, by Elias Petropoulos," review by John Taylor, *Jewish Currents*, Vol. 39, No. 1 (425), January 1985, pp. 14-15.

Article by Viktoras Netas, *Ελευθεροτυπία*, 19 February 1985.

"Η λαογραφία του αστέως: Τέσσερις ημέρες με τον Ηλία Πετρόπουλο" (Urban Folklore: Four Days with Elias Petropoulos), by Yiorgos Allamanis, *Ήχος & Hi-Fi*, March 1985, pp. 46-51.

"Einer klagt an" (One Man Files a Complaint: About Petropoulos's Appeal to the West German Minister of Justice to Prosecute the Family and Assistants of the Nazi Doctor Josef Mengele), unsigned, *Die Zeit*, 16 August 1985.

"Ηλίας Πετρόπουλος: αποκλειστική συνέντευξη" (Elias Petropoulos: Exclusive Interview), *Ιχνευτής*, No. 5, October 1985, p. 12-19.

Article by Phoebe Delphis, *Γιατί*, October 1985.

Article by Costas Tsoclis, *Μεσημβρινή*, 5 February 1986.

"Οι Εβραίοι τις Θεσσαλονίκης" (The Jews of Thessaloniki), by Yiorgos Allamanis, plus interview, *Σχολιαστής*, No. 36, March 1986, pp. 53-55.

Article by Yannis Thanassakos, magazine of the Auschwitz Foundation, June 1986.

Article in *Η Καθημερινή*, 6-7 July 1986.

"Cunta, 'Rebetika" kitabımı pornografik diye toplatmış tı" (interview in Turkish by Mehmet Akif), *Cumhuriyet*, 15 October 1986.

"Zonder *érotas* schrijf je geen regel: De folklorist Elias Petropoulos en zijn liefde voor het triviale" (Article in Dutch about Petropoulos's Work) by Flip Lindo, *Lychnari*, No. 1, March 1987, pp. 25-26.

Unsigned review of *A Macabre Song*, *Ιχνευτής*, No. 19, March 1987, p. 2.

"Οι ηλίθιοι είναι αήττητοι" (Imbeciles are Invincible), article by Christos Zabounis, plus interview, *Eva*, 9 April 1987, pp.43-49.

"Πέντε ερωτήματα στον Ηλία Πετρόπουλο" (Five Questions for Elias Petropoulos), *Ιχνευτής*, Nos. 22-23, June-July 1987.

Article in *Θεσσαλονίκη*, 20 June 1988.

Article by Vassilis Kontopoulos, *Οδός Πανός*, Summer 1988.

Article in *Η Εβδόμη* (Καβάλας), 8 July 1988.

"Αντί επιλόγου" (Anti-Epilogue: Petropoulos replies to a survey, taken by Polydefkis Papadopoulos, about contemporary Greece and its relationship to Europe), *Ta Νέα*, 22 August 1988. (Republished in *Καπαντατήδες και μαχαιροβγάλτες*.)

"Ο Βασίλης (Βασιλικός) κι ο Ηλίας (Πετρόπουλος) βρεθήκανε στο Παρίσι κι ανοίξανε μια συζήτηση" (Vassilis [Vassilikos] and Elias [Petropoulos] Meet in Paris and Start Conversing), *Ιχνευτής*, Nos. 38-39, November-December 1988.

"Research on Rebetika: Some Methodological Problems and Issues," by Ole L. Smith, pp. 177-190, *Journal of Modern Hellenism*, No. 6, 1989.

Article by Gerd. Höhler, *Frankfurter Rundschau*, 10 January 1989.

"Istanbul diyen tek Yananlıyım" (article and interview in Turkish by Şehmus Güzel), *Ikibine Doğru*, 26 February 1989, pp. 48-51.

"Elias Petropoulos : Ein Chronist gegen das Vergessen" (Elias Petropoulos: A Chronicler writing against Oblivion), by Armin Kerker, *Die Horen*, No. 153, Spring 1989, pp. 155-158.

Article by Yiannis Douvitsas, *Τα Νέα*, 22 May 1989.

Article by Yiorgos Biziouras, *Γυναίκα*, 24 May 1989.

Article by Dim. Gionis, *Ελευθεροτυπία*, 27 May 1989.

Article by Costas Taktsis, *Εντευκτήριο*, July 1989 (quoting a letter from 1972).

"Kaliarda," by John Taylor, *Encyclopedia of Homosexuality*, edited by Wayne Dynes, New York: Garland, 1990, volume, pp. 656-657. (See also "Greece, Modern" by William A. Percy and John Taylor, pp. 501-504.)

"Το δαιμόνιο του Πετρόπουλου" (Petropoulos's Devilish Genius) by Demosthenis Kourtovik, *Ελευθεροτυπία*, 14 March 1990.

"Αποκάλυψη Ιωάννου κατά...Η. Πετρόπουλο" (The Book of Revelations According . . . to Elias Petrokpoulos), *Η Αυγή της Κυριακής*, 8 September 1990.

"Συνέντευξη περί πορνογραφίας" (An Interview about Pornography), by Elpida Skouphalou, *Επτά*, October 1990. (Republished in *Ιστορία της καπότας.*)

"Der Kerl von der Gasse: Ein Besuch bei Elias Petropoulos in Paris" (The Cad from the Alley: Visiting Elias Petropoulos in Paris), by Peter Mosler, *Frankfurter Rundschau*, 19 January 1991.

"Quintette grec," by Vassilis Alexakis, *Le Monde*, 16 August 1991.

"Επαναστατική λαογραφία" (Revolutionary Folklore), by Nikos Dokas, *Κυριακάτικη Ελευθεροτυπία*, 27 October 1991.

"Τα τρία τινά" (review of Petropoulos's translation of Aretino, and interview with Petropoulos and Costas Tsoclis), by Nana Kostidhaki, *Επτάμισι*, 15 November 1991, pp. 68-71.

Interviewed by Liljana Kotevcka-Plevnes, *ΕΠΟΧΑ* (Skopje), 14 March 1992, pp. 34-36.

"New Evidence on Greek Music in the USA: [Richard] Spottswood's Ethnic Music on Record," by Ole L. Smith, *Journal of the Hellenic Diaspora*, Vo. 18, No. 2, 1992, pp. 97-109.

"Ηλίας Πετρόπουλος, ο ερωτικός ποιητής" (Elias Petropoulos, the Erotic Poet), by Philippos Philippou, *Η Εποχή*, 9 January 1994.

"Ψαλιδίζω γυναίκες γυμνές" (I Cut Up Naked Women), by Vasilis Kalamaras, *Κυριακάτικη Ελευθεροτυπία*, 2 October 1994.

"Cultural Identity and Cultural Interaction: Greek Music in the United States 1917-1941," by Ole L. Smith, *Journal of Modern Greek Studies*, Vo. 13, No. 1, May 1995, pp. 125-138.

"Ο μεγάλος ασεβής των Ελληνικων Γραμμάτων" (The Great Blasphemer of Greek Literature), interview by Philippos Philippou, in the magazine *Έψιλον* of *Κυριακάτικη Ελευθεροτυπία*, 28 January 1996.

Article in *Η Εποχή*, by Philippos Phillipou, 21 April 1996.

Joint interview of Petropoulos and the Turkish artist Yüksel Arslan, *Miliet* (Istanbul), 3 January 1997.

"Η λογοτεχνία της Θεσσαλονίκης" (The Literature of Thessaloniki), *Η Καθημερινή* (Επτά Ημέρες), 2 February 1997.

"Νίκος Γαβριήλ Πεντζίκης" (Nikos Gabriel Pentzikis), *Η Καθημερινή* (Επτά Ημέρες), 2 March 1987.

Article in *Η Εποχή*, 30 March 1997.

"Η Χαλκίδα του Σκαρίμπα" (The Chalcida of the Writer Yiannis Skaribas), *Η Καθημερινή* (Επτά Ημέρες), 6 April 1997.

Interview by G. Allamani, *Μετρό*, 18 April 1997.

Article in *Ελευθεροτυπία*, by Β. Κ. Κ., 21 April 1997.

"Θεσσαλονίκη, η εικαστική της φυσιογνωμία" (Thessaloniki: The Figuration of Physiognomy), *Η Καθημερινή* (Επτά Ημέρες), 15 June 1997.

Article by Vassilis Vassilikos, *Τα Νέα*, 1 July 1997.

Article by Vlassis Angtzidis, *Ελευθεροτυπία*, 18 September 1997.

Special Elias Petropoulos issue of *Μανδραγόρας*, Nos. 18-19, October 1997-April 1998. (An essential special issue, including biographical information and articles or tributes by Maria Dousi, Angeliki Kostavara, Phoebe Yiannisi, Jacques Lacarrière, Aristeidis Antonas, Anakreon Kanavakis, Gerasimos A. Rigatos, Marika Thomadakis, Ersi Sotiropoulou, Costas Tsoclis, Sarantis Karavouzis, Yiannis Kondos, Kostas Kremmydas, Angelis Diplas, Nikos Houliaras, Alexandra Bakonika, Philippos Philippou, Dionysis G. Hionis, Notis Mavroudis, and Kostas Voukelatos.) See especially the interview "Ισχυρότερη μνήμη είναι η μνήμη της καρδιάς: αποσπάσματα από μαγνητοδωμένες αναμνήσεις" (A Stronger Memory is that of the Heart: Fragments of Tape-Recorded Remembrance), pp. 6-30.

"Η Ελλάδα είναι κουραστική χώρα" ("Greece is a Tired Country"), interview in *Bestseller* (Thessaloniki), No. 16, May-June 1998, pp. 48-64. (The magazine has entirely reproduced the handwritten answers to this extensive interview.)

"Σύτομες πληροφορίες περί του Ηλία Πετρόπουλου" (Some Concise Information about Elias Petropoulos), by Elias Papadimitrakopoulos, *Αποκείμενα*, Athens: Nefeli, 2000, pp. 120-123. (First included in the special issue of Μανδραγόρας.)

"Hommage à Elias Petropoulos et Ante Popovski," by Christophe Chiclet, *Confluences Méditerranée*, No. 2, 2004, pp. 191-196. (https://www.cairn.info/revue-confluences-mediterranee-2004-2-page-191.htm?ref=doi#xd_co_f=ZDUwMDMzNDItY2ZiYi00NTNiLWJlZmQtMTYxZDRkOWU1NjIy~)

"Poetry, Anti-Poetry, and Disgust (Elias Petropoulos)," by John Taylor, *Into the Heart of European Poetry*, New Brunswick, New Jersey: Transaction Publishers, 2008, pp. 170-172. (Original English version of preface to Ποτέ και τίποτα.)

Special Elias Petropoulos issue of *εν Βόλω*, No. 28, January-March 2008. A second essential issue, with articles by Mary Koukoules, Kostas Kremmydas, Evangelos Avdikos, Yiannis A. Pikoulas, Alexis Vakis, Philippos Philippou, Andreas Pagoulatos, Manos Stephanidhis, Phoebe Yiannisi, Natalia Vogeikoff, and Vasia Karkayianni-Karabelia.

"Η Μακεδονία του Ηλία Πετρόπουλου" (Elias Petropoulos's Macedonia: An Interview with Jordan Plevnes), *Κυριακάτικη Ελευθεροτυπία*, 8 February 2009.

"The Art of Antipoetry", by John Taylor, *The Antioch Review*, Volume 67, No. 3, Summer 2009, pp. 594-601.

"Ομιλείτε την Καλιαρντήν;: Ο Ηλίας Πετρόπουλος στην χώρα των ανδρών" (Do you speak Kaliarda?: Elias Petropoulos in the realm of men), by Dimitris Papanikolaou, *The Books' Journal*, 7 May 2011.

"Τα καλιαρντά του Ηλία Πετρόπουλου: η ορατότητα και το περιθώριο της ομοφυλοφιλικής εμπειρίας" (Petropoulos's Kaliarda: Visibility and the margins of homosexual experience), by Terminal 119, in *Σώμα - Φύλο - Σεξουαλικότητα ΛΟΑΤΚ Πολιτικές Στην Ελλάδα* (Body, gender, sexuality: LGBTI politics in Greece). Athens: Plethron, May 2012.

"Ο υπόγειος κόσμος του Ηλία Πετρόπουλου" (The Underground World of Elias Petropoulos), by "Lifoteam", *Lifo:* www.lifo.gr, 17 July 2013.

"Ηλίας Πετρόπουλος. Η ζωή και το έργο του." (Elias Petropoulos. His life and work.), by Spyros Staveris, *Lifo:* www.lifo.gr, 3 September 2013.

"Η Πάολα Ρεβενιώτη καταγράφει τα Καλιαρντά" (Paola Revenioti records the Kaliarda), by Alkisti Georgiou, *Lifo*: www.lifo.gr, 27 January 2014.

"Mapping/Unmapping: The Making of Queer Athens", by Dimitris Papanikolaou, in *Queer Cities, Queer Cultures: Europe Since 1945*, 23 October 2014.

"Ηλίας Πετρόπουλος: 20 μοναδικά φωτογραφικά ντοκουμέντα" (Elias Petropoulos: 20 unique photographs), by Fontas Trousas, *Lifo:* www.lifo.gr, 3 September 2018.

"10 βιβλία που απαγορεύτηκαν στην Ελλάδα" (10 books that were banned in Greece), by Fontas Trousas, *Lifo*: www.lifo.gr, 5 September 2018.

"Ένα ντοκιμαντέρ για τον Ηλία Πετρόπουλο, τον άνθρωπο που ιστόρησε το ελληνικό περιθώριο" (A documentary on Elias Petropoulos, the person who historicized the Greek margins), by Kalliopi Legaki and Maria Yedekou. *Lifo:* www.lifo.gr, 22 January 2019.

"Anthropologie de la décadence aux marges de l'hellénisme: une biographie intellectuelle et politique d'Elias Petropoulos," by Christos Panagiotopoulos, *Bérose - Encyclopédie internationale des histoires de l'anthropologie*, Paris, IIAC-LAHIC, UMR 8177, 2019. (http://www.berose.fr/?Anthropologie-de-la-decadence-aux-marges-de-l-hellenisme-une-biographie)

Obituaries and tributes:

"Η στάχτη μου να σκορπιστεί στους υπονόμους του Παρισιού" (Disperse My Ashes in the Sewers of Paris), *Ελευθεροτυπία*, by Vassilis K. Kalamaras, 5 September 2003, pp. 32-33.

Announcement of death in *Libération*, 11 September 2003: "Elias Petropoulos, / ce grand ami du diable / avec son coeur d'ange / assez grand pour contenir / tous les maudits du monde, / ne fait plus partie des vivants / par son corps / depuis mercredi dernier, / mais reste toujours vivant et / combattif par ses écrits et par / les souvenirs de tous ceux qui / ont eu la chance de le connaître."

Announcement of death in *Le Monde*, 12 September 2003: "Elias Petropoulos, / 1928-2003, / écrivain et poète, / l'enfant terrible des lettres grecques, / auteur d'une merveilleuse anthologie / des chants grecs, *Rebétika*, / du *Manuel du bon voleur*, / et de *l'Histoire de la capote anglaise*, / nous a quittés en nous disant: 'La grammaire des baisers est aussi nécessaire que celle des mots.'"

"Χαίρε, Ηλία!" (Farewell, Elias!), by Kostis Papayiorgis, *Αθηνόραμα*, 11-18 September 2003, p. 16.

"Η μοναδικότητα του Πετρόπουλου" (Petropoulos's Uniqueness), *Ελευθεροτυπία* (section "Politismos"), by Dimitris Gionis, 14 September 2003, p. 28.

Tribute in the magazine *Έψιλον of Κυριακάτικη Ελευθεροτυπία*), 14 September 2003, pp. 78-79.

"Ilias Petropulos: Écrivain et poète de la Grèce de l'ombre" (Elias Petropoulos: The Writer and Poet of the Shadowy Side of Greece), by Jacques Lacarrière, *Le Monde*, 14-15 September 2003, p. 24.

Tributes by Ira Feloukatsi, Jacques Lacarrière, Vassilis Vassilikos, and K. Verghopoulos, *Ελευθεροτυπία*, 15 September 2003, pp. 22-23.

"Αφιέρωμα Ηλίας Πετρόπουλος" (special pages devoted to Petropoulos), *Ταχυδρόμος*, No. 186, 20 September 2003, pp. 36-40.

"Le Poète et l'égout" (The Poet and the Sewer), by Jacques Vallet, *Anartiste*, No. 3, November 2003, pp. 12-13, website of the Éditions Hermaphrodite (www.hermaphrodite.fr), and in Μετά / *Après* (see above).

ACKNOWLEDGMENTS

A few passages in this book have been excerpted, adapted, revised, and expanded from the following articles:

1) "Elias Petropoulos: The *Mounópsira*," *Maledicta*, Vol. 5, Nos. 1-2, 1981, pp. 11-24. (Greek translation: *Ιχνευτής*, No. 5, October 1985, pp. 20-28.)
2) "Elias Petropoulos: A Presentation," *Journal of the Hellenic Diaspora*, Vol. 8, No. 4, Winter 1981, pp. 7-28.
3) "Elias Petropoulos: Folklorist-in-Exile," *Greek Accent*, Vol. 3, No. 9, May-June 1983, pp. 25-27, 46-47.
4) "L'architecture: mémoire populaire," *Le Fou Parle*, No. 24, May-June 1983, pp. 58-59. (In French.)
5) "Benávis ta kaliardá?", *Gay Books Bulletin*, No. 9, Spring-Summer 1983, pp. 14-19.
6) "Un album de souvenir [*Les Juifs de Salonique: In Memoriam*, par Elias Petropoulos]," *Les Nouveaux Cahiers*, No. 74, Autumn 1983, p. 80. (In French.)
7) "Kaliarda Revisited," *The Cabirion*, No. 11, Fall-Winter 1984, pp. 10-11.
8) "*The Jews of Salonica: In Memoriam*, by Elias Petropoulos," *Jewish Currents*, Vol. 39, No. 1 (425), January 1985, pp. 14-15.

9) "Preface" to *Never and Nothing*, by Elias Petropoulos, Athens: Nefeli, 1993, pp. 9-14. (In Greek.) The original English version of this preface was first published as "Poetry, Anti-Poetry, and Disgust (Elias Petropoulos)" in my book *Into the Heart of European Poetry* (New Brunswick, New Jersey: Transaction Publishers, 2008, pp. 170-172) and is reproduced here, as chapter LXXXIII, with the kindly authorization of Transaction Publishers (now part of the Taylor-Francis / Routledge publishing group).

10) My essay on the art of Dimitris Souliotis, published in book form as *Dimitris Souliotis*, Athens: Titanium Gallery, 2007.

BOOKS BY JOHN TAYLOR

The Presence of Things Past
Story Line, 1992

Mysteries of the Body and the Mind
Story Line, 1998

The World As It Is
Cedar Hill, 1998

Some Sort of Joy
Cedar Hill, 2000

The Apocalypse Tapestries
Xenos, 2004

If Night is Falling
Bitter Oleander Press, 2011

Now the Summer Came to Pass
Xenos (e-book), 2012

The Dark Brightness
Xenos, 2017

Grassy Stairways
The MadHat Press, 2017

Remembrance of Water & Twenty-Five Trees
Bitter Oleander Press, 2018

A Notebook of Clouds & A Notebook of Ridges (with Pierre Chappuis)
The Fortnightly Review, 2019

Criticism:

Paths to Contemporary French Literature
Transaction, Volume 1, 2004

Paths to Contemporary French Literature
Transaction, Volume 2, 2007

Dimitris Souliotis
Titanium / Yiayiannos Gallery, 2007

Into the Heart of European Poetry
Transaction, 2008

Paths to Contemporary French Literature
Transaction, Volume 3, 2011

A Little Tour through European Poetry
Transaction, 2015

As a polyglot translator and literary critic, **John Taylor** (b. 1952) is one of the main bridges between contemporary European literature and English-speaking countries. His essays on European poets have been collected in his books *Into the Heart of European Poetry* (2008) and *A Little Tour through European Poetry* (2015). He has translated many French, Italian, and Modern Greek poets. He is the author of eleven volumes of short prose and poetry, most recently *Remembrance of Water & Twenty-Five Trees* and a "double book" co-authored with the Swiss poet Pierre Chappuis, *A Notebook of Clouds & A Notebook of Ridges*.

www.ingramcontent.com/pod-product-compliance
Lightning Source LLC
Chambersburg PA
CBHW020856020526
44107CB00076B/1868